WILD AND CRAZY GUYS

WILD AND CRAZY GUYS

*How the Comedy Mavericks of the
'80s Changed Hollywood Forever*

Nick de Semlyen

Crown Archetype
New York

All rights reserved.
Published in the United States by Crown Archetype,
an imprint of the Crown Publishing Group, a division of
Penguin Random House LLC, New York.
crownpublishing.com

Crown Archetype and colophon is a registered trademark of
Penguin Random House LLC.

Published by arrangement with Picador, a division of Macmillan Publishers
International Limited in the U.K.

Grateful acknowledgment is made to Playboy Enterprises International, Inc.,
for permission to reprint archival *Playboy* magazine material. All rights
reserved.

Library of Congress Cataloging-in-Publication Data is available upon
request.

ISBN 978-1-9848-2664-0
Ebook ISBN 978-1-9848-2665-7

Printed in the United States of America

Book design by Jen Valero
Jacket illustration by Tim O'Brien

10   9   8   7   6   5   4   3   2   1

First Edition

To Dad

Tragedy is the shattering of the forms and of our attachments to the forms; comedy, the wild and careless, inexhaustible joy of life invincible.

JOSEPH CAMPBELL

Comedy is the art of making people laugh without making them puke.

STEVE MARTIN

CONTENTS

PROLOGUE

NOBODY SAW THE punch coming. Least of all Chevy Chase.

It was February 18, 1978, another ice-cold evening in New York, which had just endured its most ferocious blizzard in thirty years. The three-day nor'easter, dubbed "Storm Larry," had closed schools the previous week, and Central Park remained blanketed by snow. Many chose to stay home that night. Outside 30 Rockefeller Plaza in midtown Manhattan, however, a long line of people waited patiently, stamping their feet and rubbing their hands. After all, freezing weather was well worth braving in order to catch an episode of *Saturday Night Live*, on a Saturday night, live.

Eight floors up in the Art Deco skyscraper, throughout the corridors behind Studio 8H, there was a chill in the air that had nothing to do with snow. The incredibly popular comedy troupe known as the Not Ready for Prime Time Players were busy prepping for their next big night, the eleventh show of season three. Dan Aykroyd was getting into the zone for his first sketch, a typically demented number about a salesman pitching a device for crushing moths. John Belushi was stomping through the halls like a buffalo, as always seemingly free of nerves. New boy Bill Murray, who'd had a shaky start, even receiving hate mail from viewers, was practicing his New England accent. Later that night he'd be playing Bobby Kennedy in a silly "chow-dah"–packed bit about JFK and RFK trying to bug the home of Martin Luther King.

And then there was Chevy.

Suave, handsome, and pumped up with braggadocio, Cornelius "Chevy" Chase had been the first *SNL* star to really hit it big. In 1975, the cover of *New York Magazine* had proclaimed him "The Funniest Man in America." The general consensus was that he agreed. He had come to dominate the first year of the show, introducing every episode but one, smirking his self-created catchphrase—"Good evening. I'm Chevy Chase, and you're not"—pratfalling up a storm, and playing the Landshark, a *Jaws*-riffing oceanic predator who targets sexy women.

Then, he had disappeared. Officially, his reason for quitting midway through season 2 was a new relationship. His girlfriend Jacqueline Carlin, Chase explained, didn't want to move to New York. But his fellow comedians felt he'd deserted them, heading for L.A. and a slew of movie offers. Especially after staff writer Tom Davis reported back to them what Chase had provided as his reason for leaving: "Money. Lots of money."

So Chase's return to *SNL*, this time as guest host, was leaving a bad taste in the collective's mouth. As the cast spent Monday to Friday honing the Chevy-heavy series of skits—as well as spouting nonsense as "the Reverend Archbishop Maharishi O'Mulliganstein DDS of the Church of Confusion," he'd be reprising his signature character, President Gerald Ford—there was much whispering behind his back, especially by Belushi.

The week almost passed without incident. But on Saturday night, shortly after eleven p.m., it all came to a head. Chase was en route to the stage for the cold open, clad in his classic Ford costume: suit, tie, brown leather shoes. Not long earlier, Murray had needled him as the two men had makeup applied; now, when Chase stuck his head into the dressing room where Murray and Belushi were sitting on a sofa, the exchange was even spikier.

"There was no love lost between those guys," says comedian Dave

Thomas, who was there visiting Aykroyd. "Especially at that time, when it was fueled by extreme competitiveness, alcohol, drugs, and fame. Who's the most famous? Who's the funniest? Who's the best? I still think what happened that night could have been avoided, but Chevy is a provocateur. Chevy says things that make people angry."

To the shock of everyone in the vicinity, the conversation between the three men suddenly escalated into hand-to-hand combat. Murray lunged forward at Chase, a mad glint in his eye, his fist connecting with his opponent's famous face.

"It was a huge altercation," says director John Landis, another eyewitness to the melee. "They were big guys and really going at it. They were slapping at each other, screaming at each other, calling each other terrible names. The best insult, which made a huge impression on me, was by Bill. In the heat of anger, he pointed at Chevy and yelled, 'MEDIUM TALENT!'"

Murray remembers it differently. "It was really a Hollywood fight; a don't-touch-my-face kinda thing." He shrugs. "Chevy is a big man, I'm not a small guy, and we were separated by my brother Brian, who comes up to my chest. So it was kind of a non-event. It was just the significance of it. It was an Oedipal thing, a rupture. Because we all felt mad he had left us, and somehow I was the anointed avenging angel, who had to speak for everyone."

The intensity of the blows alters from account to account. But the quality of the verbal burns, as the two future titans of comedy went at each other like hissing street cats, remains consistent.

"I'm gonna land Neil Armstrong on your face if you don't shut up," snarled Chase, targeting his enemy's acne-scarred skin.

"Why don't you go fuck your wife?" Murray hit back, implying that Chase's spouse wasn't getting much action at home.

And then it was all over, the pair pulled apart and Chase dispatched to begin the show.

It's a great story, the stuff of legend. But it's more than that. This moment marked the beginnings of a decade-long duel between two of the most bankable stars of the 1980s. Murray and Chase were about to be unleashed on the world in a major way, with towering triumphs and colossal defeats ahead of them both. And they weren't alone. Many of the alumni of *SNL*, as well as its Canadian equivalent, *SCTV* (*Second City Television*), would soon burst onto the Hollywood scene, competing with one another, collaborating with one another, and creating hilarious, box-office-smashing movies in the process.

Most of them would prosper. Some would fade away. A few would destroy themselves. But as a combined force they would bring about a new golden age of comedy. And there was nothing "medium talent" about it.

HOLLYWOOD COMEDY in the 1970s can be encapsulated with one image: a wimp in specs. Sure, there were other things going on, like the wackadoodle works of Mel Brooks, Peter Sellers's slapsticky *Pink Panther* flicks, the anarchic narco-japes of Cheech and Chong. Across the pond, the Monty Python boys were catapulting cows and upsetting Catholics with their big-screen antics. Burt Reynolds successfully transformed himself from brooding action man to smirking action man with the first of his car pictures, the phenomenally successful *Smokey and the Bandit*.

But of all the comedians working at the time, it is Woody Allen who best sums up the vibe of the decade: neurotic, introspective, and muted. While Vietnam raged and Nixon toppled, America produced many of its greatest dramas, from *The Godfather* to *Taxi Driver*, reflecting a sizeable counterculture churning with disaffection. The box-office charts for the 1970s are filled with dark, violent, even nihilistic movies: *The Exorcist*, incredibly, grossed more than *Rocky*. Funny movies were in scanter supply. Allen rightly received much acclaim, winning (but not turning up to accept) Best Picture and Best Director Oscars for 1977's *Annie Hall*, but otherwise the comedies that hit big tended to feature Reynolds, Clint Eastwood, and/or an orangutan.

Slowly, though, things were changing. The storm that had rocked the nation throughout the '70s was passing. Ronald Reagan, a former Hollywood star himself who had appeared in fluff like *Cattle Queen of Montana*, would soon be president, bringing with him an undentable, contagious sense of optimism and an economic boom. As Vietnam wound down, TV news footage of protests and body bags was replaced by upbeat shows like *Happy Days* and *Three's Company*. The future, all of a sudden, seemed bright. America was ready to laugh again.

And, as luck would have it, exactly the right people to make it laugh were moving into position.

Lounging on his sofa in Aspen, Steve Martin caught the premiere of *Saturday Night Live* when it aired on October 11, 1975. "It came on and I thought, 'They've done it!'" he was to recall. "They did the zeitgeist, they did what was out there, what we all had in our heads, this new kind of comedy."

Martin, the self-styled "Wild and Crazy Guy" who would go on to not only host *SNL* fifteen times (to date) but make some of the most iconic comedies of the 1980s, had immediately recognized kindred spirits. Many huge stars would be launched from the show, including Dan Aykroyd, John Belushi, Chevy Chase, Bill Murray, and Eddie Murphy. Meanwhile, up in the chillier and considerably less glamorous environs of Toronto and Edmonton, John Candy and Rick Moranis were working alongside people like Martin Short, Eugene Levy, and Catherine O'Hara, cutting their teeth at *SCTV*.

Together they made up a sprawling, smart, subversive collective. And all very different from Woody Allen—even if Moranis, himself a slightly built chap in specs, did a spot-on impersonation of the Woodster. Their approach to comedy was freewheeling, hip, and fearless. And whether their on-screen mission was to save the world from supernatural forces, get the girl, or make authority figures fizz with rage, they were about to inherit the Earth.

Try to imagine what cinema would look like without them. Collaborating with behind-the-camera talents including John Landis, Ivan Reitman, Carl Reiner, and John Hughes—and fellow stars such as Tom Hanks, Robin Williams, and Goldie Hawn—this new wave would produce a litany of big, brash blockbusters and evergreen oddities: *National Lampoon's Animal House*, *The Jerk*, *The Blues Brothers*, *Caddyshack*, *48 Hrs.*, *Trading Places*, *The Man with Two Brains*, *Beverly Hills Cop*, *Ghostbusters*, *Fletch*, *Coming to America*, and *Scrooged*, to name but some. That list alone makes a compelling case that this period is as good as things have ever gotten for big-screen comedy.

Quentin Tarantino certainly thinks so. "I think the '80s is the worst decade, with the '50s being the second worst, in the history of Hollywood," the director said in 2015. "The only movies from the '80s that I find myself really, really hanging on to, oddly enough, are the silly comedies. They're the ones that you have the most affection for. You can debate that they're great filmmaking, but I remember when I did *Death Proof*, we had a whole thing going on in the crew where we just kept saying stupid lines from comedies of that era. *Doctor Detroit*, any of those *Saturday Night Live* movies. We filled the whole day."

THIS IS THE STORY not only of how these classic movies were made, against the odds and frequently under the influence, but how their stars handled the perils and pitfalls of fame. Murray, Murphy, Martin, and company all hurtled onto the A-list, becoming global celebrities pursued by paparazzi and fending off, or accepting, frequent offers of sex and drugs. Not bad for a bunch of guys—and despite the early promise of Gilda Radner, it was exclusively the men who hit big—who generally looked more like maintenance staff, or appliance salesmen, than members of the Rat Pack.

There was plenty of fun, as these stars lived out an extended adolescence, getting paid obscene amounts of money to goof about in lavish screen fantasies. But when you're flying so high, the pressure is immense, and even the seeming perks could become nightmarish. "When I started playing stadiums, I did have girls trying to get into my room a few times," Steve Martin recalls. "But it wasn't a fun thing like you'd imagine. You don't want someone knocking at your door at two a.m. when you're exhausted and trying to get to sleep."

Everyone acclimatized to the lunacy in different ways. Rick Moranis wound up retiring in the early 1990s. Eddie Murphy embraced his celebrity with both hands, strutting around in a red leather boiler suit for the stand-up set *Eddie Murphy: Delirious* and employing a full-time entourage. Johns Belushi and Candy died tragically young. Bill Mur-

ray sailed through rumpled but uncrumpled, seemingly doing whatever he damn well pleased.

As for Chevy Chase, it was a somewhat rough ride. As his career
jolted up and down, this way and that, like a switchback roller coaster,
he battled addictions to painkillers and cocaine. But if he didn't survive the '80s unbruised, at least he learned some humility along the
way. "I'm not too proud of any of them," he said in a 1989 video interview, when asked about his run of films to date. "I feel like Lee Marvin
did, a little bit. He said, 'I've made a lot of junk and my life is junk,'
then took a swig from a bottle. I don't really feel that way, but I don't
have any major pride in them. I think the best pictures tell a story, and
if there's anything I've had trouble with in my pictures, it's the stories."

For a moment, he has become Cornelius Chase, sincere and introspective. Then he looks into the camera, arches an eyebrow, and
becomes good old punchable Chevy once more. "Incidentally, just because I say they're awful, doesn't mean you shouldn't see 'em. . . ."

WILD AND CRAZY GUYS

1
MR. CAREFUL AND MR. FUCK IT

THE CHARACTER DESCRIPTION was simple: "Cookie Monster Meets Harpo Marx." Not so simple: finding a human being who could pull it off.

In fact, the task was keeping John Landis, twenty-seven years old and a hyperactive typhoon of energy himself, up at night. As director of Universal's frat-house comedy *National Lampoon's Animal House*, Landis knew he had to bag the right person for the pivotal role of John "Bluto" Blutarsky, the biggest animal in a movie stuffed with them. Bluto was id incarnate, a Rabelaisian slob with the potential to boost the picture to new outlandish heights. "He's a cartoon," was Landis's take on it. "He is appetite."

Early in the summer of 1977, the director made a short list of potential Blutos. On it were three names: rock star Meat Loaf, Broadway actor Josh Mostel, and *Saturday Night Live*'s John Belushi. Really, though, only one of those felt right.

"The other guys were backups," says Landis. "All of my energy was going into trying to lock down John."

Belushi was keen to crank up his movie career, which thus far consisted of a voice role in *Tarzoon: Shame of the Jungle*, a wretched 1975 animated comedy that extensively features a masturbating monkey. *Animal House* seemed like a no-brainer. But the barrel-chested Albanian was the dictionary definition of unpredictable. He was a decent guy, quick to hug and easy to warm to. If a kitten fell asleep on his chest, he'd wait rather than wake it. At the same time, he'd come out of the womb looking for trouble.

In sixth grade, his gym teacher announced in class that he was the worst student in the school; so exasperated was she, she then kicked him in the balls. At *SNL*, he was a human hurricane, a wild man who referred to shows as "goddamn suicide missions." When his cast mates had whispered about how much they hated sharing the billing with Jim Henson's Muppets, Belushi yelled that he wanted to shoot the felt abominations with a gun. Around the same time, sick of a recurring skit involving a silly costume that he felt made him look fat, he griped to a *Rolling Stone* reporter: "You cannot put an actor in a bee costume and say, well, that funny dress will make up for the weak writing. Sure, they'll laugh at the antennae once or twice; after that, forget it, it's repetitive shit. *I hate the fucking bees!*"

All of this unsettled the executives at Universal. Belushi's antics might fly in the seat-of-your-pants world of late-night live TV, but could somebody that volatile be trusted to behave on a movie set, with millions of dollars at stake? Belushi himself kept hemming and hawing. It would be his first real movie role and he wasn't sure it was the right move.

Landis was undeterred. He saw Belushi as the successor to nimble clowns like Fatty Arbuckle and Jackie Gleason, a gruff teddy bear with a hugely expressive face. As for that edgy energy, which inspired Tony Hendra, director of the stage show *Lemmings*, to say, "I chose him because he projected the feeling of a homicidal maniac"? Well, that could be harnessed, hopefully, if the star was kept away from booze and drugs.

Picking somebody safer would be, to use Belushi's favorite slang word, "suck-o."

Finally, after much greasing up of both the star and the studio suits, Belushi was secured. Landis then found himself facing the opposite challenge: how to *get rid* of someone from *SNL*. He'd considered Bill Murray for the role of nice guy Boon and talked to Dan Aykroyd about playing biker D-Day. But Aykroyd decided to stay put on the show, not wanting to leave Lorne Michaels shorthanded. There was no such issue with Chevy Chase, now a free agent, and whom Universal was more than happy to cast. In fact, Landis was issued an edict from on high: hire Chase, or else.

Landis wasn't about to be told what to do.

A lunch was arranged at a swanky Los Angeles restaurant. Producers Ivan Reitman and Matty Simmons were there, plus Universal vice president Sean Daniel. And in the middle, chomping on a big cigar and flanked on either side by an agent, sat Chevy Chase, waiting to be told why he should make this little movie and not *Foul Play*, a $44 million caper with Goldie Hawn.

"There's a marvelous Hollywood saying: 'Do you know the difference between a brownnose and a shithead?'" says Landis. "The answer: 'Depth perception.' Chevy was just being impossible and they're all kissing his ass. So when it comes to my turn to talk, I said, 'Listen, Chevy, our picture is an ensemble, a collaborative group effort like *Saturday Night Live*. You'd fit right in, whereas in *Foul Play*, that's like being Cary Grant or Paul Newman, a real movie-star part. Don't you think you'd be better off surrounded by really gifted comedians?'"

It was a bit of reverse psychology worthy of Brer Rabbit. As Reitman furiously kicked Landis under the table, Chase sat back, puffed out cigar smoke, and considered. Then he took the bait. He announced that while he'd love to work with them someday, he had decided to make *Foul Play*.

IN HOLLYWOOD'S EYES, as well as Chase's, *National Lampoon's Animal House* was far from a sure bet. The script had originated with Chris Miller, a Madison Avenue advertising executive who'd been fired for putting marijuana in his soup during a business lunch. He started writing short stories; one of these, titled *The Night of the Seven Fires* and based on his fraternity initiation at Dartmouth College, was a bawdy shocker that featured one freshman drunkenly puking on another's penis.

The bigwigs at *National Lampoon* magazine saw so much potential that they not only printed it in their October 1974 issue but decided it had the makings of the first ever Lampoon movie. Miller, Harold Ramis, and Doug Kenney got together to bash out a 114-page treatment, a document so stuffed with ideas it was later described as "*War and Peace* on speed." Over the next few years, it mutated through eighteen drafts, picking up the title *Laser Orgy Girls*, before finally becoming *Animal House*.

The president of Universal, Ned Tanen, was exactly the type of puffed-up establishment square the Lampoon guys specialized in deflating. Nevertheless, he decided with some reluctance to green-light the project. "Everybody is drunk, or high, or getting laid," he grumbled to the writers at an early meeting. "I'd never make this movie—except you're the *National Lampoon*." The story slowly softened (a projectile-vomiting sequence was cut, at Landis's behest) and a good-versus-bad narrative emerged, with the party-loving outcasts of Faber College's Delta House pitted against the stuck-up stiffs in Omega. All while the authority figure Dean Wormer raged, "No more fun of any kind!" Universal expected a modest hit at best.

The controlled chaos of the writing room, where Miller, Kenney, and Ramis typed with one hand while holding joints with the other (they called this "marijuana production"), continued on-set. Turning up at the University of Oregon, the only campus that had welcomed the controversial production, several young cast members, including Tim Matheson, Karen Allen, and Bruce McGill, decided to check out a real frat party. They ran into a group of drunk jocks spoiling for a fight, and a pummeling ensued. John Belushi, arriving the next day from New York, had to be talked out of heading to the frat house to get revenge.

John Landis set out to turn the production into a fraternity itself. He organized an "orientation week," during which the cast watched a World Series game in Belushi's hotel room and enjoyed a series of rowdy dinners. Then began the thirty-day shoot. It was a tough sched-ule, an average of thirty-five set-ups a day with just a single camera, forcing the team to race from set to set to capture the tale's sexy pil-low fights, toga parties, and horse-based slapstick. The fact it drizzled almost the entire time didn't help. Landis's biggest challenge was to keep up the collective energy.

"THAT SUCKS!" he'd bellow at his actors mid-take. "IT WAS AWFUL! BE FUNNY! BE FUNNY!"

When that didn't work, Landis would fling pens at them. "I was trying to create an ambience of high energy and chaos," he was to ex-plain. "Because that's the movie."

Belushi struggled with stamina more than most. He still had *Sat-urday Night Live* to worry about: his hellish weekly itinerary involved working on *Animal House* from Monday to Wednesday, then taking a puddle-jumper plane to San Francisco and the red-eye on to New York, rehearsing and performing the show, then flying back to Oregon at six a.m. on Sunday. This was the biggest break of his career so far, and he was dead on his feet.

On paper, the role didn't look so daunting. Bluto has fewer than fifty lines of dialogue and is never on-screen for long: he's forever mak-ing big entrances and explosive exits. Belushi was getting paid only $35,000, prompting him to complain, "Bullshit money, no points, but I'm gonna be a fucking star anyway, those cheap bastards." But he knew just how critical he was to the movie's success. Bluto is the heart of *Animal House*, a shambling hippo of a man who had to be as lovable as he is wild.

It was the only way they'd get away with scenes like the one in which he climbs a ladder to spy on an undressing sorority girl. After some lurid topless shots, the ladder slowly topples backward, Bluto's erection having pushed him away from the building. What makes it not only palatable but funny is the fourth-wall-breaking look to the camera that Belushi delivers before the fall, eyebrows waggling like randy caterpillars. "He made everyone in the house a co-conspirator," was Landis's take on it. "And it was a great moment because it took the edge off."

Belushi was the only cast member given permission to go off script, and he rewarded his director's trust. Fearsomely committed when he believed in a project (on *Lemmings*, he'd sometimes turn up high on Quaaludes and ask his colleagues to punch his kidneys to clear his head), he threw himself ferociously into the role. From his first appearance, in which he pisses on two new guys' shoes while clutching a gargantuan goblet of beer, to the end-credits roll, which reveals that Bluto will one day become a senator, it's a performance studded with iconic moments. Some were guided by Landis, like Bluto's attempt to cheer up Flounder (Stephen Furst), before which the director suggested to Belushi: "Imagine you're trying to make a baby laugh." But the legendary food-fight sequence, filmed in a single morning at the Erb Memorial Student Union, was wholly improvised by Belushi.

"See if you can guess what I am now," Bluto tells a huddle of Omegas, having loaded his tray with half of the canteen's comestibles. He stuffs mashed potato into his mouth, stares his enemies down for five seconds, then thumps his fists into his cheeks, splattering them with an icky mess. "I'm a zit. Geddit?"

Cue an almighty fracas, soundtracked by the Chris Montez tune "Let's Dance" and capped off by Belushi turning to the camera and yelling, "FOOD *FIIIIGHT!*" At this point in the film, during screenings all across America, popcorn would be flung in the air with wild abandon.

The star's grin suggests he knew it would happen.

ALTHOUGH IT'S SET back in 1962, *Animal House*'s shit-kicking vibe connected with '70s America in a huge way. Vietnam was history, young people were ready to have fun again, and here was a trumpet call for the good times ahead. "The audience went berserk," remembers Matty Simmons of a test screening in Denver. "After the movie ended they were standing on their chairs, applauding and screaming. I was there with Sid Sheinberg, the president of Universal, Ned Tanen, Ivan Reitman, and Landis; we walked out single-file and nobody said anything. It was so crazy, what had just happened."

All over America, toga parties broke out. Greek fraternities became cool again. Audiences hollered and went back for more, rocketing the movie to the number-one slot at the box office in June 1978. The final tally was an astonishing $141.6 million. The film had proven to be revolutionary, comedy's answer to *Easy Rider*. As Reitman reflects, "It was the marking point. I always felt it changed the comedic language. Before *Animal House* they were all watching Bob Hope and Dean Martin and Jerry Lewis. *M*A*S*H* was the transitional one—a little bit of both—and then this was the first film really made by kids who were postwar and in their early twenties, with a different way of expressing what's funny."

It felt like the floodgates were open. Something new and exciting was happening.

Whatever it was, John Belushi was right in the middle of it. Dazed by the outbreak of Blutomania, the star treated himself to a pair of expensive Bally shoes from Switzerland, then hired a limousine to ride around Manhattan and look at the lines snaking around movie theaters. People were going back to see it again and again.

"I like Bluto a lot. He's someone that could have been my friend," he'd said at a press junket a few weeks before. Now everyone else wanted to be Bluto's friend. During an out-of-town trip with Aykroyd, Belushi stopped the car and began knocking on the ground-floor windows of an elementary school. Before long, the windows were up and the whole school was chanting, "BLUTO! BLUTO! BLUTO!"

Even more satisfyingly, Belushi had overtaken Chevy Chase, the rival he often described as a "brick." *Saturday Night Live* producer Bob Tischler said: "John was sure he would be the first person to become a star. It just killed him when Chevy was the first." Chase had bagged the bigger movie, and the bigger salary, but now the overweight underdog had his revenge. Around this time, the two ran into each other in the bathroom at a club in New York's East Village. Belushi sniped at Chase, "I make more money in movies than you, *boy*." Chase forced a smile, washed his hands, and moved on.

Belushi had gotten attention before, but mostly from the cracked end of the spectrum: one female fan repeatedly sent him tampons stuffed with pot. Now he was big-time: when he was roaming Washington, DC, one day and decided on impulse to visit the White House, he was admitted even though he'd forgotten to bring any ID. And his phone was ringing off the hook, A-listers offering congratulations and opportunities. One of the callers was more famous than most: Steven Spielberg. And he had a job offer.

LIKE LANDIS, Spielberg had sat in the audience at *Saturday Night Live*. On a show broadcast in February 1976, he actually made it on-screen during a Peter Boyle monologue, chewing gum and wearing an Indiana Jones–style fedora. Spielberg had been particularly tickled by Belushi's Richard Dreyfuss impression during a *Jaws* skit in an earlier episode. Perhaps, if the right project came along, he'd find a part for him.

Soon enough, the right project did come along—or so it seemed. Spielberg was skeet-shooting with John Milius, the writer of *Apocalypse Now*, at the Oak Tree Gun Club in California's Santa Clarita Valley, when Milius handed him a script for an ambitious World War II comedy, set the day after Pearl Harbor.

Written by Robert Zemeckis and Bob Gale, it had gone through many titles—*Tank*, *The Night the Japanese Attacked*, *The Rising Sun*, *Japs*—before landing on the thoroughly prosaic *1941*, but it may as well have been called *It's a Mad, Mad, Mad, Mad War*. There were dozens of characters, huge set pieces, and the most exuberant punctuation Spielberg had ever seen: even the stage directions came festooned with exclamation marks. Spielberg, who had never attempted a comedy before, was drawn to it like a shark to a beach. As he was to explain, "I really thought it would be a great opportunity to break a lot of furniture."

Before the demolition began, Spielberg assembled an impressive cast. He failed to secure John Wayne, who considered the story to be anti-American, but did bag Toshiro Mifune, Christopher Lee, Slim

Pickens, Ned Beatty, and Robert Stack. None of whom, admittedly, were renowned for their comedy chops. For that, Spielberg looked to New York.

Milius considered *Animal House* to be the best American movie since *Patton*, while Spielberg not only saw it three times over the summer of 1978 but regularly wore one of its promotional T-shirts. "It reminded me of my own college days at Cal State Long Beach," he told Landis when he bumped into him at an L.A. sushi restaurant. "Ken Kesey did one of his acid tests at a toga party we had. We filmed these pledges stealing traffic lights, and all my best friends ended up in the hospital." What better way to get some of that *Animal House* magic into *1941* than to enroll Bluto himself?

As it happened, *1941* had a part that seemed perfect for Belushi: a testicle-scratching, Coke-glugging bomber pilot called "Wild Bill" Kelso. There was even some neat synchronicity: in *Animal House*, Bluto had demonstrated a shaky grasp of history, speechifying, "Nothing is over until we decide it is. Was it over when the Germans bombed Pearl Harbor? Hell no!" Now fans could enjoy seeing Belushi pitted against a Japanese submarine crew. Though, for all we know, Wild Bill might have thought they were Krauts.

If Belushi was reluctant to play another crazed slob—or to shuttle back and forth again between *SNL* and a remote movie set, this time in Los Angeles—he didn't show it. After protracted negotiations, he received an official offer while at a screening of Akira Kurosawa's *Throne of Blood* in L.A.; he'd been grunting along with Toshiro Mifune, the inspiration for his iconic samurai character on *SNL*. Belushi walked outside with his friend Mitch Glazer, a dazed look on his face, bought a taco, and strolled silently to a grimy underpass before announcing, "I got the Spielberg movie." In fact, he had not only been hired for *1941*—which, in a strange cosmic coincidence would co-star Mifune—but been offered a three-picture deal with Universal, promising him $350,000 for *1941* and even more for the later pictures. In short, he'd never have to worry about money again. "He reached in his pocket and pulled out a crumpled $20 bill, arched his eyebrow and smiled," Glazer recalled. "Then he started slowly tearing the 20 and tossing little bits of green confetti out over the ditch."

"Thank you, L.A.," Belushi whispered. "Thank you, Hollywood."

AS *1941* RAMPED UP to start shooting in October 1978, the star shared his good fortune with his loved ones. He bought his immigrant parents, Adam and Agnes, a ten-acre ranch in the Cuyamaca Mountains outside San Diego. As for his closest friend, Dan Aykroyd, Belushi saw *1941* as an opportunity to take their partnership to the big screen.

By this point, Aykroyd and Belushi were inseparable. They shared a cramped dressing room at *Saturday Night Live*, where books like *Famous Tank Battles of World War II* (Belushi) and *Better Management Through Computers* (Aykroyd) lined the shelves. Panties that had been mailed to them by female admirers were nailed to the wall, as was a photograph of Aykroyd gripping two pump-action shotguns.

They loved working together on and off *SNL*—for a 1976 NBC special, they'd barged into the bedroom of reclusive Beach Boys front man Brian Wilson, dressed as the "Surf Police," then frog-marched him into the ocean. And they loved hanging out together, whether sharing a bunk bed on the seventeenth floor of 30 Rock or taking weeklong road trips to probe the nooks and crannies of America. During one of these, funded by *Rolling Stone*, they installed a ludicrously pricey sound system in their rented Chevy Caprice at the magazine's expense before prank-calling editor Jann Wenner. Putting on a Deep South accent, Aykroyd claimed to be "Sheriff Leander Perez" from the Louisiana police force, yelling that the two comedians had just killed someone with the car. Wenner's blood pressure started shooting up, until Aykroyd broke character with a snigger.

Grandson of a Royal Canadian Mountie and the owner of webbed feet, Aykroyd was very different from Belushi, whom he affectionately nicknamed "Thing," "the Black Hole in Space," and "the Bear Man." Where Belushi was an impulsive, freewheeling spirit, Aykroyd was self-disciplined to a fault; as Belushi summarized, "He's Mr. Careful and I'm Mr. Fuck It." Aykroyd played up his deadpan persona, telling one reporter, "I'm just hard inside. I've got a lot of armor . . . and I like it. I enjoy it. I'm continually meeting people who are trying to free me and free my emotions and warmth. I try to fight it."

Still, he was edgy in his own eccentric way. Despite growing up as a Catholic kid in the calm environs of Hull, Quebec, his father a straitlaced government official, he quickly developed a flair for trouble. He would torment the teachers at his seminary school in Ottawa, joined a gang called the Black Top Vamps in college, and later fell in with thieves and bootleggers. He told his long-suffering parents he wanted to be a funeral director, until he saw an embalming and changed his mind. At age fourteen he lost his virginity and was arrested for drunkenness, though not on the same night. At seventeen he spent a summer in the Northern Territories, totally isolated, roasting squirrels over a campfire for dinner.

Aykroyd turned up for his *Saturday Night Live* audition dressed as an English gentleman, sporting a bowler hat, umbrella, and briefcase, but was more frequently to be found in leather. "A remarkable, wonderful, wacky motorhead," in the words of John Landis, he read books on hydraulics and collected motorcycles, filling in dead air at the end of one *SNL* episode by petitioning the audience for spare parts for his 1971 Electra Glide Harley Davidson Police Special. Cruising down the freeway was how he got the highs Belushi sought elsewhere.

"If it weren't against the law," he told Gene Siskel of the *Chicago Tribune*, "I'd ride without my helmet."

Curiously for someone with such an anarchic streak, he was also obsessed with the law. At Carleton University in Ottawa he took college courses in correctional policy and deviant psychology, as if he was trying to figure out his own brain. Mitch Glazer compared him to a cross between a state trooper and an android. Former girlfriend Rosie Schuster said his ultimate fantasy would be to commit the perfect crime, then arrest himself. Many of his friends were convinced he was attuned to a bizarre frequency nobody else could detect. "You look at the floor and see the floor," he said to one of them. "I look at the floor and see molecules." Sometimes late at night, in his and Belushi's room at 30 Rock, he would take out a stash of gold coins and make strange gibberish sounds like incantations, awakening other people on the floor.

Downstairs, in front of the cameras, Aykroyd proved himself to be a utility player with astonishing range. He could absorb information like nobody else, and channel anyone from Sigmund Freud to Jimmy Carter. But many of his finest moments at *Saturday Night Live* came courtesy of his array of rapid-fire salesmen. Over four seasons he shilled such alarming fake products as Rothko's Puberty Helper (a giant sack for concealing children), Bag o' Glass (exactly what it sounds like), and a surgical tool called Mr. Skin Grafter.

Most famous of all was his 1976 "Bass-O-Matic" sketch, in which he hard-sells a piece of kitchen equipment that makes disgusting-looking fish smoothies. While it went on to achieve classic status, the skit provoked a letter of complaint from an angry viewer. Aykroyd was unperturbed: "She objected to liquefying dead lower species, I guess. I wrote her back with a long dissertation on the properties of matter and mass and molecular change."

Spielberg didn't take much convincing before he agreed to put Belushi's pal in *1941*. He and Aykroyd would go on to become friends, with the director giving him a cameo in *Indiana Jones and the Temple of Doom* and naming the family dog in *Poltergeist* "E. Buzz," after a particularly sleazy character Aykroyd played on *SNL*. In *1941*, though, as tank commander Frank Tree, the comedian didn't get much to do. Only one scene really showcased his machine-gun mouth, as he rat-a-tatted off technical data about a 40mm antiaircraft gun, his expression suggesting he was getting high off his own jargon.

If he was disappointed about the size of the role, or playing second fiddle to Belushi, Aykroyd didn't show it. It was only his second visit to Los Angeles; the first time, six years earlier, he'd slept in a ditch near San Clemente. Now he was in a luxury hotel, shooting a big movie with his best bud.

"Man, we're in it together!" he enthused to Belushi. "You've got the P-40 and I've got the fuckin' M3 tank. Man, between us we're the heaviest ordnances in the movie!"

ONE DAY, AS SPIELBERG SHOT a scene in which Wild Bill clambers out of his P-40, Belushi lost his balance and pitched forward, headfirst. "There was a lot of morning dew on the wing of his plane and his foot slipped," the director recalled. "Luckily his fall was broken. But unfortunately it was broken by a human being who happened to be standing there. It didn't even faze John."

Like most people, Spielberg sometimes wondered if Belushi was indestructible. The comedian seemed able to stay up all night, then turn up on-set still cracking jokes. Wild Bill's outré introduction, in which the nutso airman lands his plane in Death Valley, loots a grocery store, fires his gun at a poor passerby, then chases after his runaway P-40 with explosions going off behind him, is the perfect representation of Belushi's fireball energy.

But as the shoot proceeded, it became apparent that the star was getting plenty of chemical assistance. *Saturday Night Live* writer Michael O'Donoghue once reflected, "John's got a real Judy Garland personality sometimes; he wants to grab the world and snort it." His drug habit had even made it onto *SNL* itself, during a sketch in which he was asked to name three countries and responded with, "Belgium . . . Belgium . . . and Kansas City." On *Animal House* he had been on his best behavior, sequestered away in a nice rented apartment with his wife, Judy. But on *1941*, in the druggy environs of L.A. and with more loose bills than he knew what to do with, Belushi went wild.

More and more frequently, the entire crew would stand around waiting while Belushi failed to emerge from his trailer. Spielberg eventually snapped, marched up to the star's honey wagon, rapped on the door, and confronted the star. It temporarily roused Belushi from his bleary stupor, but before long he was back on the powder. Not even

Aykroyd, Belushi's self-appointed parole officer, could keep him clean. "I get incredibly straight, authoritarian and intense. It usually does the trick," he'd revealed in 1977. A year later, the trick was no longer working.

"Working with John Belushi was in itself a motion-picture story," is about all Spielberg will say on the subject these days. "I mean, that's a whole other story."

TIME MAGAZINE PITCHED *1941* in a preview as *"Animal House* Goes to War." Spielberg even gave John Landis a cameo in the movie, as a motorcycle messenger, as if to try to link the two movies as much as possible. But any illusions that this would be a similar success story were shattered at preview screenings, where audience members held their hands over their ears, worn down by the relentless wall of sound and frenetic visuals.

It didn't find any more favor with critics. *Newsweek* headlined their review "Spielberg's Misguided Missile." Pauline Kael compared the experience to having her head stuck in a pinball machine for two hours. After reading the trades, Aykroyd and Belushi turned up at Spielberg's house to try to cheer him up. "Fuck the critics," Belushi said. "It's got so much stuff in it, so much up on the screen, the fucking critics can't sort it out."

The movie's reception was a blow to the egos of the big names involved. "On about the 145th day of shooting, I realized that the film was directing me, I wasn't directing it," Spielberg ruefully confessed of his first failure. "It just outgrew its own Calvins and became this Great White Elephant." As for Belushi, on his thirty-first birthday some friends presented him with a black badge inscribed JOHN BELUSHI. BORN 1949, DIED 1941. He laughed and pinned it to his shirt.

While *1941* reinforced Belushi and Aykroyd's Ernie-and-Bert dynamic, with John the exuberant agent of chaos to Dan's precise authority figure, it unwisely kept them apart at all times. There's only one moment in which the pair even acknowledge each other's presence:

as Belushi clambers onto a submarine near the end of the movie, and Aykroyd, paddling in the water below, salutes him. That's it. Back in New York, however, the pair were cooking up a concept that would team them up properly.

If, that is, the lunatic thing ever got made.

THE JERKS

A 1978 EPISODE of *The Carol Burnett Show* features Steve Martin, clad in a three-piece suit and starched white shirt, attempting an experimental routine. "Now, a lot of dogs watch TV, but there's nothing really on that they can enjoy," he declares. "So I've worked up a comedy act for dogs. I know that sounds sort of ridiculous, but I tried the act on some neighborhood dogs . . . and they were on the *floor.*"

The camera zooms out, revealing Martin's audience: a St. Bernard, a Labrador, an Estrela, and a Lhasa Apso. Promising "no canned barks," he launches into a set that features the gag, "It was raining cats and dogs the other day. I know because I stepped in a poodle." The mutts are unimpressed. So Martin starts madly playing a dog whistle like a kazoo, at which point two of them leap at him, tripping him to the ground. "Good night!" he yells, a gangly tangle of limbs.

The four-minute skit was a typical piece of Steve Martin shtick: precision-tooled but with an air of exhilarating chaos. More so than any of his contemporaries, Martin was a one-man variety show. He juggled, made balloon animals, did card tricks, performed magic. But he did all of it with a thick dollop of irony. Adopting the persona of a slick, preening show-biz guy, he honed a high-voltage club act that mesmerized crowds.

"Our acts are similar in that we have no segues and go from disassociation to disassociation," said Robin Williams in the late '70s. "But his act is different. He broke the barrier. It's like rock 'n' roll comedy."

Born in Waco, Texas, but raised in California, Martin had a difficult relationship with his father, which caused him to become an independent teenager. He worked for eight years at Disneyland, helping out at a magic store in Fantasyland and learning the ropes, literally, as a lasso twirler in Frontierland. He became a self-taught entertainer, poring over copies of books like Joe Laurie's *Vaudeville* and Dariel Fitzkee's *Showmanship for Magicians*. And although he studied philosophy at Long Beach State and considered teaching the subject, he ultimately decided to put his curiosity about the human psyche to a different use.

What he meticulously crafted throughout the '70s was a postmodern style that his friend Rick Moranis later labeled "anti-comedy." He shunned punch lines, opting instead to address audiences with surreal lines such as "Does anyone know where I can get a pair of cat handcuffs?" or "Hello, I'm Steve Martin and I'll be out here in a minute." As he explained to a reporter, "Another comedian will do anything to get a laugh. But in my act I think it's abstracted back to the point where the *idea* of someone doing anything for a laugh is funny, not the action. That's the way I like it."

It was a bold, even groundbreaking theory, but for a long while didn't appear to be a successful one. Martin had a long residency in a tiny club called Bubba's in Miami, performing to fewer than a hundred people a night. During a visit to Toronto, he found himself telling jokes next to a salad bar. One Monday night in 1975, owing the bank $17,000 and profoundly dejected, he did an avant-garde set in San Francisco to a crowd comprised mainly of a Japanese tour group, who spoke no English. Laughter was not forthcoming.

Martin collected his paltry fee, wandered into the city's red-light district, and decided to pay $50 for sex in a massage parlor. The girl took the money, but gave him only a desultory dance and told him to jack himself off. In too much of a funk to argue, the comedian collected his coat and headed back into the street. He later cited this as the most depressing night of his career.

"I call them the war years; it was a tough time," says Martin, whose hair turned prematurely gray in his early twenties. "The abiding memory is of the cumulative travel and sort of self-imposed loneliness. I remember every bad review. I can still remember the pain of doing a lousy show and feeling just awful. But I didn't have anything else to do. I had no options."

Little by little, as he plugged away, things started to change. As if a dial were being turned, audiences were tuning into his frequency. And then, in October 1976, the West Coast comic flew to New York to host *Saturday Night Live*, booked in by a reluctant Lorne Michaels. Martin did two monologues straight out of his act, plus a spoof commercial for a dog that was also a watch, called Fido-Flex. The *SNL* effect was instantaneous. The next Monday, in Madison, Wisconsin, he turned up for a show to find a 6,000-seat concert venue completely packed. "I walked onstage and was greeted with a roar of such intensity that I remembered feeling both pleasure and fear," he recalled. "I was like an athlete at the college play-offs, flooded with adrenaline."

Steve Martin and *Saturday Night Live* went together like peanut butter and jelly. He immediately warmed to the oddball troupe (despite the leather-clad Dan Aykroyd, when invited by Martin to go clothes-shopping at Saks with him, telling him, "Uh, man, that's not my thing") and was to return to the show again and again. Among the subsequent creations was his goofy tune *King Tut*, the funkiest anthem ever written about an Egyptian pharaoh, and Yortuk and Georg Festrunk, aka "Two Wild and Crazy Guys," lady-obsessed Czechoslovakian brothers played by Martin and Aykroyd.

Given a national platform, Martin's popularity rocketed. He sold 5 million copies of his comedy albums. In 1977 he released a book, a collection of droll essays and short stories called *Cruel Shoes*, which became a bestseller. His TV specials got huge ratings. And all the while Martin kept crisscrossing America, selling out giant auditoriums, without a salad bar in sight. Playing some nights to a sea of forty thousand faces, he was closer to a rock star than a traditional comedian. So he started behaving like one, performing outrageous bits of boundary-pushing theatre. "This isn't comedy," gasped a *Rolling Stone* reporter. "It's campfire recreation for the bent at heart. It's a laugh-along for loonies. Disneyland on acid."

Some nights Martin would come down off the stage and run around the aisles, stopping to give people neck massages. After performing at a Georgia university, on a dizzy high, he led a horde of fans to a drained swimming pool, told everyone to get in and then crowd-surfed across. In Tennessee, he took another horde to McDonald's, ordered three hundred hamburgers, then changed the order to a single French fry.

It all made a man who had once busked for change with his banjo ridiculously rich. "I bought some pretty good stuff," he faux-bragged on his first comedy album, *Let's Get Small*. "Got me a $300 pair of socks. I got a fur sink. Oh, let's see . . . electric dog-polisher, that was a good one. Gasoline-powered turtleneck sweater. And of course I bought some dumb stuff too, you know!"

But despite it all—the fame, the fortune, the French fry—Martin was increasingly unhappy. Away from the stage, he was actually soft-spoken and intellectual, nothing like the human tornado people expected.

"The act is funny on stage, but if that guy was in your living room, you'd throw him out," he said later. "There's nothing more obnoxious than a guy who is on all the time." Before one gig, he was picked up from the airport by two excitable female fans in a Volkswagen. Folded into the backseat, badgered to tell jokes, he spent the ninety-minute journey awkwardly explaining that he was really just a shy guy from Orange County. He didn't party with groupies or get high—unlike his *Saturday Night Live* buddies he said no to drugs, having suffered a marijuana-induced panic attack during a viewing of *The Producers* in 1968. Instead, he'd flee to his motel room after a show, too cranked up on adrenaline to sleep but with nowhere else to go.

To compound matters, the world of stand-up was no longer a challenge. He was still having fun figuring out ways to make crowds gasp—at the 1979 Grammys he announced the names of the Best Male

Singer nominees while wearing a tuxedo jacket but no trousers; a few weeks later, at the Academy Awards, he came on to present the Oscar for Special Achievement in Visual Effects wearing a blue hood that, on TV, made it look like he had no head. But the shows themselves felt like an endless victory lap. "What I realized was that I wasn't getting laughs like I used to. I was getting cheers," he mused in the mid-'80s.

But for a number of years he had been formulating an escape plan. A brief foray into moviemaking, writing and starring in an eight-minute 1977 short called *The Absentminded Waiter*, had netted him an Oscar nomination. Not bad, considering it had been shot in two days for $96,000. The idea of making a feature film started to look more and more appealing.

Wild and crazy had worked onstage. Would it work on-screen?

THERE WAS ONE QUICK BIT in Martin's routine that never failed to kill. "It wasn't always easy for me," he would tell the audience, shaking his head. "I was born a poor black child." Coming out of Martin's mouth, this potentially offensive non sequitur was weirdly charming. "There was no whiter man than Steve," says Carl Reiner with a laugh. "He even had white hair."

Martin had worked alongside Rob Reiner, Carl's son and the future director of such Hollywood classics as *The Princess Bride* and *When Harry Met Sally*, as writers on *The Smothers Brothers*. But Carl Reiner knew him mostly, as everyone did, from his guest stints on *Saturday Night Live*. "He was so different," says the director. "He approached jokes, but never really told them. He had this wild energy—I don't know where it came from. I remember this magician thing he developed called Flydini, which he did on the Carson show. He zipped his pants down and produced things from his fly: eggs, birds, trinkets. You couldn't believe what he pulled out of his pants."

The two men got together in 1978, aiming to pull something more substantial out of their pants: a movie for Martin. Along with Carl Gottlieb, the screenwriter of *Jaws* who had ended up directing *The Absentminded Waiter*, they sat in a small writers' cubicle in an ancient two-story wooden building on the Paramount lot. But inspiration was not forthcoming. "My memory is that it was just days of staring blankly at paper," says Gottlieb. "We had a couple of IBM Electrics and a stack of yellow pads and a glass full of sharpened pencils, and that was it. None of us had any idea for what this movie should be. 'What do you think?' 'I dunno, what do you think?' We were dead bored."

Then, after a couple of weeks, inspiration struck. Martin mentioned that throwaway line from his act—"I was born a poor black child"—and suddenly a plot seemed obvious. *Easy Money*, which was quickly retitled *The Jerk*, was the tale of Navin Johnson, a cretin who has grown up as a member of an African American family, not realizing he's adopted. In several ways his journey mirrors that of Martin himself. Navin struggles for a long time, doing odd jobs (in a joke that didn't make the final cut, he's hired as a "buffalo-counter" in Beverly Hills; after several days one finally turns up). Eventually, he gets lucky and goes from being a poor idiot to a very wealthy one, enjoying all the amenities of L.A. "Can you believe this?" he rails to his date at a fancy restaurant, glaring at his escargot. "First they didn't have the bamboo umbrellas for the wine. And now *snails* on the food!"

The first draft was funny stuff, but Paramount, where there had just been a major regime change, blanched and passed. Martin and Reiner took the project across the street to Universal instead. When Gottlieb went on to another gig, the pair got busy with a major rewrite, with the help of Martin's old *The Pat Paulsen Show* cowriter Michael Elias. Director and star, in particular, made each other laugh, a lot. "We just hit it off," says Martin. "I was writing gag after gag, and he shaped it into a story. Carl gave it structure." Just as Martin's stand-up had ironically lampooned the medium of stand-up itself, so *The Jerk* would be an abstract send-up of cinema. Or as Martin put it: "It wasn't a parody of a particular kind of beginning, middle and end. It was a parody of the whole idea that a movie should *have* a beginning and a middle and an end."

With a $4.6 million budget to play with, the team got busy realizing their vision. One day Martin read about a $3 million home on the Sunset Strip, owned by a young pair of Saudi Arabian newlyweds, which was so horrendously decorated that their neighbors had complained. He and Reiner canceled plans to build Navin's tacky mansion on a soundstage and rented the house for $50,000 a week instead.

"The sheik and his bride were like the most bad-taste couple in the world," says Gottlieb, who returned to the project to cameo as gloriously monikered villain Iron Balls McGinty, a man with, yes, metal testes. "I visited one day and kept saying of some bit of outré interior decor, 'Where did you find this?' And he would shrug and say, 'It was here.' They had painted the statuary outside and pasted pubic hair on the nudes. Eventually the couple were recalled back to Saudi Arabia and there was a mysterious fire and the place burned down."

Each morning throughout the forty-five-day shoot, Martin and Reiner car-pooled, riding together to Universal Studios and brainstorming jokes like the famous "shit from Shinola" exchange. "Some of the funniest stuff in the movie came out of those drives," Reiner remembers. "Every once in a while Steve would come up with something that wasn't in the script and I'd say, 'We've got to get that in.'"

Martin was used to performing alone on a stage, not interacting with other performers. So several of his cast mates in the movie ended up being people with whom he was already comfortable: his girlfriend, Bernadette Peters, was hired as the sweet woman with whom Navin falls in love, while Reiner himself stepped in to play the director who sues him. This helped the first-time actor overcome his nerves and stay playful.

"There was one thing I never, ever forgot," says Reiner. "It was the scene where Steve was about to kiss Bernadette. He had never kissed a girl before on-screen and was about to kiss her on the lips. But I whispered, 'Lick her face instead.' He immediately went over and really licked the side of her face. To her credit, she didn't break. She gave the perfect reaction. That's one of my happiest memories from that show."

The Jerk came together with a minimum of pain: so many shots were nailed on the first take that the movie wrapped three weeks early and under budget. However, any illusions that it would be a home-run success were shattered by a disastrous test screening in Florida. Martin was hastily dispatched on an extensive tour of America to publicize the movie. It was not something he enjoyed, hating that he had to repeat himself endlessly. Making the experience worse was a faux pas he uttered while speaking to a writer from *Playboy*. Asked the question, "What's the most nowhere place in America for you?" Martin named Terre Haute, a backwater Indiana city in which he had done an unsuccessful gig. With outraged Terre Hautians making their displeasure known, Universal, looking to tamp down the controversy, sent Martin back there to make nice with the locals.

The comedian's grand tour of the city included a look around the local manure plant and a ride on a tractor, as throngs of angry folks gathered holding signs that read WELCOME DEAN MARTIN and NOWHERE USA WELCOMES STEVE ALLEN. Martin made nice, grinning for the cameras, accepting a $20 gift certificate for Jones and Bezy Tractor Sales, and announcing that they'd get to see *The Jerk* before anyone else. He got his revenge a few years later, however: in the climax of 1982's *Dead Men Wear Plaid*, Terre Haute gets destroyed by cheese mold.

Another unusual stop on the *Jerk* tour was at the Comedy Store on L.A.'s Sunset Boulevard, where the final round of a nationwide Steve Martin look-alike contest was taking place. Wearing a $2,000 pink suit, possibly so as not to be confused with the six contestants, Martin sat in the audience, did some good-natured heckling, and eventually picked a winner: Mark Phillips, a diabetes researcher from Nashville. The evening concluded with all of the impersonators dancing alongside their hero onstage.

As a final push for the movie, he and Reiner decided to do something unprecedented and suitably silly: host a glitzy world premiere not for *The Jerk*, but for its two-minute trailer. Keeping poker faces on throughout, they arrived at the Village Theater in Westwood in limos and did interviews on the red carpet, Reiner attesting that the trailer was "a director's dream—it came in on time and $94 under budget." Inside, the lights dimmed as Martin made a brief speech, the trailer played, and then, fewer than five minutes after the event had begun, the audience poured back out onto the street.

The actual movie, all ninety-four minutes of it, opened on December 14, 1979, to harsh reviews. "*The Jerk* is all gags and very little comedy," sniffed Roger Ebert in *The Chicago Sun-Times*. "We get a sense that the cast and crew arrived at a location, found the script bankrupt of real laughs, and started looking around for funny props." Almost across the board, it was unfairly decried as an unsophisticated, lightweight trifle, a waste of everyone's talents.

It was, at least, a big hit, making $73.7 million and ensuring that Martin's movie career wasn't dead in the water. He was now the owner of two houses, one in Aspen and another on the California coast, with a stunning view of the Pacific Ocean. An art enthusiast who bought his first piece (a print of the Hollywood sign by Ed Ruscha) at the age of nineteen, he had filled one room of his L.A. home with his burgeoning collection, sometimes sitting in it for hours at a time, gazing at his purchases. He had a beautiful girlfriend who was becoming a star in her own right. From the outside, it looked like the thirty-five-year-old had everything. But he was sensitive enough that the negative press stung.

"I remember being in Hawaii at the end of the '70s for a promotional event," Martin says. "*The Jerk* had just come out and was very controversial at the time. And Peter Sellers came up to me at this event and said, 'I know you're under a lot of criticism right now, but I know what you're doing.' It was really nice, a big moment for me."

STEVE MARTIN HAD WRITTEN a tiny part in *The Jerk* for Bill Murray: a flamboyant interior decorator who offers to do up Navin's mansion. While shooting it, Murray strolled up to Carl Reiner and whispered, "I don't know why you're doing this scene. You don't need it." The director came to the same conclusion, cutting it in post-production.

Murray, who had attended the world premiere of the trailer and kicked back at the after-party with Martin, took the opportunity to get pretend revenge via *Saturday Night Live*. "Steve Martin is a friend," he announced from behind the "Weekend Update" desk. "As a matter of fact, I was in the movie but got cut out of it. That doesn't influence my opinion. The movie is a *dog*." He went on to pan *1941*, out in theaters the same week. "War: what is it good for? Absolutely nothing, and so is *1941*. . . . Steve Spielberg is good with the mechanical shark and the flying saucer, but the guy wouldn't know funny if it bit him in the underwear."

One of nine siblings ("Ed, Brian, Nancy, Peggy, Laura, Andy, John, and Joel," he liked to rattle off), Murray's formative years were spent in Wilmette, Illinois. Even more insubordinate than the young Aykroyd or Belushi, he was kicked out of the Boy Scouts before even being issued a uniform. It cost him when it came to the casting of his school play. "I'm still bitter about this," he says. "It was a grade-school nativity play and I was beaten out for the role of the innkeeper. Matt Klein got it instead. I ended up being in the choir and we had to wear these cardboard halos. I don't know why I wasn't chosen as the innkeeper, or Joseph. I suppose I wasn't holy at the time."

Murray's was a Catholic household, but a rowdy one. "No drunken audience could ever compare to working our dinner table," he said in 1981. "If you got a laugh, it was like winning a National Merit Scholarship." His father, Edward, was a thin, quiet, diabetic man, a lumber salesman by trade, who could still administer a mighty smack; Bill would study him scientifically, figuring out how to make him laugh, not least so he could talk himself out of trouble when he got busted for something. "One of my strongest childhood impressions," he wrote in his slim 1999 golf book cum memoir *Cinderella Story*, "is falling off my chair at the dinner table while doing a Jimmy Cagney impression. I hit my head very hard on the metal foot of the table leg, and it hurt terribly. But when I saw my father laughing, I laughed while crying at the same time. I guess that was some kind of beginning."

With his mother, Lucille, not often prone to jollity either, the Murray Christmas tree had few exciting gifts beneath it come December. Mostly the kids got school clothes. Once Brian wrapped up some wooden blocks from Edward's lumberyard for a joke. Another year, Bill, feeling lazy, wrapped up some cashew nuts in tinfoil.

At this point, the notion of a career in entertainment didn't occur to him. Instead he wanted to be a doctor, perhaps because of his father's illness, as well as the polio one of his sisters suffered from. But few could imagine him occupying any position of authority. He routinely defied the Jesuit priests at Loyola Academy, a Roman Catholic school where discipline was meted out roughly. One time an assistant principal slammed him into his locker, something he claimed left the combination imprinted on his spine. Another teacher, a burly ex-boxer, customarily socked him in the solar plexus if he misbehaved in class.

Each punishment only made his anger simmer closer to the boil. "I was an underachiever and a screw-off," is how Murray remembers those days. "Studying was boring . . . I was basically causing trouble all the time." His favorite book told the tale of Davy Crockett, who ran away from home as a child, something the young Murray dreamed about doing himself. And when his father died when he was seventeen, he retreated into his shell even more. "At that point, the only decent relationship I had in the house was with the dog. I'd walk the streets of Evanston all night long."

He was a loner, a brawler, a joint smoker. He dropped out of college after one year, trying his hand at landscaping, pizza making, and construction work. In September 1970, on his twentieth birthday, Murray was overheard at Chicago's O'Hare Airport joking to a fellow passenger that he had two bombs in his suitcase. Security confiscated the case, which contained no explosives but instead five bricks of Jamaican marijuana. Murray spent his birthday evening in jail; the bust made the front page of the next day's *Chicago Tribune*. He was spared serious prison time as a first-time offender, instead being placed on probation for five years.

To anyone looking on, it seemed like the youngster was on a grim downward spiral. Yet Murray's anarchic sense of humor, the exact thing that had landed him in hot water with airport security, was to prove his salvation. Invited to fill in for his brother Brian on a Second City tour, he was a hit with audiences, his wild improvisational riffs and ferocious commitment to whatever bit he was doing inspiring roars of laughter. He transferred to New York, joined the *National Lampoon* crew—John Belushi, Gilda Radner, Brian, Harold Ramis, Joe Flaherty—and quickly acquired a taste for the lifestyle.

"We drank Champa Tampas . . . Champagne and orange juice," he later recalled. "It's a great drink to work on because it's got that sugar pump, and it's nice and cold. And the air-conditioning was no good in that place, and we were just drenched with sweat. After three shows on a Saturday night, you'd literally have to wrap up your shirt in a paper bag and put it inside a plastic bag."

Despite this new lease on life, Murray's edge remained razor sharp. According to people attending a performance of *The National Lampoon Show* in New York, after folksinger Martin Mull talked loudly throughout Murray attacked him backstage, bellowing, *"I'll kill him! I'll kill that fucker!"* He grabbed Mull by the neck and had to be restrained by Belushi. Another night, in Toronto, where the audiences were rowdier, he dragged a drunk heckler out into an alley and pummeled him, breaking the guy's arm. "He's fearless and physically strong, so if anybody wants to start a fight with him he'll go, 'All right,'" says Dave Thomas, who was there. "He's not shy about throwing his fists around."

Murray was gaining a reputation as an unpredictable force of nature, sometimes kind and sweet, sometimes dangerous. As a kid, his nickname had been Sleepy, bestowed on him after he kept nodding off on the baseball field. "That's why they made me the catcher," he explains. "So I wouldn't fall asleep." But Dan Aykroyd, who had been given a personal tour of Chicago by Murray on their first meeting, drinking cans of beer as they drove around the city, came up with an inspired new moniker: the Murricane. "Because he can come at you with hurricane force," says Ivan Reitman, one of the many who would use the nickname. "Both in terms of the comedy that he creates around himself, and also if he's unhappy with you the kind of anger he can generate."

Murray's raw talent made it virtually inevitable that he'd follow his buddies onto TV. And sure enough, when Chevy Chase unexpectedly left *Saturday Night Live*, Murray was drafted in as a replacement. He arrived in New York in true Bill Murray style, driving his battered old Nash Rambler all the way from California. But he was hardly an instant smash, as Chase had been. His first appearances were unremarkable: Murray got stuck in insignificant parts in sketches, and when he did get lines he often flubbed them. He began to feel like a lemon, unappreciated by the writers and show runners. "I became the second cop," he reflected years later. "I was getting paid, but I was playing that second cop every week."

Finally, he decided he'd had enough. He talked to Lorne Michaels, and they came up with a sketch in which he would address the viewing audience directly. On March 19, 1977, shortly after Dr. John performed his song "Let's Make a Better World," the show cut to Murray sitting behind a desk. Wearing a smart red sweater, his hair neatly combed, he looked somberly into the camera and delivered a three-minute monologue. "I'm a little bit concerned. I don't think I'm making it on the show. I'm a funny guy but I haven't been so funny on the show. My friends say, 'How come they're givin' you all those parts that aren't funny?' Well, it's not the material. It's *me*. . . ."

He went on, explaining that his father died when he was seventeen and that all he wanted was to make him proud. "I just want to make it as a Not Ready for Prime Time Player," he said with a frown. "When that's done, I'll be able to stand here on a Saturday night, in the middle of Rockefeller Plaza, New York City, New York 10020 . . . and say, 'Dad? I did it.' He'd like that."

Murray's father *had* died when he was seventeen, and it had all the makings of a genuine plea. But beneath the sentiment there was just a flicker of a smirk. That night the *SNL* audience witnessed three minutes that were somehow phony and sincere simultaneously, as well as funny, truly original, and weirdly charming.

In other words, vintage Bill Murray.

IVAN REITMAN TRIED the number again. *Ring-ring. Ring-ring. Ring-ring.* Finally, he put the telephone receiver down. All around him was the sound of laughter, but that only made him feel worse. His nightmare was intensifying.

Meatballs was cooked up out of envy. Reitman had wanted to direct *National Lampoon's Animal House* himself—after all, he had spent two years of his life working on the script and had done more than anyone to secure John Belushi for the project. But Universal had nixed the idea, unimpressed by Reitman's only directorial credit: the $12,000 horror-comedy *Cannibal Girls*. So Reitman ended up producing, with John Landis bagging the gig instead, and the lion's share of the glory. "I thought John had done a great job directing the film, but I was frustrated," Reitman admits. "It was fine and everything to be the producer, but really my creative desire was to get back to directing. So I called up a couple of my friends in Canada, Dan Goldberg and Len Blum, and said, 'Let's go make a film.'"

The three buddies had all gone to summer camp in Ontario, and it occurred to them that the environment would be fertile fodder for a knockabout comedy. They started scribbling the screenplay in March 1978, aiming to be shooting it in early August: a lightning-fast incubation period that afforded the project far less finessing time than *Animal House* had had. There was no time for second-guessing. The original title, *Summer Camp*, turned out to already be the name of a film, so they switched it to *Meatballs*, a culinary camp staple. The premise, meanwhile, was essentially *Animal House Jr.*, the tale of two rival camps at war with each other: cheapo but good-hearted Camp North Star versus wealthy, sneery Camp Mohawk. There was a Bluto figure in the form of Tripper Harrison, Camp North Star's slobbish head counselor. Reitman even called up *Animal House* composer Elmer Bernstein, asking him to make music for his movie too.

As summer began, Goldberg drove all over Canada, pleading with real camps to let them shoot on their grounds, since the $1.5 million budget wouldn't allow them to build their own. He got no after no, until Camp White Pine, up in Haliburton, Ontario, agreed. It was a huge obstacle cleared, giving *Meatballs* free sets and five hundred inexpensive extras, in the form of the real White Pine campers.

But an even bigger problem remained. With the first day of filming rushing up, the movie still didn't have a star. Some of the cast had heard that Dan Aykroyd would be playing Tripper, but in reality there was only one person Reitman wanted. And Bill Murray was not playing ball.

In fact, he was watching other people playing ball. "That summer

Bill was following some triple-A baseball team around the country," recalls Reitman. "I had worked with him the year before on the Lampoon show, so I did have a decent personal relationship with him, but it was incredibly hard to get him on the phone. I knew that he was spectacularly talented, so without him knowing it we designed *Meatballs* with him at the center. But the problem was that he really wasn't inclined to work that summer."

Reitman tried everything, sending copies of the script to baseball stadiums where he suspected Murray would show up, and pleading with Murray's lawyer to pass on messages. The brief responses that came back were hardly encouraging: "Bill's thinking about it," "Bill's not sure." As August arrived, the director moved up to Camp White Pine to prepare for the arrival of cast and crew, still without a bite on his line.

As he tried Murray's home number again and again from the camp phone, he slipped into an increasingly dark mood.

"It wasn't like I didn't audition anyone else," Reitman says. "I auditioned a lot of people. But the voice I'd had stuck in my head as I worked on the script was his, and I just couldn't see compromising on it. I had this terrible feeling that unless I had Bill, the film was not going to work. And I just wasn't going to allow that to happen."

The truth was that while other cast members at *Saturday Night Live* leaped at the chance to star in a movie, Murray was trepidatious about the idea. At the time he was living in a $300-a-month loft on New York's Upper East Side, with no TV, no stereo, a bare double mattress on the floor to sleep on, and a refrigerator he unplugged because its loud hum was giving him headaches. Compared to John Belushi's and Dan Aykroyd's new luxury homes in Martha's Vineyard, it was a lousy state of affairs. But the idea of becoming more famous scared the hell out of him.

"One advantage [of joining *Saturday Night Live* late] was that I was able to watch my friends going through the fame thing before I did," Murray told T. J. English in 1988. "I learned a lot about it by watching them. When I met Dan and John after that, boy, were they different. I thought, 'Oh Jesus. When you get famous, something weird happens to you.' It's just a mechanical thing. When everyone starts kissing your butt, you just walk bent over."

So while he golfed and snarfed down baseball-stadium hot dogs over the summer of 1978, he grappled with the decision. Then, finally, he made up his mind. The day that filming began on *Meatballs*, Murray's lawyer called Reitman back, confirming that the star was in. On the second day of filming, the man himself strolled into Camp White Pine, clad in a Hawaiian shirt and red shorts and clutching a dogeared copy of the script. "At least I knew he had read it," says Reitman, "or at least couriered it around with him everywhere he went. And he just showed it to me and sneered, in that wonderful way he can, and said, 'You know, this is kinda crap.'"

At *Saturday Night Live*, Murray read off cue cards. He quickly made it clear that he wouldn't be doing the same on *Meatballs*. In fact, he began most scenes by reading the script, then tossing it on the floor and saying, "I got this." He not only improvised over half of his lines, but insisted on wearing the clothes he'd turned up in, rather than the prepared costume. And instead of fighting it, Reitman generally let Murray roll.

It worked, turning the movie into a delivery system for the star's slovenly, party-blitzed charms. The line that would become the movie's philosophical core, "It just doesn't matter," uttered by Tripper to help the kids in his charge realize that it's OK to lose as well as win, came from something Murray said to Reitman in a coffee shop. The character's unorthodox seduction technique, grabbing female counterpart Roxanne (Kate Lynch) in a wrestling move, was based on the star's real-life (and decidedly socially primitive) method of courtship.

But Murray's most significant effect on the story concerned the friendship between Tripper and troubled youngster Rudy (Chris Makepeace). The original script for *Meatballs* focused on the antics of the CITs, young camp counselors played by Canadian unknowns. But the scenes between Murray and Makepeace proved so sweet and funny that Reitman ordered extensive reshoots to expand on that part of the story. Just as Tripper teaches Rudy how to play cards, jog, and burp, so Murray showed his young co-star how to shave. Their relationship was the same on-screen and off, and *Meatballs*, most unexpectedly, became a movie with an oversized heart.

"It turned out far better than we expected," says Reitman, "but when you hire Bill Murray you never know quite what's going to happen. Even back in those days he was the nerviest and most confident person in any group. If he saw a group of people standing on the street, he'd go up to them and engage them in dialogue, or start hollering, in that 'honker' voice he ended up using as the gardener character in *Caddyshack*, 'Watch out! There's a lobster on the loose!' And these strangers would laugh, instead of thinking of him as dangerous. He could take over situations through the magic he wove."

While trying to woo Murray in pre-production, the director had promised that if the movie stunk, it would disappear, not hurting his career. In fact, the messy, low-budget Canadian comedy was a hit—not an *Animal House*–size one, admittedly, but a $50 million charmer that had kids cackling in theaters and imitating Tripper's wrestling moves.

It would spawn three increasingly desperate sequels, but Murray wouldn't star in any of them. His stint at camp was over. He was ready to face the big wide world.

HIT IT

ON THE CORNER of Hudson and Dominick, just south of New York's Greenwich Village, sat a four-story tenement building. With darkened windows and garbage cans overflowing outside, it wasn't much to look at. In any case, this was a truly filthy part of town, industrial and bleak. Passersby would hustle past without giving the place a second glance.

If only they knew.

Those who had received an invitation would venture down the dark alley to the building's side. There, at a small door wreathed in shadows, they would utter the pass code, "Big Jake summoned us." The door would creak open, giving them entry to a real-life Ali Baba's Cave of Wonders: the Blues Bar.

This after-hours joint was the brainchild of John Belushi and Dan Aykroyd, designed as a place to let their hair down after tapings of *Saturday Night Live*. A former garage where Aykroyd had once stored his Harleys, it had been converted into a private bar, although it likely would have made any health-and-safety inspector blanch. The wallpaper was peeling off. The ceiling was crumbling. As for the bathroom facilities, you'd be better off using a trash can on the street outside.

The toilets in the 505 Club, Aykroyd's former after-hours joint in Toronto, had been so grim that Aykroyd had once heard a scuffling sound as he perched on a seat, and looked down to see a slimy rat scrabbling up toward his privates. The facilities in his new place were equally terrifying, despite him placing a red plastic rose in the women's room—a none-more-Aykroydian touch.

At least one woman did venture in: Laraine Newman, member of the original *SNL* cast. "When I saw *Trainspotting*, they had a sign: 'The Filthiest Toilet in Scotland,'" she recalled. "Well, the toilet at the Blues Bar was the filthiest toilet *anywhere*. It was so vile. Nothing short of Turkish torture with a hole in the ground."

Its many hygiene issues aside, the covert speakeasy quickly became the most rocking joint in town. You might find a Hollywood star like Richard Dreyfuss lounging in the corner, an A-list director like Francis Ford Coppola holding court, or a rock god like Keith Richards taking a turn behind the bar, pulling pints of Heineken. The drinks were all free, as was the jukebox, stuffed with rare tunes. There were musical instruments on demand, in case guests like David Bowie or ZZ Top got an urge to jam. And there were drugs—lots of drugs. Parties went on until well after dawn.

Here, Belushi and Aykroyd could do whatever they liked. And what they liked to do more than anything was play the blues. Aykroyd was the earliest adopter: he'd learned to play the harmonica at sixteen and had since accrued an encyclopedic knowledge of the works of James Cotton and Pinetop Perkins. Belushi grew up preferring hard rock. He drummed with Animal-from-the-Muppets enthusiasm in a high school band called the Ravins; his vinyl collection was smothered with Cream. But an encounter with Curtis Salgado during the *Animal House* shoot instilled in him an enthusiasm for blues that soon became a hurricane-strength obsession. "I couldn't stop playing the stuff!" Belushi enthused a year on. "Magic Sam, Lightnin' Hopkins, Junior Wells—I walked around playing that shit all the time." He bought hundreds of records, creating towering stacks of them all over his home, often playing only a minute of one before he'd excitedly put on another.

But listening to it wasn't enough. The pair began performing blues sets themselves, first at the Blues Bar, then as a warm-up act at *SNL*. They approached it as they would a skit, creating characters to enhance the performance. The look was inspired by an outfit Belushi had worn once to play Roy Orbison: white shirts, black serge suits, ribbon ties, porkpie hats, and sunglasses. "The glasses are crucial, man," explained Aykroyd. "The band has got to have the right look or the whole thing won't work. It's essential that we get Ray-Bans, model number 5022-G15."

Finally, the act got a name, suggested by *Saturday Night Live* bandleader Howard Shore: "the Blues Brothers."

Aykroyd and Belushi were accustomed to mocking everyone and everything. But their new endeavor was irony-free. They took the music seriously, deadly seriously, and although blues was currently out of vogue in America, their reverence started to rub off. Lorne Michaels allowed the Blues Brothers on *SNL* proper in 1976, on the condition they perform in bee costumes. "Boy, that was a dog performance," Belushi later winced. By the time they appeared again on November 18, 1978, they were big enough to open the show, with a finely polished act.

Poker-faced, Joliet "Jake" Blues (Belushi) and his brother Elwood (Aykroyd) stride onstage, Elwood's wrist handcuffed to a briefcase. Jake produces a key and opens the case. Elwood removes a Marine Band harmonica. As the intro music finishes, Jake does a clumsy cartwheel across the stage. Then they proceed to play a storming rendition of Sam & Dave's *Soul Man*, Belushi bellowing into the mike, Aykroyd breaking into a peculiar, frenzied dance-stomp as if he's battling a torrent of fire ants.

The shtick killed, and not just in New York. Around the same time, the Blues Brothers opened for Steve Martin at the colossal Universal Amphitheater in Los Angeles. Backstage, while Martin nibbled fresh fruit and raw vegetables, Belushi gulped beer and yelled for a chili dog. "We haven't eaten one meal sitting down in three days," he explained to an onlooker. "Can't take the time. I haven't changed my socks or underwear in four days. This is the blues, man."

Then he and Aykroyd hit the stage, Belushi executing a less clumsy triple cartwheel, to find six thousand fans stomping their feet. Among them were Mick Jagger, Henry Winkler, Walter Matthau, and Jack Nicholson—all wearing Blues Brothers buttons. The show was a roaring success: somebody dashed into Aykroyd's trailer afterward and stole his Ray-Bans. "When they finished, half the audience got up and left," remembers Dave Thomas. "And then Steve came out and I felt terrible for him. It was like, 'What the hell?!'" It was an even bigger hit on record: an edit of the nine Amphitheater shows was released as an album, *Briefcase Full of Blues*, selling 3.5 million copies worldwide.

"It was incredible," says John Landis, who got married on the day of the opening and took the entire wedding party to the gig. "At that moment, John and Danny were the stars of the number-one TV show in the country, John was the star of the number-one movie in the country, *Animal House*, and they had, as a recording act, the number-one record in the world." What had happened to Chase and Belushi had finally happened to Aykroyd too. "At *SNL*, Lorne was always warning all of us, 'Your lives are going to change. It's public access now. You're part of the *matsuri bayashi*; you're one of the dancing girls owned by the state,'" Aykroyd remembers. "Lorne warned us and warned us."

Not everyone was impressed. "It's too good to be a parody, and not good enough to be good for what it was," sniped Jerry Garcia of the Grateful Dead, who performed on the same bill at one festival. But it was clear that what had started as a gas had become a phenomenon. A movie was inevitable.

NEGOTIATIONS WERE FIERCE. Don Simpson, the legendarily wild Hollywood producer, turned up at *SNL* one week in an attempt to woo Jake and Elwood to Paramount. Other studios left pleading voicemails. But it was Universal who was, once more, to take a risk on the stars. Belushi was promised $500,000, Aykroyd $250,000. "Those guys were like bloody meat in shark-infested water," said studio vice president Sean Daniel. "We wasted no time in making the deal."

Belushi was to be reunited with his *Animal House* director. John

Landis had used that movie's success to try to kick-start an action-comedy called *The Incredible Shrinking Woman* with Lily Tomlin. He was well into pre-production in 1978, building miniature sets, designing costumes, and obtaining permission to not only stage an assassination on the steps of the Capitol in Washington, DC, but shoot a chase with a gorilla through the Smithsonian. Then Tomlin's new film, a romantic drama with John Travolta called *Moment by Moment*, came out. It was such a box-office calamity that it not only torpedoed Travolta's white-hot career, putting him on the skids until 1996's *Pulp Fiction*, but compelled Universal to slash the budget of *The Incredible Shrinking Woman*. Landis flew into a panic, which was cut short when the studio shut the project down altogether. Fortunately, the Blues Brothers were waiting. A hasty deal was made in early 1979: Aykroyd, Belushi, and Landis could make what they wanted, on the condition it met its release date in June 1980.

There was only one problem: there was no script.

Aykroyd, the keeper of Blues Brothers lore, had never written a screenplay in his life. In fact, he'd never read one either. Still, he'd spent many a night at the Blues Bar pondering what a Jake-and-Elwood movie might look like. He had two somewhat surprising touchstones in mind: Bernardo Bertolucci's five-hour Italian political drama *1900* and Stanley Kubrick's candlelit period piece *Barry Lyndon*. Neither of those films is a comedy; both, however, are mammoth in scale.

As Aykroyd tapped away on his typewriter, everyone waited. And waited. And waited. "I was going crazy, because it's Danny who works in mysterious ways," says Landis. "Finally, he threw the script over the garden fence of Bob Weiss, the producer. And it was huge, the size of a phone book. In fact, as a gag he'd put it inside the cover of an actual phone book."

Titled *The Return of the Blues Brothers*, it was credited to a robot called the Scriptatron XL 9000 and clocked in at 324 pages, roughly three times the size of a normal screenplay. Aykroyd's imagination was like an out-of-control fire hose, twirling around in all directions, ideas spraying out, and his first screenplay was overflowing with material: lengthy subplots for all eight members of the Blues Brothers band, plus weird digressions on Catholicism, recidivism, and automobile engines. "It might be a little too big for the studio to make," he admitted, when someone managed to track him down.

Time was of the essence. Landis frantically tackled the document, trying to make it filmable, slashing scenes and paring down the more peculiar digressions. Though unwieldy, Aykroyd's script was also brilliant, fleshing out the sullen siblings' backstory—they were raised by nuns at an orphanage and turned on to blues by Curtis, a musician named in tribute to Curtis Salgado—and giving them a clear objective, to raise money to save said orphanage. It also featured the biggest car chase in cinema history, the beats of which were now plotted out by Landis. "I wrote a heavy, urban experience," said Aykroyd. "What he did was to put a little Disney flash into it, you know what I mean? And the blend worked really well."

With locations rapidly scouted in Chicago, the project was ready to begin. Perhaps if the clock hadn't been ticking, the Universal executives would have asked a few more questions. But the project, now simply called *The Blues Brothers*, had gained unstoppable momentum. "They just said, 'Go!'" recalls Landis. "There was never a budgetary process of any kind. We were just shot into space."

For now, everyone was smiling. So much so that in July 1979 Universal placed a jokey announcement in *Variety* and the *Hollywood Reporter*. "It's too late," it read. "Production has begun."

THE MOVIE'S PLOT saw Jake and Elwood track down each member of their band and convince them to play, by any means necessary. In one of the most famous scenes, they hunker down in a restaurant where trumpeter Mr. Fabulous (Alan Rabin) is working as a maître d', and they cause chaos—"How much for the women and children?" growls Jake at fellow diners—until he gives in and leaves with them. The sequence is not as outlandish as one might think. When the Blues Brothers first began to come together as a serious concept, Belushi took charge of musician recruitment—a project he approached in typically unorthodox style.

"He phoned around three in the morning and woke me out of a sound sleep," recalled Donald "Duck" Dunn, session bassist for Stax Records. "He said he was John Belushi and he was gonna make me rich and famous."

Being Belushi, he succeeded in sweet-talking every person on his and Aykroyd's wish list. The Blues Brothers band was stuffed with the best session musicians in the business. As for the roster of cameos they lined up for the movie, it was a staggering list of song-and-dance legends: James Brown, Aretha Franklin, Cab Calloway, Ray Charles, and John Lee Hooker. Although it wasn't as hard to bag them as one might expect. "In 1979 the big acts were ABBA and the Bee Gees," says Landis. "Ray Charles was doing well—he was doing country-and-western at the time—but rhythm-and-blues was totally out of fashion. That was one of the reasons we were able to get everyone with a phone call. It was a unique situation where Danny and John used their celebrity to focus attention on these brilliant artists."

The Blues Brothers was not just to feature songs; it was a full-on musical, the likes of which just weren't made anymore. On a freezing October morning, a crowd of extras congregated in a poverty-stricken Chicago ghetto, to perform a Busby Berkeley–style dance number to "Shake Your Tail Feather." Franklin performed a barn-burning version of "Think," although her inability to lip-sync caused problems in the editing room. For the big finale, Jake and Elwood's orphanage-saving mega-gig, Landis filled the Hollywood Palladium with radio-competition winners, all of them enraptured at seeing their heroes live onstage. Aykroyd and Belushi got them even more amped by initiating a pretend auction, asking for bids on a live goat, a Styrofoam cup, and Aykroyd himself. (Asked how much he was going for, he shot back, "Seven dollars and ninety-eight cents' worth of chemicals. Just cut me open and see.") Looking out into the audience, Belushi cooed, "What an attractive crowd! They pass out those hash joints I rolled?"

If the film had just been musical numbers, its shoot would have been tough but manageable. But the makers of *The Blues Brothers* wanted it all. Aykroyd had been able to indulge his motor-head tendencies to the max while writing the script: the Bluesmobile, a 1974 Dodge Monaco

440 ex–police cruiser, was very deliberately a vehicle from before the dawn of unleaded gas. It also had magical powers, capable of performing almost any stunt, a fact the film seemed determined to prove. An early scene sees it leap over a rising bascule bridge, for no apparent reason. Later, it trashes a shopping mall and forces a squadron of Illinois Nazis into a river.

And then there's the climactic chase. "It's 106 miles to Chicago, we got a full tank of gas, half a pack of cigarettes, it's dark and we're wearing sunglasses," summarizes Elwood. "Hit it," orders Jake. Cue a clattering demolition derby, packed with hair-raising stunts and choreographed as if the cars are performing an asphalt ballet.

As those scenes began to be shot, the production finally got people's full attention, both at the studio and everywhere else. "The story became: *Hollywood out of control!*" recalls Landis. "$24 million was the magic number in terms of budget, because that was *Cleopatra*. That was the number that sunk Fox, that forced a studio to sell its back lot. And at that time, there were five Hollywood films in production that surpassed it: *1941*, *Blues Brothers*, *Heaven's Gate*, *Apocalypse Now*, and *Star Trek*. We were getting so much heat in the press. But it's undeniable that we were ginormous. We were doing these massive military operations with 110 cars going over 100 miles an hour in downtown Chicago. We had hundreds of extras and stunt people. And gosh, in one scene we had almost five hundred PAs. We had to make sure there was someone with a walkie-talkie at every possible alley or entrance to this street, because it took the cars three blocks to get up to full speed."

Poor Ned Tanen, the Universal chief who had gotten palpitations from *Animal House* and suffered through *1941*, was having another rotten time. Every morning, he had to sit through a tense phone conversation with his superior, Lew Wasserman, who was becoming increasingly irate over the film's soaring budget. The calls generally began with Wasserman yelling, *"Goddammit!"* Tanen had looked foolish early on, when he announced to journalists that the film would cost $11 million; in reality it had burned through that amount already. And he'd had to endure a Category-5 Wasserman tantrum after word reached L.A. that Belushi and Aykroyd had boosted Nazi uniforms from Wardrobe and driven around Chicago in them.

A visit to the set failed to lower Tanen's blood pressure. After looking around the "War Room"—a chamber strewn with charts for upcoming action sequences—he headed back to the airport with an ashen face. Both he and Wasserman had suddenly woken up to what kind of bizarre mongrel they had on their hands: a stupendously expensive musical-comedy spectacular, with outdated songs and stars whose eyes were permanently covered by sunglasses. Wasserman's daily telephone greeting became "*Goddamn* that director!"

In fact, Belushi was more to blame for the delays than Landis. *1941* had seen him lapse into bad behavior; now, he was in full-on Galactus mode, gobbling LSD, amphetamines, and Quaaludes. Part of the film's budget was set aside for cocaine for night shoots, the only time Aykroyd would join in too. According to guest star Carrie Fisher, who had hosted the *SNL* episode that the Blues Brothers opened, and who was playing Joliet Jake's jilted lover, Belushi scored mescaline from a girl who cleaned the fish tank at a local bar. Although Belushi was such a hero in Chicago that he could hail police cars like taxis anytime he wanted a ride, he was becoming increasingly lawless. Four days of shooting had to be abandoned entirely due to his being unable to perform. And even when he was capable of delivering lines, he wasn't exactly in peak form. "It turned out those dark glasses were a good thing," says Landis. "It wasn't our intention, but it worked out well that you couldn't see John's eyes."

Belushi's misdeeds have been chronicled at length in Bob Woodward's book *Wired*. Landis, however, insists that's an exaggerated account. "It's crap. Forgive me, but it's crap. It opens with this sensational account of an altercation between me and John that's written like Mickey Spillane. But John did have a terrible problem on the movie. *Animal House*, he was clean and wonderful in every way. He was just a very sweet guy, who became an addict. And it was terrifying. It's like a drowning person: you jump in the water to try and save them and they punch you in the face. There's just nothing you can do."

BY SUMMER 1980, *The Blues Brothers* had acquired a new nickname in the industry: *1942*. And not because Landis had returned the favor and given Spielberg a cameo, as a tax clerk who gets dozens of gun barrels stuck in his face. The final budget for the film had clocked in at around $32 million, almost triple Ned Tanen's claim to the press. Eighteen months earlier, everyone had been cheering for Jake and Elwood, dressing up in imitation costumes. Now it looked like their big-screen adventure could very well end up being one of the costliest flops of all time.

Paranoia began to set in. "The critics will gun us down," announced Aykroyd, after watching the final cut twice in twenty-four hours. "They will kill us. They want to see us fail. They will singe Belushi and singe me. We'll get hit by the barrage and we'll really feel it, but there will be a day when John Belushi and Danny Aykroyd movies will be fuckin' history."

Preview screenings for exhibitors and bookers had not gone well. "They were wearing white shoes and smoking cigars!" reported Landis after one. "Fifty percent hated it. 'Too many car crashes. . . . The plot makes no sense. . . . Too many *nee-groes.*'" So he and Aykroyd hunkered down in the edit suite to undertake damage control, cutting the film into a more commercial shape. Gone was their dream of having an interval in the middle. A scene explaining how the Bluesmobile gets its supernatural qualities went in the trims bin. Even a $300,000 explosion was yanked out of its reel: this was no time for sentimentality. The run time was reduced by twenty minutes, down to a shade over two hours.

Even so, multiplex owners were sniffy: Mann Theaters refused to show it in Westwood, a prosperous white neighborhood, and it secured only around 600 bookings across the country, nothing like the 1,400 a big-budget movie usually got.

It turned out that Aykroyd was right in his doomy prediction. The critics did get their biggest guns out, and shrapnel flew everywhere.

"A $30 million wreck, minus laughs," went the first review, from the *Los Angeles Times*. The volley from the East Coast was even more brutal. "A ponderous comic monstrosity," proclaimed Gary Arnold in the *Washington Post*, before zeroing in on the moment where Belushi lowers his Ray-Bans for the only time in the movie: "Never, never, never should anyone, especially a performer with expressive eyes, be allowed the imbecilic drollery of concealing them from a motion picture audience." Even the soundtrack got assailed, Dave Marsh of *Rolling Stone* calling Aykroyd and Belushi's spin on African American music patronizing.

But Jake and Elwood had survived Nazis, rednecks, and the entire Illinois law-enforcement community. Their mission from God sure as heck wasn't going to be stopped by espresso-sipping critics. Accompanied by a blizzard of merchandise (including a tie-in book by Belushi's wife, Judy), *The Blues Brothers* hit screens on the agreed-upon date: June 20, 1980. And though it couldn't compete with box-office rival *The Empire Strikes Back*, it did become one of the year's top-ten hits, making $57 million in the United States and an even bigger figure overseas. Ray-Ban Wayfarers, which had been on the verge of getting axed by the company, suddenly became a must-have item. The musicians featured in the film found themselves in demand again. America had officially caught the blues.

This deeply odd amalgam of crunching automobile action, soulful music, and chilly urban desolation, with criminal heroes who rarely talk, actually worked. Like *1941*, it was a film that roared with excess, but in this case too much of a good thing turned out to be just the right amount. Instead of the desperation of Spielberg's movie, *The Blues Brothers* has a laidback confidence, despite its tumultuous production. Landis and Aykroyd would not be so lucky when it came to the 1998 sequel, *Blues Brothers 2000*. "It was very, very, very truncated and fucked up by the studio," says the director. "By the time they were done with us, they'd castrated the whole thing. They insisted it be PG-rated, which meant no profanity. They insisted it have a child. They were essentially doing everything they could to make us not make it."

Even if that hadn't been the case, what would a Blues Brothers movie be without John Belushi? Even hobbled by narcotics, he and Aykroyd made a powerful double act—it was hard to imagine one without the other. With a hit movie under their belts, they looked ahead to the '80s, making plans for their next step. Neither they, nor their legions of fans, suspected that their days together were numbered.

DR. GONZO AND THE GOPHER

CHEVY CHASE FELL all the way to the top. He was the prince of the pratfall, the lord of lunges, a stumblebum extraordinaire. After years of practice he had his moves down pat. One moment he was striding forward with a cocky grin on his face, the next his six-foot-four frame was plummeting through the air, arms akimbo, diving, diving, en route to a hard collision with the ground. Even when you knew it was coming, the trip looked real.

It also looked painful, because it was. Chase often joked that his publicity photos should come with a set of X-rays.

His love of physical comedy was inherited from his father. A writer and editor, Ned Chase liked to stop and cock his leg like a dog when he passed a fire hydrant. He also had a good gag for when visitors came to the house: he would go into the bathroom, leaving the door ajar, and slowly pour a large pitcher of water into the toilet, until anyone listening was convinced he had a bladder the size of a paddling pool. "My father was the funniest guy I ever met," Chase was to say. "I'm not sure if I stole his stuff or if I inherited it."

Despite this admiration for his dad, and his later screen image as a breezy, handsome, suntanned dude, Chevy's early life was deeply un-happy. His mother, Cathalene, had a nervous breakdown when he was a baby; his parents divorced a few years on. Her second marriage was more durable but a disaster for Chevy and his brother Ned Jr., who were regularly abused by both their mother and stepfather. A small act of rebellion would see them confined to a closet. Even if they hadn't broken one of the many household rules, they could be woken in the middle of the night and slapped, for no apparent reason.

"I lived in fear all the time, deathly fear," Chase says in his memoir, *I'm Chevy Chase and You're Not*. "I was just working to survive a life where if I got home at 6:30 and dinner was at 6, I got beaten for that."

It was an odd life: Dickensian levels of misery alternating with Ivy League privilege. Paternal grandfather Cornelius Chase, from whom Chevy got his real name, was enormously wealthy, and so the young Chase would spend holidays aboard a 200-foot yacht, or watching ser-vants scuttle about the mansion. It looked like that fortune would pass down to him. But it was not to be. Instead, Cornelius divorced his own wife, fell in love with a Zen Buddhist, and ultimately bequeathed most of his riches to a temple, leaving little for Chevy.

Chase did, however, attend a series of exclusive schools, where he quickly established a reputation as a smart-mouthed brat. Chase's antics, which saw him kicked out of both Riverdale prep school and Haverford College, were many and varied. He carried a knife. He lit his farts. On one occasion, he bit an overweight kid named Alan.

Most famously, although there is still disagreement over whether it actually happened, he brought a cow up to the second floor of a dor-mitory building at Haverford, knowing full well that cows can only ascend stairs and not come down them. "I can't discuss that—that's not fair to the cow or the cow's family," Chase stonewalled on the *Today* show in 2009 when the subject was broached, before conceding, with a sly grin, "There was a cow, on an occasion. I'll just say that much."

Like Bill Murray, Chase had early ambitions of getting into medi-cine. But once he realized how easy it was to make people laugh, he dropped that notion and decided to become a comedy writer instead. He churned through a succession of unenjoyable jobs—cabdriver, fruit picker, wine-store salesman—scribbling away all the while, writing a *Mission: Impossible* spoof for *Mad Magazine* in 1970 and working for the Smothers Brothers shortly after. They were lean, difficult years. Chase would later tell the story of the time he caught his wife, Susan, cheating on him in the cockroach-infested, one-bedroom apartment they shared in New York. The couple split up and he was left alone with his tabby cat Swipe (short for "Asswipe"); one of his subsequent girlfriends had an Irish setter that would take Swipe's entire head in its mouth and gently gnaw on it.

Chase could relate to Swipe's predicament. He felt underappreciated and bitter, the success he craved perpetually out of reach.

"There's this intense reverse elitist backlash view of a preppie like me who picks his nose for a laugh," he told Mitch Glazer of *Crawdaddy* in 1978. "Without knowing the years I lived on the Lower East Side in holes where the roaches would open the door for me. Literally. Do they know that I've had my jaw broken, my front teeth knocked out and every finger on my hand broken in fights?"

Things were rough, but slowly getting better. As the '70s went on, Chase glided from writing into acting, joining an experimental theater company called Channel One, which performed largely to a stoned audience, then teaming up with John Belushi and Christopher Guest in *National Lampoon's Lemmings*. Chase got big laughs as a Hells Angel with Tourette's, yelling, *"Shitfuckpissprickpussycockfart!"* Those laughs got even bigger when he started tumbling around and off the stage, perfecting the acrobatic falls he'd performed at school to make fellow students laugh. In the spring of 1974, Chase decided to go see *Monty Python and the Holy Grail* at the Los Angeles International Film Festival. In the line, as Chase cracked jokes and did impressions, he happened to get the attention of *Saturday Night Live* boss Lorne Michaels, then in the process of putting together the original cast. Michaels was impressed, and even more so when, on a rainy night out with Chase, he saw the fall guy in action.

"He goes into a pothole, does a complete ass-over-teakettle into this immense pothole, and comes out of this thing just soaked," remembered NBC executive Dick Ebersol. "Lorne looks at me and says,

'Now, how could you say no to somebody who was crazy enough to do that?'"

Each episode of the first season of *SNL* was to start with Chase crashing to the ground in some new and spectacular way. "Chevy's falls were incredible: ungainly and graceful at the same time," enthuses Carl Reiner, director of *The Jerk*. While Chase's persona was that of a super-relaxed, suntanned smoothie, he committed to his physical comedy with fearsome intensity. On September 18, 1976, he appeared as his legendarily clumsy take on President Gerald Ford, debating against Dan Aykroyd's Jimmy Carter. The skit finished with Chase toppling forward along with his lectern, a stunt that went badly wrong. "The prop guy, his name was Willy Day and he was about eighty-eight, and he'd forgotten to take out a middle portion of the lectern," remembered Chase. "So when I fell into it, I went right into a board. It hit me right in the tonsils. I was in the hospital for a week, peeing blood."

By this point Chase had become so essential to the show that he opened the next week's episode from the hospital, via telephone. Besides his Gerald Ford impression, which involved neither a wig nor makeup, his most famous appearances on *SNL* were on "Weekend Update," for which he would sit behind a desk, look into the camera, and spin real-life headlines into gags. The side effect was that he quickly became the show's most well-known star. One day on a bus to work he realized the other passengers were all staring at him. Another time, as he took a lunch break in December 1977, he wandered down Sixty-First Street and saw his own face looking back at him from the covers of a dozen *New York* magazines.

"Look," he said, dumbfounded, to the vendor at the newsstand.

"Yeah, that's you," confirmed the guy. "You're famous."

It changed everything. His *Saturday Night Live* cast mates started talking to him less, especially John Belushi, who had craved that stardom for himself. They thought he was becoming an obnoxious egomaniac, and the backstage tension began to bleed into the show, with one sketch seeing his colleagues stick pins into a Chevy Chase voodoo doll. It might have bothered him, but he had other things on his mind, like the beautiful women who were suddenly smiling at him from across every room. "I know that I had sex appeal," Chase later smirked, "because I know how much sex I had."

The boyish bumbler had become a man, and it began to feel like New York was holding him back. He decided his future was in Los Angeles.

ONE OF THE FIRST THINGS Chevy Chase treated himself to in L.A. was a car. Not just any car, but a gleaming silver Porsche Turbo Carrera, which he drove at reckless speeds through the Hollywood Hills as he puffed on a cigar. He couldn't get enough of the vehicle. Although his new wife, Jacqueline, a model and aspiring actress from New Jersey, referred to it derisively as "the silver penis."

That relationship, which Chase had claimed was the reason he'd left *SNL* and headed west in the first place, was soon to crash and burn. After a wild wedding in December 1976, at which Belushi got so drunk that he made out with Chase's mother, domestic serenity was soon shattered by a series of loud fights. During one, Jacqueline threw a colander at Chase's head. They were to divorce in 1980.

His professional life, at least, was on firmer ground. He had struggled for a while with his increasing fame, saying in 1976, "Acting's the most tenuous, gratuitous profession imaginable. I hate how self-indulgent actors become, that they lose all perspective. You're unable to see yourself anymore except as what agents and the press tell you you are." Two years later, he had done a one-eighty, stating, "It's bullshit to think that wanting to be a star is bullshit. Why shouldn't I want to be a star? Isn't the idea of any job upward mobility?"

In 1977, at age thirty-four, he was a huge TV celebrity, about to move into cinema, with rich deals being dangled in front of him. He would voice no regrets about turning down *National Lampoon's Animal House*. "I met with John Landis and we just didn't get on too well. I didn't think he could handle it," said Chase a half decade on, his memory of that fateful restaurant meeting differing from the director's. "The second reason I turned down *Animal House* is that I had already lived it in real life. And in real life, we were funnier and wilder and stranger than anything you saw in that film."

Paramount had more luck when they offered him *Foul Play*, a San Francisco–set caper written and directed by Colin Higgins (*Silver Streak*). The role of wry cop Tony Carlson looked like an ideal showcase for Chase's charms, a leading role that paired him with national sweetheart Goldie Hawn and let him do some trademark Chevy slapstick: in his first scene, Tony knocks over drinks at a cocktail bash.

No matter that Harrison Ford had already turned the part down.

Foul Play began shooting on location at the end of 1977, conveniently close to home. The plot was frothy, complicated nonsense, pitting Tony and a librarian (Hawn) against an albino bent on assassinating the pope, with a killer dwarf thrown in for good measure. But Chase's trademark confidence, which he had effortlessly mustered up on *Saturday Night Live*, was draining away. He agonized about scenes, fretted over how he looked in close-ups, and badgered his cast mates for advice, exasperating even the patient Hawn. "It's not an easy thing to overcome when that camera zeroes in on you," he admitted. "I couldn't stop from twitching over certain straight lines."

One of those lines in particular raised Chase's blood pressure. It required him to tell Hawn, "You have the most beautiful green eyes I've ever seen." It had to sound sincere, not goofy, and he felt it came out phony every time. The twitch on his mouth went into overdrive. Years on he would claim that the line still haunted him, a reminder of his inability to inhabit a role.

Unbeknownst to Chase, Steve Martin had also read for the part. Asked by *Playboy* after the film's release whether he felt relieved that he'd flunked his audition, Martin replied tersely, "Made me realize I don't want to do murder mysteries."

Foul Play is not edgy or cool like *Saturday Night Live*, and it's definitely not *Vertigo*, the Hitchcock film that inspired its Bay Area setting. Chase was embarrassed when he saw the finished product at the premiere. His ego had suffered its first major bruise.

Another quickly followed, as Chase decided to make his second film, *Oh! Heavenly Dog*.

Even on paper, it can't have looked good. Built as a further vehicle for Benji, a golden-furred mutt who had achieved box-office success with the 1974 film that bore his name, the idea was to cross-breed a crime story with cutesy canine fun. The character earmarked for Chase, a private investigator named Benjamin Browning, would be stabbed to death ten minutes into the film, and have his soul transferred into a stray dog so he could finish his case. It was already a weird and morbid setup. It got a lot more so with the decision to shoot in a gloomy and rain-lashed London, and if it was aimed at families, it's hard to fathom why it's littered with curse words—"Shit! Jesus!" says the Chevy-dog, before accusing a bus driver of being racist—or features scenes in which Benji first ogles Jane Seymour, then jumps into a bath with her.

As an experimental five-minute *Saturday Night Live* skit, it would have raised eyebrows but been quickly forgotten. As a feature film, sold heavily on Chase's name, it was a protracted humiliation, barely scraping together $6 million in takings. "The last thing I wanted to do was—quote, unquote—my dog movie," he said with a shrug in 1980. "But what an oddity to be able, when you're a grandfather, to have a kid on your knee and say, 'Oh yeah, I was a fireman for a while and once I played a dog in a movie.'" Decades on, he still refuses to watch it.

It wasn't a completely disastrous opening salvo: *Foul Play*, at least, was warmly received, making $44 million at the box office. But it was hardly the killer double-whammy Chase needed to justify the hype— and his $1.25 million asking price.

A LITTLE DISTANCE EAST, Bill Murray was having his own problems. One summer afternoon saw him paying a visit to the home of Hunter S. Thompson, in Aspen, Colorado. He had only met Thompson a short while before, and the legendarily debauched journalist

had taken a shine to him. This affection manifested itself in a peculiar way: during a conversation about Harry Houdini, Thompson
lashed Murray's hands and feet to the cast-iron garden chair he was
seated on, dragged the helpless comedian over to the swimming pool,
and hurled him in. Murray nearly drowned before someone dove in
and pulled him out.

His trip to Aspen wasn't a social call. Hollywood had decided that
the time was ripe to make a film about the man known as "Dr. Gonzo,"
a *Rolling Stone* contributor and a scribe so hard-living he made Ernest
Hemingway look like Edith Wharton. On one occasion, Thompson
sprayed a can of mace around a restaurant, until everyone was coughing so hard they had to evacuate. Another time, he celebrated Jack
Nicholson's birthday by leaving a frozen elk's heart on the actor's door-
step. After ringing the doorbell, Thompson scurried back to his car
and blasted a tape recording of a pig being eaten alive by bears.

Naturally, the Dunhill-puffing, tequila-chugging, chemically en-
hanced Thompson was buddies with John Belushi: the writer once
said that more fun could be had in twenty minutes of Belushi's company than you'd have in twenty years with most other people. In fact,
the concept of "gonzo"—originally South Boston Irish slang used to
describe the last man standing after a marathon drinking session, but
in Thompson's case a reference to his kamikaze lifestyle—was something that applied to many of the male performers at *Saturday Night
Live*. "In the first half of the '70s, feminist and gay rights were coming
out," said *SNL* writer Rosie Shuster, "but the New Macho guy started
to emerge in the second half of the '70s, and that was very much alive
on *Saturday Night Live*."

That included Murray, who jumped at the chance to star in the
Hunter S. Thompson movie, *Where the Buffalo Roam*, when intended
stars Belushi (set to play Thompson) and Aykroyd (secondary character Oscar Zeta Acosta, aka "the Brown Buffalo") jumped ship to make
The Blues Brothers instead.

Where *Meatballs* had been a throwaway lark, *Where the Buffalo
Roam* was a chance for Murray to prove he had dramatic chops. So in
pre-production he began shadowing Thompson, obsessively studying

his mannerisms, from the way he clenched his long black cigarette holder between his teeth to his habit of pouring lighter fluid into his mouth, lighting it, and belching a blaze of flame past an onlooker's ear. He turned down Dr. Gonzo's frequent offers of hard drugs, but did start to share his bottles of Wild Turkey.

"It finally got to where I could drink with him, although I can't now," Murray said in 1988. "It was an interesting experience. He came out and lived in the house where I was staying in Hollywood, so I was basically living twenty-four-hour days. No shit. But that made the performance work too. I really had him cold."

One weekend, Bill and Brian Murray decided to head out of town, so they asked Dave Thomas to babysit Thompson. "They were worried that Hunter might kill himself or do something stupid," says Thomas. "So I spent this bizarre couple of days at the Sheraton Universal with him. Bill was incredibly committed to studying Hunter: he even did the voice, which I thought was a terrible mistake, because Hunter mumbled. He was not articulate."

Perhaps inevitably, given its subject, *Where the Buffalo Roam* rapidly began to slide off the rails. Shooting on the Universal lot and out in the desert beyond L.A.'s borders, Murray stayed in character, talking in his guru's trademark mumble-bark and chain-smoking Dunhills. But Thompson himself, skulking around the sets and occasionally firing off machine guns in the parking lot, was unimpressed by the bigger picture. He drawled that the film should be renamed *The Death of Fun*, and considered bringing in his own crew to make a film about the film being made about him. Midway through the shoot, he made up dozens of badges with the legend GONZO GUILT, and secretly distributed them among the crew until everyone had one except for director Art Linson.

Thompson and Murray worked up their own dialogue for several scenes, including a restroom confrontation between the hero and Richard Nixon. But a tug-of-war began between them and Linson that was to drag on into post-production. Murray recorded a narration for the movie, hoping to clarify the action; the director removed it without telling him.

One night in December 1979, well after midnight, Thompson called his illustrator friend Ralph Steadman. "Ralph, it's me, Hunter," he rasped, desperately. "I'm going to Hollywood. No one must know. It's important. I'll be at the Sheraton. Bill Murray is there. We've got to get into the editing room and change the beginning and the end. The film has no message. It doesn't mean anything."

Whether they actually pulled off the Great Cutting-Room Heist is unknown. Either way, the final film pleased nobody. Universal's Ned Tanen, already a nervous wreck from the *Blues Brothers* drama unfolding in Illinois, flew back from the first preview in San Jose with his head between his knees; when Linson tried to talk to him, he covered his ears with his hands. Others were less reticent with their opinion. "An embarrassing piece of hogwash utterly devoid of plot, form, movement, tension, humor, insight, logic or purpose," wrote David Felton in *Rolling Stone*. "The cultural revolution of the Sixties is reduced to a Three Stooges routine." Thompson was even more direct: "Horrible pile of crap. Murray did a good job. But it was a bad script. You can't beat a bad script." After seeing the rough cut, he'd threatened to attack Linson with a baseball bat.

It was a disappointment for Murray also, who had immersed himself in his second film to an alarming degree, but only received middling reviews. Even worse, he'd succeeded in pissing off his colleagues back at *Saturday Night Live*. His return trips to New York had seen him stalk around 30 Rock with dark glasses and a darker mood, still in character as Thompson, throwing temper tantrums and grousing about the hosts, the cameramen, the quality of the writing. Brandishing a cigarette holder in his hand, he would sometimes walk out of 30 Rock on Friday night and not show up again until late Saturday afternoon.

Eventually Murray's old, mostly genial personality returned. But Thompson lurked in his psyche for a long time to come. In the late 1990s, when Johnny Depp signed up to play Thompson in *Fear and Loathing in Las Vegas*, he tracked down Murray and asked him about his experience. "I wanted to know how long this was going to stay with me," said Depp. "And he told me, basically, it took him five years."

CHEVY CHASE HADN'T SEEN Bill Murray since their scuffle backstage at *Saturday Night Live*. But a year on, as he glided around a ritzy Hollywood party, Chase spotted his old nemesis loitering by the swimming pool.

He could have sloped away, avoided another confrontation. Instead, Chase put down his drink and marched toward Murray, a furious glare on his face. Murray tensed up. But just as he reached him, Chase dropped to his knees and began to unzip Murray's pants, miming preparation for a blowjob. Murray cracked a smile at Chase's sophomoric bit, then both of them started to laugh.

They hardly became friends; a great deal of tension remained. But hostilities reduced just enough for the two stars to agree to star in a movie together. It probably helped that their characters weren't to share a scene. And it can't have hurt that Warner Bros.'s *Caddyshack* looked like it had a decent shot at capturing some of that *Animal House* magic. Not only was it dreamed up by two of the writers of that movie, Doug Kenney and Harold Ramis, but it shared the same slobs-versus-snobs dynamic, this time transposed to a members-only golf course, the fictional Bushwood Country Club.

Both Bill Murray and his brother Brian, the latter of whom joined Kenney and Harold Ramis on the *Caddyshack* writing team, had worked at Indian Hill Country Club in Illinois in their teenage years. It was a low-paying and often demeaning way to make some holiday cash—not least because the extremely rich people whose bags they were lugging around, at $3.50 a pop, were not allowed to tip. The Murrays sometimes found themselves wading into muddy ponds, risking a turtle bite or a disease of the foot. Whoever they returned the ball to would nod, then say, "Can you wash it for me, please?"

Ramis had actually met the young Murray for the first time when he bought food from him at the ninth-hole snack bar. Many of the movie's elements were pulled from their lives: hero Danny Noonan's large family was based on the crowded Murray household, while the scene where a Baby Ruth chocolate bar is mistaken for a floating turd was inspired by a real prank Bill and Brian pulled at their high school swimming pool.

Still, despite his suitability for the project, Murray was the last to sign on, for what was written as a cameo. His character, brain-frazzled assistant groundskeeper Carl Spackler, shares attributes with a bit part he'd played in an *SNL* skit called "Theodoric of York: Medieval Barber"—the twisted lip, the slack face, the honker voice. Although it's never spelled out, Carl is clearly a Vietnam veteran, equipped with camo hat and plastic explosives. And he's nuttier than a squirrel's stash. "Forgive me," he says when charged by his boss with ridding the course of gophers, "but if I get rid of all the golfers, they'll kill me and throw away the key."

As written, Spackler was a silent presence in the film. That quickly changed, when one of the writers turned to him and said, "Any ideas?" Murray had a few. "I thought there should be a whole bizarre world for this guy," he later explained. "'Let's make a bunker,' I said, and the set decorator got it right away. 'And let's make some explosives out of clay.' I just sort of walked around the shack for fifteen minutes and it started jumping into my head."

What the star dreamed up was a mad duel of wits between Carl and a gopher, in which the harebrained human is outwitted at every turn by his furry quarry. The critter had originally been set to make only a brief appearance, and the glove puppet that had been built clearly wasn't going to cut it. So Ramis auditioned real animals, even a rowdy ferret, before commissioning special-effects artist John Dykstra to construct an animatronic gopher, its face capable of grinning, giggling, and coughing smoke. (The chittering vocals added in post-production were pinched from the TV series *Flipper*.) Incorporating a blowpipe, a gun, and finally squirrel-shaped bombs, the battle rages on and ultimately destroys the golf course with a climactic explosion. Murray's walk-on role turned out to change the entire structure of the film.

As for Chevy Chase, the character of millionaire playboy Ty Webb had been written specifically for him, tapping into his aptitude for white-bread cool, but he was given equally free rein to improvise.

Murray free-styled legendary bits like the "Cinderella Story" monologue; Chase ad-libbed nonsense Zen aphorisms like "See your future. Be your future," throwing off co-star Cindy Morgan in one take by snorting a hefty pile of salt.

As their respective scenes got funnier and funnier, the balance of the film started to shift. What was intended to be a coming-of-age story, about young caddy Danny (Michael O'Keefe), was becoming a vehicle for the two *Saturday Night Live* veterans.

Marooned together for fourteen weeks in a motel at Florida's Rolling Hills Country Club—the weather swampy enough to inspire bug-eyed comedian Rodney Dangerfield to quip, off-camera, "Hoo, Florida, it's a sauna with gnats!"—the young cast and crew cut loose. There were parties every night and copious drug taking; Dangerfield showed up two days before filming with a suitcase filled with weed, exceeded in size only by the one Chase wielded when he arrived the day after. There was to be much rolling at Rolling Hills, and more potent narcotics were in equally free supply. "Robin Williams has said, 'Cocaine is God's way of telling you you're making too much money,'" said National Lampoon veteran Matty Simmons. "God spoke loudly on that shoot."

The twenty-two-year-old Trevor Albert had been sent to the set to help out producer Jon Peters, but ended up working for Harold Ramis. "It was a recipe for calamity and hijinks," he recalls. "Because when you put all these people together on a resort golf course, the lines between work and play become fuzzy. I would have to wander down the hall at six forty-five a.m. for a seven o'clock call, finding out why people weren't already heading to the set. And that was challenging to say the least. It was easy to get the people who were asleep in the hall, but harder to get people who were asleep in their rooms."

As special guest star, Murray was on-set for only a few days, and largely kept his distance from Chase. Until one night, around three a.m., when there was a banging on Chase's door. He got out of bed and opened it, to see Bill and Brian standing there, looking sheepish, wondering if he had any spare weed. He sent them next door to Dangerfield's room, where they found a large paper bag. "Heavy enough to carry a baby's head," recalled Chase. "Rodney said, 'Take it. That's all my pot. Enjoy.' So they took it and they left. And it turned out that that bag contained nothing but seeds. Nothing but pot seeds, with only a smidgen of actual smokeable pot in it. It was as if he'd been waiting for someone to ask him. He wasn't going to give his away, that's for sure."

The atmosphere was loose and lawless, but Ramis did pay attention to one studio note: the movie *had* to have the two ex-*SNL* titans cross paths. A quick scene had actually already been shot with Chase and Murray squeezed together on the seat of a large mower with dangerous-looking blades; as they trundled into position, Chase had told his co-star to take it easy, prompting Murray to deliberately take a hard right, pitching him onto the ground. But the scene was viewed as inadequate, so over lunch Kenney, Ramis, Murray, and Chase thrashed out a new sequence in which Ty's golf ball rolls into Carl's decrepit abode. Then the pair were set loose, for the only moment in movie history to feature both.

Chase was nervous about crossing swords with Murray in full honker mode. "He just scares you because he looks like he's out of control—and he is half out of control anyway." And everyone else crowded around, wondering what the hell was going to unfold, and if it was going to feature another near miss involving a blade. "There was a sense that anything could happen," remembers Albert. "Both were unpredictable. Everyone was thinking: Are they going to get along? Is this going to work? There'd been talk about Bill and Chevy's relationship and whether they were cordial or fighting or whatever."

In fact, the two run-throughs of the scene went without a hitch. Fortuitously, the action involved the two stars smoking their very own version of a peace pipe: an enormous doobie, stuffed with Carl's special blend of "Kentucky bluegrass, featherbed bench, and northern California sinsemilla." And their double-act proved a shambling delight, a goofy scenario in which the rich golfer is trying his hardest to escape, while his deranged host continues to be terrifyingly friendly, at one point suggesting Ty handicap his opponent by slicing their hamstring.

"I'll drop by. You drop by my place any time," says Ty nervously, eyeing the exit.

"What's your address over there? You're on Briar, right?" replies the intense Carl.

"Briar, uh-huh . . . Two," Ty lies.

"You got a pool over there?"

"We have a pond in the back. A pool and a pond. A pond would be good for *you* . . ."

Chase was relieved both to have got some magic in the can, and to have walked away without being brained. "I didn't know that Bill was going to come at me with the wine and the joint," he said years later. "What makes Bill great and funny is his danger. And that's a reality in his life too. So you're there to do a scene with Bill on the golf course and you may have had a little thing a few years earlier, you better watch out. You might be hit by a club. He's funny, but it's not that funny to get a big gash in the back of your head."

But while that scene was a triumph, the movie's release was not. The publicity tour was a disaster, culminating in a press conference at which Dangerfield was stoned, Kenney passed out at the table, Murray was hostile, and Chase told a meek Canadian reporter, on camera, to go fuck himself. All of this may not have helped the reviews, which were tepid in the extreme. The *New York Times* was kinder than most, calling *Caddyshack* an "amiable mess," a critique Ramis admitted he agreed with. *Caddyshack* aspired to be *Animal House* and fell short, grossing $39.8 million, less than a third of the earlier film's total.

He and Warner Bros. were immensely disappointed. Yet as the years rolled on, the movie's dialogue, everything from "Oh, rats' farts!" to "Na-na-na-na-na!," would continue to be endlessly quoted by fans. In the end, *Caddyshack* would prove as impossible to dislodge as that damn gopher.

5

A RISE AND A FALL

FILM CRITIC PAULINE KAEL said it best: "John Candy is perfectly named. He's a mountainous lollipop of a man, and preposterously lovable."

A roly-poly giant, six foot three and sometimes weighing in at as much as three hundred pounds, Candy liked to greet his pal Dan Aykroyd by lifting him up with one hand and hauling him over his shoulder. And even that wasn't the limit of his power. "Once, backstage at Second City, he picked Aykroyd and I up horizontally like logs and spun us," recalls *SCTV* cast mate Dave Thomas. "To this day I can still see Danny's face, cackling as he spun around the room. John was not a podgeball. He was physically very strong. Onstage I could run at him, jump into the air, lift my legs up, and tuck my arms, and he would catch me like a football or basketball. He'd barely rock on his heels."

Aptly born on Halloween—he liked treats so much as a child that people called him "Sweet Tooth"—Candy lost a parent at the age of four, when his father, Sidney, a thirty-five-year-old Toronto car salesman, died of heart disease. From then on he was raised, and fed extensively, by his mother, Evangeline, his aunt, and his grandparents. "My grandmother was Polish, so we had a lot of cabbage rolls and coffee," he recalled. "I guarantee you, no one ever walked into the house who didn't get fed."

Candy initially wanted to be a football player—he was so big that nobody got past him—but a busted knee put an end to that. He worked for a while as a Kleenex salesman, driving around in a brown Pontiac and a brown suit. He did a stint in a factory, mixing yellow and white road paint. But increasingly he felt the lure of the stage. Having drifted into a bunch of odd acting jobs, including a Colgate commercial and a production of David Freeman's *Creeps* at Toronto's Tarragon Theatre, he found the experiences liberating. "There's relief in acting," he mused years later. "There's an escape within a character, the ability to get lost and take up another life. I think I may have become an actor to hide from myself." He hadn't gotten many dates at school, but he knew he was funny. And here was an outlet for his frustrations.

Encouraged by Aykroyd, a fellow Ontarian, Candy auditioned for the Second City improv troupe in 1972. He got the job. Despite an unfortunate early incident in which he was knocked out onstage after colliding with another actor, he proved a dynamo, capable of astonishing, high-energy physical comedy. "John liked to have a drink now and again," said Aykroyd, "and sometimes he'd go onstage after having a couple, and it would be unpredictable." But unlike Belushi or Murray, Candy never lost his temper. "He was the most playful and childlike of the Second City cast," says Thomas. "Onstage he had an imaginary room, with everything in a certain position. There was a file folder over here, a shelf up there where he kept his blowgun. Everything was in its place and it was always there. So once you knew John's room you could play with him in there, and the audience could see it too, because John established it so well."

Beneath Candy's whimsy was a streak of raw ambition. Throughout the mid-'70s, he hurtled around America with Second City, performing everywhere from Chicago to Pasadena. Up in Toronto one day, he took a drag on a cigarette, tossed it on the ground, and said, only half-seriously, "One day I'm going to own this town." His cast mate Joe Flaherty gave him the nickname "Johnny Toronto." It stuck.

Even when he barely had two coins to rub together, Candy behaved like a high-roller, wearing expensive suits and hiring limousines to take him to auditions. His air of importance succeeded in winning him jobs. He even found himself headlining a movie before any of his *Second City* compadres, making him the Chevy Chase of *SCTV*—although admittedly that movie was *Find the Lady*, a dire Canadian farce in which a gong sound effect plays every time its Chinese character enters a scene. The other roles weren't much better, Candy mainly playing blubbery, blabbering creeps.

Much more satisfying was *SCTV*, the Second City crew's TV show, which began in 1976. Without the production values, the star power, or the live-broadcast element of *SNL*, its main appeal was its warmth. The huggable Candy fit right in. "A lot of *Saturday Night Live* was very abrasive, what I call bad-boy humor," he said. "*SCTV* was never that way. It was too easy to go that route. You should be comfortable with the people in a picture or on a television show. You should care about them."

SCTV's hook was ingeniously meta. It purported to be a local-network broadcast from the fictional town of Melonville, making this a television show *about* television. A typical episode could feature everything from clips of fake late-night movies (Monster Chiller Horror Theater) to commercials for ludicrous products (Al Peck's Used Fruit). The cast, which included Eugene Levy, Harold Ramis, and Catherine O'Hara, played multiple characters, while Candy ran wild with creations like the obnoxious Johnny LaRue and polka clarinetist Yosh Shmenge. He also proved capable of channeling celebrities like Pavarotti or Orson Welles, his take on the portly auteur responding to any kind of direction with frosty ripostes like, "What? I'm *on* my mark. Move your *camera*."

SCTV never got huge ratings, but those in the know appreciated its sharpness and guts. "I was in a bad hotel room in Worcester, Ohio, up late and not able to sleep, and turned on this thing that was called *Second City TV*," said Tom Hanks. "The first episode I saw was the *Leave It to Beaver* episode, where John was playing Beaver. It was like hearing the Beatles for the first time."

It was cutting-edge stuff, but minus the drugginess of *SNL*. Down in New York there were blizzards of cocaine; in Toronto, the snow was real. It was a far more relaxed and congenial troupe, the hub of which was a cozy house at 1063 Avenue Road, in which Candy and his wife, Rose, lived from 1976 to 1980. A night owl, he'd often sit up until dawn with a rum and Coke in one hand and a Marlboro Light in the other, yakking up a storm. "All of us partied there and sang there," said Candy. "It was just full of music and fun and comedy."

It was also full of food, always. Candy would sometimes order from three or four different restaurants simultaneously, so he wouldn't have to make a choice. But when he was in the mood to cook, his guests were in for a culinary adventure that was likely to be chaotic. One Thanksgiving he invited the *SCTV* cast back for dinner, but forgot to defrost the turkey and ended up putting the bird under the shower to thaw. "You never ate until midnight," says Dave Thomas. "You'd end up gorging yourself on snack food because you were so hungry, and then when the meal started it was like, 'Oh my God, Jesus, I can't eat all this.'" Eugene Levy remembers food being served even later: "You'd eat at 2 a.m., leave at 5 a.m., and later on you'd realize it was one of the greatest nights you ever had."

Candy had his vices: the Bacardi Light, the chain-smoking. But his main battle, from the beginning, was with his weight. He knew the dangers—his father's premature demise was not the only instance of heart disease in his family—and fretted often about his health. Even so, as his career took off and he gave up playing sports entirely, he started to balloon.

"I'm the one who has to look in the mirror," he told *People*, when asked if his size bothered him. "And after a while it begins to eat at you."

As his star rose, there were more and more distractions from those uncomfortable thoughts. On a visit to Hollywood in 1976 with the rest of the *SCTV* cast, Candy strutted drunkenly around a party held in their honor, Chevy Chase's head trapped under his arm. He didn't let Chase go for an entire hour and a half, eliciting riotous laughter. "For some reason I started playing wrestler with him and carried him under my arm in a headlock for a while," Candy admitted. "Or so I'm told."

Later that night, even more hammered on rum, Candy bumped into Steven Spielberg and told him, "I like your movie about the fish." Spielberg laughed at the reference to *Jaws*, then offered him a part in *1941*, despite Candy insisting, "There are any number of leeches around here who want the job more than I do." He ended up taking it, and turning up to the *1941* set almost every day for six months, though his performance got shrunk to almost nothing in post-production.

Candy also got a small but memorable role in *The Blues Brothers*, as a genial lawman on the trail of his buddy Dan Aykroyd, getting the iconic line, "Who wants an Orange Whip? Orange Whip? Orange Whip? Three Orange Whips!" All this did not escape the notice of *Meatballs* director Ivan Reitman, busy prepping his next, and significantly more ambitious, movie.

REITMAN HAD HAD HIS EPIPHANY as he looked into his bathroom mirror, shaving before the premiere of *Meatballs*. It was not exactly a holy vision, given it involved topless women and wanton anarchy, but it was a vision nonetheless. "All of a sudden the idea for *Stripes* came to me," he recalls. "At the premiere I saw Jeffrey Katzenberg standing outside the theater and said, 'Remind me to talk to you after this. I have an idea of what I'd like to do next.'"

Stripes was the tale of two slackers who decide they could do with a dose of discipline and join the army. Shenanigans ensue as they run afoul of a formidable drill sergeant, romance a pair of beautiful military cops, and end up in actual combat in Cold War Europe. It sounded ambitious, but Reitman was determined to avoid the mistakes of *1941*: he promised Columbia Pictures he'd bring the movie in for a mere $10 million. His first move was to contact the Pentagon and cut a deal. Reitman would not only rent troops and tanks for a pittance, but be allowed to shoot on a real army base. In return, the Pentagon brass would have a say in the script. This was a worrying prospect for a comedy filmmaker who aspired to edginess, akin to letting a real college dean have a say in *Animal House*, and when the objections arrived there were plenty of them. Fortunately, Reitman found they were mostly technical in nature, and, as he told a reporter, "They gave up on 50 points right off the bat." He dispatched writers Len Blum and Dan Goldberg to army bases for six weeks of research, gathering anecdotes from recruits.

As for the stars, Reitman's initial idea that this would be a Cheech and Chong vehicle faltered when the stoner comedians' manager demanded, incredibly, 25 percent of Reitman's income for his next four or five movies. The director refused, and aimed instead for Bill Murray and Dennis Quaid. When word came back from Murray that he'd prefer to do it with a friend, it became Murray and Harold Ramis.

At the time, Murray was still living in his New York loft, which he'd decorated by putting a moose head on the wall: "The biggest moose head I've ever seen. It's a sobering thought that something that big can die." But his personal circumstances had changed, as he was now in a committed relationship with an Irish girl he'd known for ten years, Mickey Kelly. They would marry during the *Stripes* shoot—twice. The first time was a ceremony performed at four thirty a.m. by a man in sunglasses in a Las Vegas chapel. The second was a much bigger affair, back in the Wilmette, Illinois, church where Murray had been baptized. Stuffed with family members, rowdy friends, and hangers-on, it was an Irish carnival that went on for days.

Perhaps it was this turn in his personal life, or the fact he was about to turn thirty, that made him start to take his career more seriously. *Stripes* saw Murray back in his comfort zone, working with friends, with a doozy of a role: a *Rocky & Bullwinkle*–watching, Tito Puente–loving, Pabst-sipping wastrel who makes good. "I don't want to be doing movies when I'm 50 years old," Murray said after the movie wrapped, but added that he worked "more efficiently than I ever worked before."

Shooting partly at Fort Knox, Kentucky, with all the military ordnance that came with it, the production felt enormous to the people making it. More than a thousand off-duty soldiers were there to be deployed as extras if Reitman willed it; there were fifty-nine drivers just to shuttle everyone around. The schedule allowed for the shooting of set pieces like a parachute drop—Ramis's character, Russell Ziskey, accidentally ingests six LSD tabs instead of diazepam—and a visit to a strip club called the Pom Pom.

The latter sequence was to be John Candy's big moment, as his hapless recruit, Ox, steps into a mud ring to wrestle with a bevy of women. But rather than being excited by the scene, Candy argued passionately that it should be cut entirely, believing it was sexist and designed to make him look like a pig in a sty. "John didn't want to do it and he was pissed off that he'd agreed to do it," says Dave Thomas. "He was like, 'Hey, I've got a lot more to offer than this. Don't make me wrestle nude women in a mud tub.' In a way, Harold Ramis lowballed John. Even at *SCTV*, he would write a load of fat jokes for John and John would do them because he was a nice guy, but it bothered him."

In the end, Reitman and Ramis won and the sequence was filmed as written. The director admits that he knew how distressed it made Candy. "It was probably because of the nakedness, because some of the girls were going to be topless by the end of it," says Reitman. "But it seemed like the appropriate level of sexuality for a film about young guys in the army, and I felt we shouldn't cop out on it, in the same way *Animal House* does not cop out of the college sexuality that it portrays. It was one of the defining changes of these comedies from the comedies of the '50s and '60s—we couldn't scale back and be frightened in our storytelling."

Predictably, the sequence became Candy's signature moment in the movie, the one he was asked about in every interview. By that time, he was able to joke about it. "I had to do it for the team," he told one journalist in 1989. "That took an extra week of shooting. For some reason, I just got a blank and couldn't get a line out there. It got boring too, believe me. You just have to get in there with six girls, wrestle them, and then, if the take didn't work, you'd have to go in and take a shower with them. The first two times I'll admit it was fun. But by the sixth or seventh time—'Scrub my back, okay? Let's get this over and done with.' It was tough."

Stripes was an anarchic film, stuffed with nudity and disregard for authority, and the Pentagon oversight didn't improve anyone's behavior on-set. "It was 1980 and the beginning of a decade that had a lot of drugs, sex, and rock 'n' roll," is how Sean Young, who plays the love interest of Ramis, remembers it. "I was never a big abuser but I certainly witnessed a lot of it [on *Stripes*]. Coke, booze, and, of course, lots of laughter." At some point in the shoot Murray and Warren Oates, who played a drill sergeant in the movie, decided to visit the ashes of character actor Strother Martin at Forest Lawn Memorial Park in the Hollywood Hills. They drank so much Armagnac that they both blacked out and woke up covered in cuts and bruises.

But if the chaotic vibe resembled that of *1941*, at least in this case a decent movie came out the other side. "A magnificently irreverent comedy that combines cleverness with grossness," raved one review, though it noted that the film lost its teeth in the army-approved third act. Reitman's camerawork had a newfound verve, considerably more impressive than the scrappy craft on display on *Meatballs*. Murray's performance oozed lazy charm, whether he's issuing asides such as "Don't eat the schnitzel. They're using schnauzer," or advancing his seduction technique from wrestling his target to tickling her with a spatula.

Most non-Canadians, though, would have left the movie theater wondering who the hell the big guy was. Candy's performance mixed laughs with pathos ("I swallow a lot of aggression, along with a lot of pizza," Ox explains to the rest of his platoon), stealing almost every one of his scenes. The project had felt personal to Candy—he had tried to join the US Marines when he was eighteen but was rejected because of an old football injury. And he had gotten to reconnect with Murray, who had taken Candy under his wing during his time in Chicago, taking him to the original McDonald's for a hamburger and baseball games at Wrigley Field.

Making over $85 million in the United States, *Stripes* was a game changer, not just for the people who had made it but the entire *SNL* and *SCTV* collective. "Old-fashioned and arrogant movie businesspeople were saying movies like *Meatballs* and *Caddyshack* would fail," said top talent agent Michael Ovitz in 2016, "and that movies with *Sat-*

urday Night Live people in them wouldn't work because, 'Why would people pay to see things they could see for free?' I'll tell you when people all of a sudden woke up: they woke up on *Stripes*."

It cemented Murray's and Reitman's reputations, and garnered plenty of buzz for Candy, although not all of it was the kind he wanted. Candy read one review in which the critic described him as "the elephant," a jibe that hurt him deeply. "Jerks like that are so obvious," he said. "They can't even be clever. Sure, I'm sensitive about my weight. I don't do fat jokes."

Candy's next job was another Reitman project, an adult animated feature called *Heavy Metal*, based on the cult magazine. Structured as a rumination on the nature of evil, it was a bizarre blend of highbrow and lowbrow, featuring music from the Royal Philharmonic Orchestra, countless cartoon breasts, and a scene in which aliens snort space cocaine. One of Candy's characters was a robot who hooks up with a voluptuous human; another was a dweeb who transforms into a muscle-bound barbarian but continues to deliver a dweeby voiceover, issuing bons mots such as "There was no way I was going to walk around this place with my dork hanging out."

As 1981 wound on, Candy's phone started ringing, and kept ringing. Asked later how his life changed during this heady period, Candy replied, of course, with a food analogy: "I went from macaroni and cheese to macaroni and lobster."

A COPY OF *HEAVY METAL* magazine can be spied in a single shot in *Continental Divide*, the John Belushi film that came out just a month after *Heavy Metal*, in September 1981. It's on the newsstand that Belushi's character, hardboiled city reporter Ernie Souchak, swings by to check out his latest big story. Somewhat implausibly, a van on the street bears Souchak's name on the side. Even more implausibly, a cab-driver recognizes him and yells out, "Hey, Souchak, hell of a column today!" For a journalist, this guy is kind of a big deal.

Continental Divide marked Belushi's second attempt to escape his comedy roots. The first, 1979's downbeat drama *Old Boyfriends*, he afterward denounced as "a piece of shit." This one, he hoped, would be better. Scripted by Lawrence Kasdan, who'd written *The Empire Strikes Back*, it was a low-key tale about a Chicago hack who finds love up in the Rockies with a reclusive eagle researcher. There was humor in it, gentle riffs involving Belushi's character wheezing his way around mountain trails, or having his Marlboro Reds eaten by a bear. But it was a long way from *Animal House*, clones of which Belushi saw popping up everywhere, like toadstools. He even dismissed *Stripes* as a pale imitation: "That's just *Animal House* joins the Army."

As prep work, Belushi read up on *Chicago Sun-Times* columnist Mike Royko, the inspiration for his character. He even visited old enemy Chevy Chase at his home in the Pacific Palisades, picking his brains about the ins and outs of romantic comedy. He took the project very seriously: he'd had bad press all the way through *1941* and *The Blues Brothers*, but here, at last, was a respectable project at which nobody could snipe.

"It was John trying to reinvent himself from the fat, obnoxious Bluto character, which is what studio executives wanted him to play, into a leading man," says Dave Thomas, who as cameras rolled on *Continental Divide* was hunkered down with Aykroyd in his and Belushi's frat house–like bungalow on the Warner Bros. lot—complete with bunk bed—working on the script for *Spies Like Us*. "It's kind of sad, really. It's a common thing that comedians get successful and then they'll walk by the mirror one day and say, 'Hey, you know what? I don't look too bad.' To me that was always the beginning of the end for a comedian, when they start to see themselves as a handsome leading man."

What nobody said, but everybody was thinking, was that surely not even Belushi could get himself in trouble up a mountain. The shoot would have a dual purpose: work and detox. After the madness of the *Blues Brothers* shoot, Belushi now had a support system in place, including an enormous ex–Secret Service agent named Smokey, to keep drugs away from him, and a karate world champion called Bill "Superfoot" Wallace, to keep his weight down. Instead of bacon double cheeseburgers, Belushi had started gorging himself on tubs of cottage cheese. He quickly dropped fifty pounds. "My mother had always told me that I'd have to suffer if I wanted to look good," he lamented.

Finally the new, streamlined Belushi headed to Colorado for the shoot. His routine was austere: he'd wake up at six a.m., have cantaloupe and black coffee for breakfast, then travel by helicopter to the remote set. "It's so quiet here you could hear a mouse get a hard-on!" exclaims Souchak as he surveys the lonely wilderness. It didn't require much acting on Belushi's part to work up that shell-shocked reaction. The parties, the limos, the booze—all gone, replaced by babbling brooks and pure air. He might as well have been dropped on the moon.

He struggled to rein himself in for line readings, resisting the urge to play Souchak as Bluto with a backpack, and finding a gentler tempo, particularly for the romantic scenes with Blair Brown. "I had to hold myself back," Belushi said shortly after the shoot wrapped. "I had to walk across a room like a normal person. Not swagger or anything— just *walk*."

But the fun that people associated with Belushi was absent from his performance; the new, sober John even looked a little scared on-screen. *Continental Divide* did badly at the box office, indicating that few people wanted to see him being mild-mannered. It was a blow, but Belushi doubled down on his resolve; visiting Steve Martin at his home in Beverly Hills, he told Martin that he saw a future for himself as a proper actor. For his next movie, *Neighbors*, he would quadruple down, stampeding into uncharted territory.

Set on Bird Lane, a cul-de-sac containing two houses, a swamp, and ominously buzzing power lines, *Neighbors* aimed for dark farce, portraying the effect a wild couple has on their new street mates. Earl Keese, a stuffy homebody with an ordered life, was an ideal fit for Dan Aykroyd. Vic, the hyper weirdo who turns up at his door one stormy night, could have been written for Belushi. Happy to be working together again, the two stars signed up for those roles with enthusiasm.

Almost immediately, however, they changed their minds. "We were in rehearsal, reading the parts, when we said, 'Hey, let's switch them and try it,'" said Aykroyd. "We've played these other roles before, and we thought going against type would be more fun."

That did not prove to be the case. Carl Gottlieb, who was briefly in talks to do a pass on the script, was one of many to feel foreboding when the casting was announced. "I was shocked," he remembers. "Belushi has the reputation of being the wild man and Danny the straight guy. In truth, it's not so simple—Danny is quite a complicated man with a lot of complicated theories about life and art. But their public persona was pretty set. And *Neighbors* was like Abbott and Costello suddenly swapping places."

Aykroyd threw himself into playing Vic, inserting creepy blue contact lenses, dyeing his hair blond, and ad-libbing bizarre lines like "Ramona and I haven't eaten all day. We could eat a baby's butt through a park bench." The character, deranged and lawless, was a throwback to Aykroyd's more outré transformations on *Saturday Night Live*: in one scene, he gleefully gobbles down edible panties belonging to Keese's daughter. Belushi, on the other hand, felt uncomfortable and uncertain about how to play Earl. He was getting $1.25 million for the movie, his biggest payday yet, but on-screen he resembled a party wagon that's been impounded, the role less a straight man than a straitjacket.

It was a miserable shoot. Screenwriter Larry Gelbart watched forlornly as Belushi and Aykroyd ran roughshod over his precisely calibrated lines, making up their own dialogue. Director John G. Avildsen, hired off the back of his success with *Rocky*, clashed with Belushi constantly. Asked to undergo a makeup transformation to look older, the star refused, allowing only some slight graying of his eyebrows. He reportedly went on to accuse Avildsen of not having a funny bone in his body, of being "a little Hitler." Finally, Belushi called John Landis midway through the shoot and begged him to take over. Landis declined.

The discord came to a head in post-production, the time at which most stars step gently away from a project. Instead, Belushi, back on drugs in a major way, attended an early screening and heckled loudly, at one point taking off a shoe and banging it on his armrest. Lately he had neglected his collection of blues records in favor of punk rock, and he decided that *Neighbors* needed an injection of earsplitting guitars. He gathered together Fear, a hardcore band with a truly hellish sound, and got them to record a song for the end of the movie. Then he went on a mission to get the cacophonous track into the film, playing the song to Avildsen and Columbia president Frank Price, while slam-dancing around their offices to illustrate its power. Both men hated it.

The Fear tune didn't end up in *Neighbors*—as a sop, Belushi convinced NBC to let the band play on *SNL*—but after a calamitous test screening Avildsen did record a new score, by *Rocky* composer Bill Conti. He also reshot the ending, after long and bitter negotiations with Belushi. Despite all the arguments and tantrums, there was still hope. The re-teaming of Aykroyd and Belushi had been feverishly awaited by fans; on November 10, a *New York Times* preview predicted it would have lines circling the blocks.

But as most inside the production had suspected, the movie proved a lemon, as weird as *The Blues Brothers* but nowhere near as likable. Roger Ebert liked it, calling the reverse casting "brilliant" and the film "an offbeat experiment in hallucinatory black humor," but most other critics went to town. David Ansen of *Newsweek* wrote, "Without question Bill Conti has come up with the year's most offensive score, a cattle prod of cartoonish cuteness that only underlines the movie's desperate uncertainty of tone." Rex Reed's review, dismissing it as a "slimy, vulgar piece of trash," inspired Chevy Chase to defend Aykroyd and Belushi on the *Tomorrow* show. "This guy's a dip. I don't like him, and he can sue me," Chase said of Reed. "Those are my friends and I don't like what he said."

If it had just been the reviews, Belushi might have bounced back quickly. But the numbers were terrible too, about a quarter of the gross of *The Blues Brothers*. "John got really mad, because it didn't open in the big way he wanted it to," remembers Dave Thomas. "I think he blamed Danny in some way, although the decision for Danny to play the wacky character and John to play the straight man was John's, not Dan's. I was there with Dan while he was on the phone with John and watched the effects of John's tirades. It was unfortunate."

IT'S ANYONE'S GUESS what movies John Belushi would have gone on to make. As 1982 began, he talked to anyone who would listen about the various ideas spinning around his head, from a remake of *Guys & Dolls* starring himself and Carrie Fisher to a Ken Russell musical in which he would play God. He had been writing a screwball comedy called *Noble Rot*, revolving around diamond fraud and a wine competition, for himself to headline. Sergio Leone had sounded him out about a supporting role in the crime epic *Once Upon a Time in America*; Belushi met with Robert De Niro, with whom he shared an obsession with Marlon Brando, several times at the start of the year. And Aykroyd, undeterred by the response *Neighbors* had received, was not only continuing to write *Spies Like Us* for them, but another vehicle, even more ambitious than *The Blues Brothers*. It would see the two old friends journey into other dimensions, saving Earth from dark supernatural forces.

But after cleaning himself up for *Continental Divide*, Belushi was back at his worst, hoovering up endless lines of cocaine, the substance he called "Hitler's drug." He traveled around in a limousine, sometimes for days on end, going from party to party. He was pale, twitchy, talking nonsense, and behaving erratically. On the evening of Valentine's Day, he talked his way into Steven Spielberg's house, even though the director was out, taking a drink from the refrigerator and leaving a note. At a movie night at the Playboy Mansion, he crawled over to Hugh Hefner's seat and finished off his host's soda and popcorn.

There were times when he was sober and in control, but these were increasingly rare. His work, inevitably, was suffering too. When Bernie Brillstein was asked by Belushi to take a look at the latest draft for *Noble Rot*, he was appalled. "It was terrible," the Hollywood manager wrote in his memoirs. "Nothing was funny. . . . The screenplay was neither fish nor fowl. It was no good. It didn't even make sense."

Then, in the small hours of March 5, a Friday, after a long evening in which he'd partied with De Niro and Robin Williams, Belushi took a fatal speedball, consisting of a mix of cocaine and heroin. He was pronounced dead at the scene. It had been less than three months since the release of *Neighbors*.

The next day, Aykroyd got a call from Brillstein as he sat at his desk in his New York office, working on the script for the supernatural comedy in which he would star with Belushi. "I was actually writing a line for John when I got the word that he died, that they found him curled up in the Chateau Marmont," Aykroyd recalls. Feeling numb, he locked up the office and walked down Fifth Avenue to Judy Belushi's house. One thought kept looping through his mind: "I can't get in a cab. I've got to keep walking." It hadn't yet sunk in that he had lost his comedy partner. His best friend. His brother.

The news felt like a gut punch to most people who had crossed paths with Belushi. "I genuinely loved him, and I'm still angry with him," says John Landis. "That was my reaction when he died. I was so furious when Danny called me. I thought, 'You *fucker* . . . I won't get to see you anymore.'" De Niro sat in his Chateau Marmont penthouse, watching Belushi *Saturday Night Live* clips on his VCR. Steven Spielberg wrote a tribute for a magazine, opining that "John represented messy bedrooms all over America. He was always the guy that we secretly want to be." John Candy, who called Belushi "the Bear," was so shocked he hired a personal trainer, resolving to get himself in shape.

As for Bill Murray, he and Aykroyd went to Belushi's property the night before the funeral. There, they fired shotguns at the moon.

6

CONFIDENCE MAN

THERE WAS ONE person considerably less shaken up about Belushi's death. "Thirty-three years old and dead from some fucking cocaine," Eddie Murphy said. "It's stupid, man. It's fucking stupid. I feel some sympathy, but then the other side of me goes, 'Jesus Christ, that's so *fucking stupid.*'"

Murphy wasn't like his *Saturday Night Live* predecessors, Belushi, Aykroyd, Murray, and Chase. All of those guys had essentially stumbled into stardom, talented but lucky to be in the right place at the right time. Murphy, on the other hand, raced after fame like a greyhound chasing a hare. Any possible distraction from his goal was ruthlessly eliminated. He didn't drink alcohol. He didn't smoke weed. He sure as hell didn't snort cocaine.

The ultimate test of Murphy's willpower came one night in New York. Belushi and Robin Williams had taken him out to the Blues Bar for a kibitzing session. After shooting the shit for a while, they decided it was time to change the pace. "They put blow out on the bar," Murphy recalled, "and they said, 'C'mon, have a sniff.'"

The young comedian looked down at the line of coke, back up

at the two icons egging him on. Then he shook his head. "Don't be a tightass," said Belushi. But Murphy remained resolute. "I was real close to doing it. But I didn't. I just didn't. That was the closest I'd ever come to experimenting with drugs."

He hadn't always been so disciplined. As a fourteen-year-old growing up in Roosevelt, Long Island, Murphy's dream had been to own a Mister Softee ice-cream truck so he could snarf free cones. But another fantasy slowly came to the fore. Down in the basement of the family house, he liked to stand in front of a full-length mirror, lip-syncing to the Elvis Presley album *Live at Madison Square Garden* and gyrating until he was dripping with sweat. Occasionally he'd sit in a chair and practice with a ventriloquist's dummy. It was unusual behavior for a boy in his early teens. His mother, Lillian, looked on with a mixture of curiosity and awe. "He looks in that mirror," she said, "and he's on a natural high."

The opinions of his other relatives differed. Eddie's uncle thought it was hilarious and bought him a gold lamé coat for his routine. Charlie, his older brother, just thought it was weird. When he caught Eddie dancing by himself one day, he asked him what exactly he was rehearsing for. Eddie had no reply. As for his father, Charles, he wasn't there at all. After separating from Lillian when Eddie was only three, he was stabbed to death by a girlfriend five years later. The tragedy had a huge impact on Murphy, who was haunted by it for decades. A friend even ventured to him once that it was the reason he didn't trust women. Murphy told them to fuck off.

The tragedy may have been partly responsible for the feverish way in which he threw himself into his practice. And before long, an opportunity came along. In July 1976, the fifteen-year-old Murphy and a friend were asked to host a regular talent show at their local youth center, though really their job was closer to crowd control. If a heckler piped up, Murphy tossed back insults, getting the crowd laughing. But after he'd done a few shows, he decided to try his luck, putting on an Al Green record and throwing some moves onstage. To his amazement, it got a riotous reception. "Girls started screaming," he marveled. "And I said, 'Shit, you can't make girls scream in a Mister Softee truck.'"

Murphy's confidence, already preternaturally high, rocketed higher. Voted most popular student at Roosevelt Junior-Senior High School, he started turning up in elaborate outfits. "When I was at high school, I used to wear a suit, a shirt and tie with a collar pin, carry a briefcase and have my cashmere coat slung over my shoulder," he told *Playboy* in 1990. "And everybody would say, 'There goes Eddie Murphy.'" That was when he was there; more often he'd cut class, heading out to scuzzy nightclubs and badgering the staff to let him go onstage. At sixteen, he was too young to drink, but old enough to make $30 for commanding a stage.

Audiences lucky enough to catch him were amazed by his self-assurance. He'd spit out obscenities with a giant grin on his face. In one routine he pretended to be mid-inauguration as America's first black president, then drop to the stage, felled by an imaginary bullet. Another night the crowd was unenthusiastic, so Murphy told them, "Hey, y'know what? In three years I'm going to be on *The Tonight Show*, so you can all kiss my ass." He walked offstage.

A myth began to build around him: the whippersnapper out to conquer the world. Robert Wachs, owner of the legendary Comic Strip comedy club in Manhattan, experienced Murphy in full force in 1979. "I'm there Monday night," he said. "All of a sudden this kid comes in, announced that he's here and that he's gonna go on. I say, 'Who are you?' 'I'm Eddie Murphy. I'm ready to go on.' I say, 'Wait a minute. We have systems around here, procedures. You don't just walk in and say, "I'm here and I'm going on." Get the hell out.' So I threw him out of the club." A short while later, Wachs was not only letting Murphy go onstage but working as his manager.

Murphy had a mantra, which he'd repeat to anyone who'd listen: "I'm gonna be a star in a year." When, in 1980, the entire cast of *Saturday Night Live* departed the show, Murphy saw the opportunity he'd been waiting for. He went to a pay phone and rang 30 Rock. Neil Levy, the show's talent coordinator, picked up and politely told Murphy they'd finished auditioning. He ended the call. But the next day, the phone rang again. And again the day after. "He would call every day for about a week," Levy recalled. "He would go into this whole

thing about he had eighteen brothers and sisters and they were count-
ing on him to get this job. And I finally decided I would see him as
an extra."

As with the first five years of the show, the higher-ups at *SNL*
planned to hire only a single black cast member, and Robert Townsend
was already in talks. But when Murphy showed up, doing a four-
minute monologue as three characters bickering in Harlem, he blew
the show's new team away. "Talent was just shooting out of him," Levy
marveled. *SNL* was at its lowest ebb, with an unremarkable lineup and
massively slashed budget. But the show's savior had just arrived.

"IT WAS JUST TOKENISM," Murphy told *Playboy* after leaving *Saturday
Night Live*. "They just threw me in there to be the black guy on the
show. They had no idea what was going to happen." To be fair to
NBC, nobody could have predicted the Murphy Effect.

As his first year began on November 15, 1980, signed on a contract
that netted him $750 a show, the nineteen-year-old kept a low profile—
on-screen at least. He'd saunter around the offices, making the writers
giggle with his profane riffs, but when Saturday night rolled around
there was rarely anything of substance for him to do. Typical was a skit
in which he and his fellow newbies sat quietly while guest host Bill
Murray gave them a pep talk, referencing such real negative headlines
as "Saturday Night Dead" and "Vile from New York," leading them in
a chant of his *Meatballs* slogan ("IT JUST DOESN'T MATTER!")
and telling him, "Eddie . . . you're black . . . and, uh, that's beautiful,
man. That's beautiful. You can do whatever you want."

Murphy didn't get a single line with which to respond, but there's no
doubt he believed what Murray was telling him. One day he took a pencil into the communal bathroom and wrote "Eddie Murphy No. 1" on
the wall. When acting coach Del Close came in to teach the cast some
improv skills, Murphy told him gently, "Hey, I'm funny. I don't have to
learn that shit." In his downtime he sat in his dressing room, watching
his videotape of Elvis's 1968 comeback concert over and over again,
studying the King's energy, his dynamism, his lightning-flash hips.

In the early hours of Sunday, January 10, 1981, he got his first chance to show off. The show was running too fast and there was five minutes of dead air to fill—no backup. Panicking, executive producer Jean Doumanian gave Murphy the green light to go onstage and perform some of his stand-up material. "His face lit up like he'd been waiting for this moment his whole life," said Neil Levy.

That's because he had. Murphy looked down at the faces in front of him and asked, "How many people in the audience have seen black people fight before?" Then he was off, cutting rapidly between a high-pitched character and a gruff one, editing out his usual cusswords as he went. Studio 8H went wild.

And quickly Eddie Murphy started to take over *SNL*. His effervescent mind and whipsaw wit meant he could roll with any deviation from the script. "If I throw up a ball, he goes for it," marveled cast mate Tim Kazurinsky. "Eddie Murphy is an otter." And his inimitable hearty laugh—"EEEEE! HEEEE! EEEEH!"—which a writer for *Time* would later describe as "a happy goose crossed with a stopped-up vacuum cleaner," was more contagious than swine flu. In his office, new show runner Dick Ebersol had a bulletin board with the week's show blocked out by segments. Sometimes he'd put up a card simply reading "EDDIE," meaning Murphy could do whatever he wanted in that slot. "Eddie has no fear whatsoever of a television camera," Ebersol gushed.

Collaborating with writers Barry Blaustein and David Sheffield, able to determine instantly whether a skit had what he called "whoosh," Murphy created an array of remarkable characters: oily huckster Velvet Jones, ghetto-dwelling Mr. Rogers send-up Mr. Robinson, even an outrageous take on Claymation icon Gumby. Virtually single-handedly, he brought not only the edge back to *SNL*, but the ratings and critical acclaim. "Eddie Murphy has stolen the show," declared a *New York Times* profile in October 1981. "What you get from Mr. Murphy is the gap-toothed grin of a guy who can't help feeling that things are turning out just as he planned them."

Soon, the "Eddie Murphy No. 1" graffiti in the bathroom had been rescrawled by the star, in pen and with larger letters. The rest of the cast watched with envy as his contract got renegotiated, earning him $4,500 per show. "When Eddie wasn't at read-through, we'd have to go find him; he'd be downstairs buying jewelry in the jewelry store," remembered Margaret Oberman.

Murphy adjusted to fame remarkably well, perhaps because he'd spent most of his life fantasizing about it. Drugs still held no allure for him, although he did indulge his one major vice: women. "I went through a stage the second year of *Saturday Night Live* where I was trying to fuck every woman who could possibly be fucked," he said. "I tried a lot. I got a lot of cooperation."

He was the biggest deal in town. And he intended to stay that way. After his first guest spot on the *Tonight* show, in early 1982, he flew back to New York with Wachs, poking at the unappetizing airline food. Eventually he put down his fork, turned to Wachs, and muttered, "This is the last time we fly coach."

WHEN HE MADE his big announcement on *SNL* that he'd been promoted from featured player to cast member, Murphy cooked up a little riff. "Am I going to be a burn-out?" he asked the audience, and America. "Am I going to go crazy, burn myself, start using drugs, abusing myself, wasting thousands of dollars on things I really don't need? I don't think so. If you're worried about Eddie Murphy going Hollywood, please don't. 'Cause I got my stuff together."

The specter of Belushi hung over the industry, a cautionary tale, but Murphy was determined to do things differently. He'd conquered TV through sheer will; he was going to rocket into the movie business the same way.

Step one: find the right project. Murphy's agent, Hildy Gottlieb, was in an on-off relationship with Walter Hill, the director of tough action films like *The Warriors* and *Southern Comfort*. And as it happened, Hill's next movie was in need of a young black lead. The tale of a burned-out cop and a small-time crook who are forced to pair up on a case, it had been in development since the mid-'70s, long before Hill got involved. Originally titled *Loan Out*, at one point it was talked about as a vehicle for Robert Mitchum and Clint Eastwood. Then Hill decided it would be more interesting to make Eastwood the cop and pair him with a black actor. "But he didn't want to be a cop," Hill says. "He already had the *Dirty Harry* franchise. So he faded into the horizon line."

The project faded away with him. But it reignited in 1982, when Paramount decided that Nick Nolte, who contractually owed the studio a movie, was perfect for the cop role. The disheveled star wasn't exactly enthusiastic, but agreed to sign up for what was now called *48 Hrs.* "He came in to meet me looking, fifteen years before the fact, like his mug shot," remembers writer Steven E. de Souza. "He's fat, he's unshaven, his hair is wild, and he says, 'Yeah, the studio's going to get me a trainer. Don't worry, I'll be in shape for the movie.'"

Now Paramount just needed a criminal. Enter Eddie Murphy, whose meeting with de Souza was the polar opposite from the Nolte encounter. He turned up early, eager to please, all done up in a suit and tie. "The fact he wore that to meet me, the writer, shows you how little he knew about the pecking order in Hollywood," de Souza says. "He was very serious and very nervous. He assured me that he could stay on-script. It was actually kind of adorable."

Hill had actually pursued a different actor for the role, Gregory Hines, before finding he wasn't available. The director flew to New York and met with Murphy in a restaurant. Sizing up the comedian, who was quiet but palpably desperate for a big break, he decided to give him a go. Hill saw talent, albeit of the rawest kind.

"It's going to be like acting with a kid or a dog," he told Nolte shortly after that meeting. "You've got to be good every take, because the one take he's great, that's the one we're going to print."

The first two weeks of the San Francisco shoot were Nolte days only, as Murphy was still taping *Saturday Night Live* in New York. Finally, the day after his last show, he flew coast-to-coast and was immediately fitted for his character's Armani suit (a quirk inspired by his outfit during his meeting with de Souza). The next morning, May 24, he was in front of a movie camera, for the very first time.

Murphy had always seemed effortless in front of a live crowd. But on location, with only the silent crew watching and no time to rehearse, he seemed to flounder. "At risk of saying, 'I told you so,' it was exactly as I had predicted to Nick," says Hill. "You'd do four takes and Eddie would be very good in one and not so good in a couple and OK on the other one. In dailies, his deficiencies were on display as well as the strengths."

Studio executives, visiting *48 Hrs.* on day trips from L.A., watched and worried. For eight or nine days there were murmurings, serious phone calls back to Paramount HQ. Then a meeting was convened to discuss options. Recalls producer Larry Gross: "The studio wanted to fire him. They said, 'We don't think he's funny. We'll recast and we'll save things.'"

It was crisis time. But Hill held firm: he'd seen enough flashes of genius from Murphy to be convinced he was just the man the movie needed. He assembled footage to show to the studio head, Michael Eisner, then ordered another pass on the script to emphasize Murphy's strengths. "We came to the conclusion that Eddie was best whenever he was competing with Nick over something in the scene," says Gross. "That activated some nerve center in him and suddenly he'd come alive and be mesmerizing. So we had to work up moments that were like a jump ball in basketball, with two guys going for the ball. It has to do with stand-up—he was incredibly responsive to provocation that was right in front of him."

The movie featured frequent verbal duels between Nolte's Jack Cates and Murphy's Reggie Hammond, as they dispense hardboiled bons mots such as "I should get my dick bronzed" and "Your ass is new-mown grass." But its signature scene featured a Murphy monologue. As originally written, Hammond entered a black bar looking for information, telling Cates, "I'll show you how to deal with the brothers." But it had been reconceived in the light of Murphy's edgy racial material on *Saturday Night Live.* Now, instead, he would walk into a country-and-western bar called Torchy's, filled with tough cowboy shit-kickers. In an incendiary set piece, the young black criminal would lay down the law, brandishing a police badge and running rings around the rednecks.

Hill saved it for near the end of the shoot, around the fiftieth day on a schedule of sixty. When Murphy walked onto Stage 3 on the Paramount lot, a space stuffed with brawny extras and adorned with Confederate flags, he was pumped up and tightly coiled. The filmmakers were nervous. Gross wrote in his diary, "Worst comes to worst, there is the editing room. We can always cut to Nick." Murphy himself, who at the crisis point had said, "I know I sucked those first few days—just somebody tell me from here on out," knew how big a deal the sequence was: fuck it up and the movie might die. But it soon became apparent that there was no need for nerves. "By that point, Eddie was in full control of his instrument," Hill says. "He was commanding that room for real."

Murphy set Torchy's on fire, with a tour-de-force five-minute routine, much of it improvised, as hard-edged as any featured in a big-screen comedy. "Listen up. I don't like white people. I hate rednecks," he says. "You people are rednecks, which means I'm enjoying this shit." He smashes a mirror. Dons a cowboy hat. Fearlessly returns the stares of the pissed-off country boys eyeballing him. Then he delivers the movie's most iconic line: "I'm your worst fuckin' nightmare, man: a nigger with a badge."

"He ad-libbed that," says de Souza. "I would have been nervous typing it."

Midway through one of Murphy's takes, standing by the camera, Hill turned to Gross and whispered, "We're rich." He knew it was the movie's showstopper. Even so, the scene was to be ferociously debated in post-production. "There were some who freaked out," says Gross. "They said, 'We have to cut this down tremendously. Eddie is spitting out obscenities and treating these people like dirt. We're going to have violence in theaters.' When we saw a cut-down version I said, 'This is twenty times more dangerous. The first cut was over the top and funny. If you do this trimmed-down version to escape the risk of offending members of the audience, I promise you it will backfire.'"

In test screenings, some people got up and left when the movie reached Torchy's. But when *48 Hrs.* was released in theaters on December 10, 1982, with the scene untampered-with, it slayed audiences, making them roar with laughter, astonished by the balls on this kid. In some screenings, during the Murphy-less opening twenty minutes, crowds started chanting, "EDD-IE! EDD-IE! EDD-IE!"

For the ebullient star, it was a Christmas miracle. Driving his first sports car around New York, Murphy had been frequently pulled over by cops, who would usually ask for an autograph once they realized who he was. Now he was up on giant screens everywhere, waving a police badge and running rings around everyone. He got a particular kick out of seeing himself in action mode in the movie's climax: he'd modeled his facial expressions on his kung-fu hero, Bruce Lee.

Less euphoric was Murphy's grandma, who had cheered him on back in his youth-club days, and who now eagerly ushered deacons from her church into a preview of *48 Hrs*. Two hours later, the group emerged, shell-shocked, and skipped the special dinner laid on by Paramount. "Oh my gosh," chuckles Hill now. "I hope their hearts survived."

THE MOVIE HAD NOT been designed for a God-fearing audience. But everyone else ate it up. "Mr. Murphy runs away with every comic situation that comes his way," raved the *New York Times* review. Another critic exalted, "Call it Bitch Constantly and the Souldance Kid. *48 Hrs*. has never gone by so quickly." Murphy had only been paid a meager $450,000, to Nolte's $1 million, but he was suddenly on the map. Hearing audiences cheering his name as it appeared on the screen gave him a drug-free high. "I left the theater like a dope addict," he said with a grin. "I was on cloud nine for two weeks." And one more amazing experience was to come.

Nolte had been set to host *Saturday Night Live* to promote the movie, but called in sick on the day of the show, after a long Friday night partying at Studio 54. Murphy stepped in to save the day. "When Nick got here and got off the plane he vomited on my shirt," he told the audience in the cold open, a grave expression on his face. "We realized Nick was too sick to do the show. . . . But I know you people tuned in to see one of the stars of *48 Hrs*. host the show and dammit, you're going to see it. Because *I'm* gonna host the show!" His face lit up. Then, instead of the traditional "Live from New York, it's *Saturday Night!*" he yelled, "Live from New York, it's the Eddie Murphy Show!" An hour later Steve Martin gate-crashed his closing remarks to mock-chastise him, crying, "Eddie, you're taking money out of my pocket! I'm a professional host!" But to anyone watching it was obvious that Murphy had transcended not only *SNL*, but the whole medium of TV. The mouthy youngster who had struggled to get a line just two years earlier was now the fastest-rising star in the West.

In quieter moments, Murphy would admit to having fears about the future. But as the offers started to flood in, quiet moments were becoming increasingly rare. "If you think of the '60s, you think of the Beatles," Murphy told *Rolling Stone* in 1983. "The '50s, you think of Elvis. I hope, when you think of the '80s, you think of Eddie Murphy."

7
NEW-MODEL CHEVY

THE START OF the new decade found Chevy Chase at a low ebb. His divorce from Jacqueline Carlin became final on November 26, 1980, with the star ordered by a judge to pay a $400,000 settlement. The best friend he would have turned to for consolation, *Animal House* and *Caddyshack* writer Doug Kenney, had died that summer, falling from a Hawaii cliff top in a peculiar incident that remains a mystery. Some believed that the erratic Kenney, increasingly drug-dependent and driven into a deep funk by what he perceived as the failure of *Caddyshack*, had leaped to his demise. But Chase refused to believe it hadn't been an accident. He had gone to Kauai with Kenney so the two of them could dry out, and the pair had parted on warm terms when Chevy flew back to the mainland. The news left Chase, himself trying to kick a cocaine habit, in a tailspin. "It was the closest to being out of control I've ever been," he was to reflect. "I was emotionally overwhelmed."

A month after Kenney's death, Chase appeared on the late-night *Tomorrow* show. And what should have been a routine bit of on-camera badinage turned into a PR nightmare. Host Tom Snyder asked a question Chase had heard a million times before: with his suave good looks and big-screen romantic capers, was he the new Cary Grant? He could have deflected the question charmingly. Instead, he decided to go for an ill-advised laugh.

"Cary Grant is brilliant, elegant, and athletic," he said. "Can deliver lines with great humor. . . ." Beat. "And I understand that he is a homo." For good measure, Chase mimed a limp-wristed affectation and lisped his next few sentences. After the taping, Snyder offered to cut the offensive joke, but Chase told him to keep it in, sure that the leading man of *North by Northwest* would see the funny side.

He did not. When the episode went out, Grant hit Chase with a major lawsuit, demanding $10 million. It was finally settled out of court for just $150,000, but the humiliating affair did nothing for Chase's image. "I don't think the whole mess ingratiated me much with the gay populace," he told *Playboy*. "So my films don't do great in San Francisco."

In fact, his films weren't doing great anywhere. After a promising start with *Foul Play*, *Oh! Heavenly Dog* had turned him into joke fodder, prompting film critic Roger Ebert to appear on *SNL* with TV partner Gene Siskel and make a wisecrack about it: "That movie split the audience down the middle. Half the people were disappointed when Chevy turned into the dog, and the other half were disappointed when the dog turned into Chevy."

Caddyshack had done OK, but it wasn't really Chase's movie; besides, the golf flick had triggered a full-on crisis of faith. While he had avoided all screenings of *Oh! Heavenly Dog*, admitting years later that he couldn't stomach watching it all the way through, he made the mistake of attending the *Caddyshack* premiere. He'd cruised through the shoot with coke-fueled confidence, but what he saw on-screen appalled him. "I just don't understand my performance," he lamented. "I went in thinking I was the funniest man in the world and could do anything. But when I saw *Caddyshack*, I realized I couldn't act."

Freaking out, he retreated to a familiar working relationship, signing up to star opposite Goldie Hawn again in *Seems Like Old Times*. The project originated with legendary playwright Neil Simon, who aimed to emulate the screwball comedies of the 1930s. Chase was to play Nick Gardenia, an accident-prone writer, who ends up on the run and hiding in the home of his ex-wife, Glenda (Hawn). Also in the movie: Charles Grodin as Glenda's beleaguered district-attorney husband, plus six dogs and two cats, presumably put there on the assumption that more creatures equals more laughs.

Originally Burt Reynolds had been in the frame to play Nick, until a misunderstanding between him and Simon, each of whom was convinced the other had cooled on the project, put the kibosh on that plan. It's hard to imagine the romantic farce working with Reynolds in the role. It certainly doesn't work with Chase. Like those screwball comedies of the 1930s, there are endless comedic misunderstandings and much running around from room to room. But *Seems Like Old Times* is more flat than fizzy, the animals making a bigger impression than the humans. Even the movie's production notes, supplied to the press, seemed more interested in the mutts (Buck, Soarky, Aggie, Jiggs, Scrapper, Peanut) and kitties (Skinny Butt, Swirls) than Chase and Hawn, excitedly proclaiming that Buck, a St. Bernard, was "a descendent of the original Buck in *The Call Of The Wild* and TV's *Topper.*"

"Goldie Yawn!" yelled the headline of a scathing review in the *Daily Mirror.* Chase barely got mentioned in most of the critiques, an also-ran in his own misfire. As for the movie, it made money at the box office, but was not the career salve Chase had been praying for. It was, he decided, time for a risk. So he turned to an unusual screenplay that had made him chortle when he'd sat down to read it one night. It was to prove his biggest disaster yet.

UNDER THE RAINBOW was the brainchild of Fred Bauer and Pat Bradley, producers of the *The Buddy Holly Story.* That Oscar-winning picture had looked back to the 1950s; their new one would go back even further, to the 1930s and Hollywood's Golden Age. The Orion Pictures project would re-create the elite Los Angeles hotel in which the cast and crew of *The Wizard of Oz* had stayed while making the fantasy classic, for an elaborate farce involving 124 oversexed Munchkins, a little-person Nazi spy, and a dog named Strudel.

Bauer and Bradley saw dollar signs, especially when they landed Carrie Fisher to play a talent agent who spent much of the run time in just bra and panties. Their enthusiasm rubbed off on Chevy Chase, to whom they offered the role of FBI agent Bruce Thorpe. He saw similarities to *Foul Play* in the antic plotting: would this be a route back to the heat he'd enjoyed in 1978?

"I read the script and thought it was hilarious," Chase said. He told his agent he was in.

Situated in West L.A., the Culver City Hotel had been open just fourteen years when it was invaded in 1938 by a small army of undersized extras. The circus dwarfs cast as *The Wizard of Oz*'s Munchkins took over the hotel, getting increasingly out of control as the shoot went on. Legend has it there were ransacked rooms, drunken sex parties, and little people swinging from chandeliers. One, who called himself the Count, fell in a toilet inebriated and couldn't get out. *Under the Rainbow* set out to re-create the chaos, with added espionage hijinks, even securing permission to shoot scenes inside the Culver itself. Orion approved a budget of $3.5 million; Bauer, Bradley, and director Steve Rash launched a vast casting call for little people to fill the hallways of the hotel, offering a salary of $100 a day. In late 1980, the shoot began.

A reporter from *Rolling Stone*, visiting the set, was astonished by what he saw. "The frame teems to the point of hallucination," he reported. "Much of the intensity comes from the little people: dwarfs in period costume in a conga line, threading their way through an elegant hotel dining room; dwarfs dressed as Munchkins in a posse, running amok through a swimming-pool set and knocking bathing beauties into the water. . . . The first time you find yourself in their midst, you stare shamelessly, uncontrollably. After a few days on the set, however, your psychological horizon lowers."

If Rash thought he could succeed where *Wizard of Oz* director Victor Fleming failed and tame the sea of tiny extras, he was wrong. Fisher, then just twenty-four, embraced the madness. Decades on, in fact, she recalled that she had scored a large amount of LSD from one of the little people. "That was probably the height of my drug days," she admitted. "I was taken from that set in an ambulance. That was kind of the cap of the whole experience."

The little people were rowdy, Fisher was unstable, and she and Chase were not getting on. What was scheduled as a 55-day shoot dragged on for 110 days. The budget shot up to nearly $7 million. Around Hollywood, the production became known as "Midget's Gate," a jokey reference to the bloated flop *Heaven's Gate*.

Says Mike Medavoy, co-founder of Orion: "I remember going on the set of that movie—I think we were a couple of million dollars over budget at that point—and the first thing I saw when I arrived at the Columbia Ranch was a bunch of people playing horseshoes. I thought, 'Man, we're over budget and these guys are playing horseshoes? There's something wrong with this picture.'"

As for Chase, he spent countless hours standing around, wondering what the hell he was doing. "They're half the size of normal people, so everything takes twice as long," he quipped of the Munchkins. "It takes twice as long for them to run across the set in a chase scene."

There was one upside to the delays: a pretty production assistant named Jayni Luke, whom Chase started getting to know. There was plenty of time for flirting, as the movie's five screenwriters argued over set pieces and historical accuracy. By the time it wrapped, Chevy and Jayni were an item. The new relationship took the sting off the inevitable bad buzz, but once again he was taking jabs from every direction. "Chevy Chase, once a potentially exciting leading man, looks perpetually embarrassed throughout this melee (and well he should)," read one review in the summer of 1981. "His performance as the romantic lead here is surprisingly wooden and devoid of Chase's usual comic sparkle," declared another.

Worse was to come. In New York back in the mid-'70s, Chase had made a low-budget film called *The Groove Tube* with a former child star named Ken Shapiro. It was forgettable, filled with puerile puns (including a commercial for the "Uranus Corporation"), and the pair had had a volatile relationship. But when Shapiro got back in contact with his old friend, now a Hollywood big shot, Chase agreed to star in his second feature film, *Modern Problems*. It was likely out of loyalty:

the script was a blatant stinker, following an air-traffic controller who gets doused with radioactive slime and gains telekinetic powers, which he uses to punish his enemies and give his girlfriend powerful, contact-free orgasms. Tonally wonky, the climax of the increasingly sour tale required Chase to channel Linda Blair's performance from *The Exorcist* as he floats above the ground, green-hued and sickly looking, snorting huge lines of "voodoo power" as if he's in a nightclub in hell.

Snuck out in movie theaters on Christmas Day, 1981, by 20th Century Fox, *Modern Problems* made a smash-grab of $26 million before poisonous word of mouth had a chance to spread. To compound matters, Chase had nearly died on-set. During the filming of a dream sequence in which the hero imagines himself as an airplane, the star had a string of landing lights wrapped around his arms. There was supposed to be padding, but at the last moment they were attached to Chase's bare skin for maximum effect.

"Look, I'm clammy, sweaty. I think there's a danger," Chase muttered.

"It's perfectly safe," someone insisted.

But it wasn't perfectly safe, and when the power was flipped on, a huge charge of electric current jolted through his body for ten seconds, leaving black burn marks on his skin. Chase screamed repeatedly, then passed out. The next thing he saw was a paramedic crouched in front of him, and crew members yelling, "What's your name? What's your name?" Smiling weakly, he quipped: "Don't you know who I am? I'm the star of the picture."

The experience put him into a very dark place. His muscles wouldn't heal fully for two years; psychologically, recovery would take even longer. For over a year, he refused to touch a light switch, asking Jayni to do it instead. He fell into a deep depression, with bouts of uncontrollable crying. When the date of John Belushi's funeral was announced, he decided not to attend, a decision that would haunt him for a long time to come. As he moped around his home, he sometimes worked off his blues by heading to the garage to hunt down spiders, burning them with his lighter.

From the golden boy of New York to the pariah of Hollywood

within half a decade, it had been the roughest of rough rides. One journalist pointed out that he'd put on so much weight that "at times he looks like a giant Pillsbury dough boy." Another noted, "Five years and six movies later, the Chevy Chase promise still seems to be on hold."

HIS CAREER was in the doldrums, but for once his relationship was going well. He and Jayni made each other laugh, and after they wed in 1982 he started to feel like his turbulent days might be behind him. Their first child, Cydney, was born in February 1983, after a marathon twenty-hour labor. Finally, Chevy Chase was a family man.

And in a strange bit of serendipity, his screen image was about to morph in the same direction. Up until this point, he'd exclusively played single guys chasing women. But the next film he was offered drastically recast him from cool-witted lothario to ineffectual husband and dad of two kids. There was still a flirtatious beauty for him to pursue, but he had as much chance of getting together with her as Wile E. Coyote did of bagging the Road Runner.

The script, called *National Lampoon's Vacation*, was based on a 1979 short story by John Hughes, which the future comedy god had written during a Chicago blizzard. Titled *Vacation '58*, it is the tale of a gruff father set on taking his family, by any means necessary, to Disneyland in California. "Dad" is a tightly wound disciplinarian, who hasn't even left the house before he's spitting with frustrated rage: "Goddamn Plymouth Motors! I should have gone with a Ford—they know how to make an ignition. These damn Plymouths!" He is Captain Ahab, Disneyland his white whale, and he'll get there if it kills him. Nothing can stop him: not a run-in with the police, not a dead dog, not even a dead aunt who has to be strapped to the car's roof rack.

The Harold Ramis–directed movie retained much of the story's plotting, but reconfigured the central character. Now named Clark Griswold, he was even-tempered, endlessly optimistic, and more than slightly foolish. For the first time, Chase would be playing someone more silly than slick, and he was at first reluctant to commit. "I knew my career was going completely downhill in comparison to the effect I had in New York City with *Saturday Night Live*," he said. "To the critical world I had gone to the lowest form of family comedies."

Ultimately he realized he didn't have much choice. Remembering the planet-shaking success of *Animal House*, the last National Lampoon movie he'd turned down, he agreed to play Griswold. The producers were delighted. "Chevy was the first one we thought of," says Matty Simmons. "It was as perfect casting as you'll ever see in a movie. Everybody has a relative like Clark—a good guy who loves his family, works hard, and is anxious to do things, but he's not the brightest bulb in the lamp. Chevy could convey all that effortlessly."

With Jayni there to encourage him, cast and crew saw a new Chase. Throughout the six-week shoot, which included stops in such scenic locales as Colorado and Monument Valley, he stopped taking cocaine and arrived at the set on time each day. When he wasn't in front of the camera, he played poker nonstop. The fact he was playing a dad, with two screen children played by Anthony Michael Hall and Dana Barron, may have helped encourage him to clean up his act. Although the kids also inadvertently caused him some pain, when he attempted to stand on his head in a moving trailer to impress them, injuring a pair of vertebrae in his back.

It might have been a family comedy, but it was a National Lampoon one, with a script that had plenty of edge. As well as nudity, there was a questionable scene in which the Griswolds drive their puke-green station wagon through an African American neighborhood and are robbed blind. The aunt and dog still get bumped off. But there were constant debates behind the scenes over where the line should be drawn, with Chase demanding script approval before the shoot. "There's one scene with homegrown pot," he explained to a reporter, "but the girl doesn't really inhale. These are pretty wholesome kids."

After a heated discussion, a shot showing a red stripe of the dead dog's blood running down the highway was left on the editing-room floor. Also cut: the entire original ending, in which Clark arrives at the amusement park (no longer Disneyland, but the fictional Walley World) to find it is temporarily closed, causing him to fly into a rage and take the park's creator hostage in his own home. It tested so badly with a preview audience that the last fifteen minutes of the film were entirely reshot at Six Flags Magic Mountain in Valencia, California. In the new version, Clark waves a BB gun ("It's a Magnum PI!") in a security guard's face, forcing him to reopen the park so that his family can have enforced fun to their heart's content.

The reshoots were great news for John Candy, who, when Bill Murray proved unavailable, was drafted in to play the security guard, starting an important relationship with John Hughes, with whom he would work on seven more movies. As Matty Simmons recalls, Candy was paid an incredible $1 million for his cameo, something which became a sore point on-set.

"He was very upset with me for teasing him about it," the producer says. "The studio made the deal and I was astounded he got that much money. So I said, 'You're spending three days here and getting a million dollars? My God, that's more than I got!' There were two or three hours where he was mad at me and scowled every time I walked by. But then we made up. I said, 'Ah, come on, you're worth everything. I'd pay you $2 million if I could . . . '"

The reshoot was less fortuitous for Chase, who became nauseated after having to ride a roller coaster over and over again. But the star had finally found a role he really clicked with: Clark, in his tortoise-shell specs and nebbish suit, was not only his most likable character to date, but the funniest. The fact he starts the movie so chipper makes it all the more hilarious when he finally snaps.

"I think you're all fucked in the head," he tells his wife and children, a maniacal glint in his eye, when they suggest the holiday be cut short. "We're ten hours from the fucking fun-park and you want to fucking bail out. Well, I'll tell you something: this is no longer a vacation. It's a quest. It's a quest for fun. I'm going to have fun and you're going to have fun. We're all going to have so much fucking fun we'll need plastic surgery to remove our goddamn smiles. You'll be whistling 'Zip-a-Dee-Doo-Dah' out of your *assholes*!"

National Lampoon's Vacation was as successful as the road trip it depicted was disastrous. It shot to number one at the box office in

July 1983, making over $60 million. Candy went on to be hired by Ron Howard for his mermaid comedy *Splash*, cast as the hyperactive brother to Tom Hanks's hero. Despite playing a sleaze who peeks up ladies' skirts, Candy continued to charm all who came within his orbit. "I just absolutely adored him," says co-star Daryl Hannah. "Tears-coming-out-of-your-eyes, pee-your-pants hilarious. I used to sit on his lap all the time and he would talk for me while I mimed what he was saying. I would just be his ventriloquist doll." With his earnings, Candy bought a ten-acre country estate outside Toronto, and a tractor (a 1947 Massey-Harris) so he could re-grade the enormous lawn himself.

As for Chase, *National Lampoon's Vacation* was his biggest hit to date. He returned to his Pacific Palisades home on a high. He had a wife he loved. He had two pet parrots, named Doug (after Kenney) and Darwin. And he had, once again, some Hollywood heat.

8
BRAIN POWER

ON THE MORNING of March 27, 1980, Steve Martin received a phone call from Stanley Kubrick. In Britain to promote *The Jerk*, Martin had spent the evening before guesting on Michael Parkinson's chat show. Wearing a pink suit and bunny ears, he'd rushed onstage and slapped an arrow-through-the-head prop on Parkinson. "And now *you're* funny," he said. Then he grabbed the host's notes, perused them, and said, "Yes. No. Yes. I don't know. Yes and no. He'll tell you the questions later—I've gotta go." The bit had made the audience howl, and it had the same effect on the reclusive director of *2001: A Space Odyssey*, who had been watching it on TV.

"He called me up and said, 'I was just sitting there and thought, 'Oh, that's who I need for this movie,'" Martin recalls. "So I went to his house in the country." That house was Childwickbury Manor in Hertfordshire, an hour north of London, a sprawling pile with twelve reception rooms and twenty-nine bedrooms. The movie was *Eyes Wide Shut*, an erotic drama Kubrick was cooking up, based on a 1926 novella called *Traumnovelle* by Arthur Schnitzler. "Kubrick described all his films as comedies," says Martin. "*Dr. Strangelove* was a serious book (it was loosely based on Peter George's 1958 thriller novel *Red Alert*), but he saw it as a comedy. *Lolita* he saw as a comedy. And so for this project he was looking for comic people and thought I might be the right guy."

Within the space of twenty-four hours, the thirty-six-year-old had gone from goofing around in rabbit ears to locking minds with the world's most revered auteur. In the hush of the vast manor, he and his host sat down for a game of chess. Later that afternoon, they visited the pool room, where Martin smelled something awful: it turned out one of Kubrick's dogs had crapped all over a nearby hallway. The filmmaker didn't acknowledge the reek. Finally, Martin was ushered into the archives, a series of towering stacks full of files. One box was marked "Hostile Press": inside was every negative review Kubrick had received.

Ultimately, this version of *Eyes Wide Shut* would evaporate; the project didn't come together for Kubrick until 1999, with Tom Cruise playing the lead role. But the eight-hour meeting was a good indication of where Martin's head was at following the release of *The Jerk*. Following the snooty critical reaction to his debut film, he was seeking legitimacy as an actor. "When I look at it now, I think I yelled through the entire movie," he said in 1983, after catching it on cable TV. Martin would always be fond of *The Jerk*, even toying with the idea of writing a sequel: "There was a funny opening. 'My mother couldn't make the payment on her land, so the bank came with a tractor and scooped it up and put it in a barn.'" But he thought it was time to evolve.

Hence his wary reaction to the offers thrust in his direction. He wanted to be thoroughly convinced that the next project was a good one. Soon enough, though, one came along that convinced him beyond doubt.

Pennies from Heaven was to be an American adaptation of a six-part BBC drama, which Martin happened to have seen on PBS when it aired in 1978. The tale of an unhappy song-sheet salesman in the 1930s, who periodically escapes his bleak life via fantastical musical dream sequences, Dennis Potter's heady mix of glitz and grim reality was, Martin thought, one of the most startlingly original things he'd ever seen. So when he heard it was being reimagined as a Hollywood picture of considerable budget, he went for it.

Al Pacino and Richard Dreyfuss were among the big names in the running for the lead role. But most stars were put off by the grubbiness of Arthur Parker, a sad little man who cheats on his wife, inadvertently drives his lover into a life of prostitution, and ultimately becomes a murderer. Martin was undeterred by any of that. Neither was he put off by the fact he'd have to dye his gray hair brown and take months of tap-dancing lessons. Hearing of his passion for the project, director Herbert Ross went to Las Vegas to watch two of the comedian's shows. He returned to L.A. convinced he'd found his Arthur. "What I saw in Steve was his ability to move," Ross said. "He's rhythmic and musical and coordinated, and somehow he's in the tradition that those numbers are in. . . . He's literally the only actor in Hollywood equipped to do a musical. Even Robin Williams, who is trained, hasn't got his technique."

Martin's manager Bill McEuen publicly fretted that *Pennies from Heaven* was a terrible career move, saying, "I just don't think he should be doing a dramatic role at this point." But the star was offered the role, and he took it, timing be damned: "The script is now, not ten years from now. So I have to do it now."

It's not hard to see what the appeal was for him. *Pennies from Heaven* is filled with references to art, re-creating famous paintings such as Edward Hopper's *Nighthawks* and Reginald Marsh's *Hudson Bay Fur Company*. There are ambitious song-and-dance sequences, with one Busby Berkeley–esque sequence mounted in a bank and another giving Martin the chance to not only hoof but strum his signature banjo. It couldn't hurt, either, that his girlfriend, Bernadette Peters, was lined up to play Eileen, a wholesome schoolmarm drawn into Arthur's doomed orbit.

A journalist visiting the set took in Martin's dyed, slicked-back hair, watched him shoot a particularly depressing scene, then asked if he was anxious his fans might reject this new-model Steve. He shook his head. "I would not allow myself to be afraid," he would say after the shoot. "When I first started doing my act, it was not normal. It was not what was expected. That's why the public caught onto it. And I said, 'If I start getting trapped by my own sameness, I'm not doing what they secretly want, which is for me to do what I want to do.'"

His confidence wasn't borne out by the reaction to the final product. On its December 1981 release, *Pennies from Heaven* did lively business in New York, but sunk around the rest of the country, making just $9 million back from its $22 million budget. That dichotomy was mirrored in the reviews. *New Yorker* critic Pauline Kael rhapsodized that it was "the most emotional movie I've ever seen." Roger Ebert, on the other hand, echoed his assault on *The Jerk* by singling out Martin for rebuke: *"Pennies from Heaven* is all flash and style and no heart. That's the problem with the Steve Martin performance, too. He provides a technically excellent performance that does not seem to be inhabited by a person."

Even more stinging was the critique by musical legend Fred Astaire, footage from whose 1936 classic *Follow the Fleet* had been woven into the film. "I have never spent two more miserable hours in my life," Astaire reportedly raged, after emerging from a screening of *Pennies from Heaven.* "Every scene was cheap and vulgar. It makes you cry, it's so distasteful."

Martin's friends Aykroyd and Belushi stood up for it, the former praising the dancing and hailing it as a bold and topical tale. But otherwise Martin felt under siege from all sides—he'd even heard that Bob Hoskins, the star of the British version, was furious not to have been asked to reprise the role. While shocked that something so heartfelt could evoke such anger, Martin refused to throw his second film under the bus.

"I loved doing *Pennies from Heaven,*" he says, decades on. "Because you have to understand that I'd been doing comedy for fifteen to twenty years, and suddenly along came the opportunity to do this beautiful film. It was so emotional to me. I loved it. I don't think it was a good career move, but I have no regrets about doing it."

At the time, he had a more colorful defense. "I must say that the people who get the movie, in general, have been wise and intelligent," he stated. "The people who don't get it are ignorant scum."

AS MUCH AS HE ADORED *Pennies from Heaven*, it was by no means his movie. His fans waited eagerly for a proper follow-up to *The Jerk*, conceived and written by Martin himself. But try as he might, the inspiration just wouldn't flow. Through the first half of 1980 he worked with Carl Reiner and George Gipe on a screenplay called *The Depression*, a comedy about the economic collapse of the United States. But at lunch one day that summer, the three men came to the glum conclusion that the economic collapse of the United States just wasn't that hilarious a topic. Six months of hard work had come to naught. Before they left the restaurant, however, inspiration struck. "Like all good things," says Reiner, "it was conjured in a panic."

The brainwave was this: what if they interspersed footage of Martin with clips from old movies, Frankensteining their own silly narrative? They batted around the idea of making a pastiche Western, before deciding that re-creating the vast vistas of Monument Valley wasn't a viable option. Instead, they settled on film noir.

"We wanted personalities," said Martin, "and all the actors we liked worked mostly in the crime thriller genre." A gumshoe spoof filmed in this way could make him part of the ultimate ensemble: Humphrey Bogart, Ava Gardner, Ray Milland, Joan Crawford, Charles Laughton, Cary Grant, Veronica Lake, Kirk Douglas, and more. It would be like that scene in *Blazing Saddles* where the cast runs through different movies, except with real films and real stars.

As Martin headed off to shoot *Pennies from Heaven*, Reiner and Gipe tracked down prints of every '40s and '50s noir they could think of, embarking on the ultimate noir binge. "We spent months looking at these old black-and-white films, screening three or four a day, saying, 'Hey, here's a funny line,' or, 'Could this insert of a dagger work?'" says Reiner. When Martin returned, the three men scrawled fragments of dialogue and plot points all over a blackboard, slowly piecing together a coherent story like a giant jigsaw puzzle.

Dead Men Don't Wear Plaid—its title inspired by a scene from the Lauren Bacall thriller *Dark Passage*—features a doofus detective named Rigby Reardon (his name an amalgam of characters from MGM's *The Bribe* and Universal's *The Killers*). As he embarks on his latest investigation ("the case of the dame with the big tits"), Rigby weaves in and out of such classics as *The Lost Weekend, This Gun for Hire,* and *White Heat,* getting shot by James Cagney and strangling Bette Davis (with Paul Henreid's hands). "We really had to contort ourselves to match what was going on in the old movies," Reiner admits. "But the story we came up with isn't any more confusing than *The Big Sleep.*"

Martin himself avoided watching any noirs: "I didn't want to act like Bogart. It's too easy to pick up his style, and I didn't want to be tugging my ear or drawling my lines." He did, however, spend a month punching up the script, adding jokes and tweaking the structure. Then he dyed his hair black again—the back of his head had to match those of actors from the old movies—and headed to Laird International Studios in Culver City for ten weeks of painstaking filming. Two actors, Matthew Laurance and Jill Jaress, doubled for whichever Golden Age star Rigby was dealing with; a host of old-school Hollywood talent, including legendary costume designer Edith Head, *Cleopatra* production designer John DeCuir, and *Raging Bull* cinematographer Michael Chapman, fiddled with their elements until the illusion was complete.

Rarely has such a silly experiment been taken so seriously. "Both Steve and I got really immersed in it," says Reiner, who had to devise a running joke about pajamas to explain why Rigby's costume keeps changing. "For that scene where he chases Vincent Price down the stairs, we re-created a sequence from *The Bribe* out on the back lot, with hundreds of extras. It looked so amazing, you would never know it was not in the original scene."

By the time it was all cut together, it was a marvel of craftsmanship. Not only that—it was funny, a paean to a bygone age of cinema that was also full of the kinds of witty riffs Martin had done onstage. Test screenings in Santa Barbara and San Diego were a huge success, with both star and director basking in the laughter. "I felt like nudging Carl," Martin said, "and saying, 'We're so smart.' It was just a good feeling. I hadn't done anything funny for almost two years. I felt in contact with the audience again."

But once again, his instincts proved wonky. *The Jerk* had been the eighth biggest movie of 1979, but in the box-office tally at the end of 1982, *Dead Men Don't Wear Plaid* floundered at number 40 with just $18 million. It had been not just beaten but thrashed by *48 Hrs.* ($76 million) and *Porky's* ($109 million). Perhaps it shouldn't have been a huge shock that young audiences shunned a black-and-white send-up of fusty old movies, but the disappointment still hit Martin hard.

Instead of distancing himself from his collaborators and trying something completely different, however, Martin did exactly the opposite. He'd thought up another way to pay tribute to a hallowed Hollywood genre—and his *Dead Men Don't Wear Plaid* director was the first person he called.

"That was a great one," Carl Reiner says of *The Man with Two Brains*. "Steve came to me with the idea. Remember a movie called *Donovan's Brain*? He said, 'Let's do a takeoff of *Donovan's Brain*.'" That 1953 B-movie, starring Lew Ayres and First-Lady-to-be Nancy Reagan (then Nancy Davis), was a slab of schlock horror with an even schlockier tagline: "A dead man's brain in a hidden laboratory told him to KILL . . . KILL . . . KILL . . ." Martin loved its crazed plot, its lurid mood, and its shots of brains floating in vats. Push it all a little further, he thought, and you'd have a comedy that, yes, would KILL . . . KILL . . . KILL . . .

Dead Men Don't Wear Plaid had been all about discipline: even Martin's performance had required an ultra-deadpan affect. *The Man with Two Brains*, on the other hand, was a chance to cut loose across the board. Martin, Reiner, and Gipe reassembled for a marathon *Brains*-storming session; this time they didn't have to invest in a blackboard to keep the plot straight, and no idea was too silly. The hero they came up with was brilliant neurosurgeon Dr. Michael Hfuhruhurr ("A lot of people mispronounce it. But it sounds just the way it's spelled. H-F-U-H-R-U-H-U-R-R"), the pioneer of cranial screw-top zip-lock brain surgery. Life is peachy for the egomaniacal MD, until he accidentally hits a beautiful woman with his car. Soon he's trapped in a sexless marriage with a scheming harridan who wants him dead; to complicate matters, he falls in love with the disembodied brain of a serial-killer victim, Anne Uumellmahaye.

That logline is demented enough. But the film piles on a relentless blizzard of jokes, from sight gags (one of Hfuhruhurr's medical hoods has bunny ears, a nod to Martin's famous stand-up prop) to word-play ("Can I get you anything else, sir? I am about to retire," a butler asks, prompting our hero to respond, "But you seem so young!"). The atomic-powered lunacy features moments of physical comedy, ridiculous riffs on Hitchcock, even gags that smash the fourth wall: when a German realizes the doctor is American, he barks an order for the scene's subtitles to stop.

"It was a wonderful amalgam," Reiner says. "On *The Man with Two Brains*, everything was funny. And we used everything Steve could do. When he's driving drunk and he's stopped on the road by the police and tested, he's told, 'Walk in a straight line.' He does that. They say, 'Do a handstand.' He walks on his hands. Then they say, 'Now sing while juggling.' And there Steve is, singing a German song while juggling. We only wrote that scene because Steve had all those skills."

Wheel of Fortune creator and talk show host Merv Griffin was cast as the serial killer—playing himself—and British horror stalwart David Warner as a mad scientist who lives in a logic-defying castle condominium. But the real coup was getting Kathleen Turner, then riding high from her debut film performance in the erotic hit *Body Heat*, as sex siren Dolores. Arriving on-set, she asked Reiner, "How far will you allow me to go?"

"How far can you go?" the director asked.

"Just watch me."

Her comedic skills proved formidable, whether she's lusting after Mexican gardeners, tormenting her husband, or gamely being flung by Martin into a puddle, inspiring the immortal line, "Into the mud, scum queen!" Her palpable glee was matched by that of her leading man. This was an unfettered Steve Martin, ultra-glib, live-wire, and back at the thundering energy levels of his live performances. As with the movies of Monty Python, it felt like anything could happen, an impression aided by the movie's R rating. At one point Hfuhruhurr gets an almighty erection: he hangs his hat on it, then accidentally breaks a pane of glass. At another, the harebrained surgeon says the words "I couldn't fuck a gorilla." It makes perfect sense in context.

The hyperactive horror parody was released in early June, and sunk fast, earning only $9 million. "I really don't understand why this comedy has been slighted," wrote one journalist. "*Two Brains* is a laughing-gas high." Those who saw it tended to love it, but that didn't make up for the fact Martin had had three strikes in a row. Friends tried to console him by pointing out that the third installment in the *Star Wars* saga, *Return of the Jedi*, was still sucking up a lot of the potential audience, but it didn't help his state of mind. "I got stunned again, and I was really depressed. I don't know why nobody came," he reflected shortly afterward. The cheering hordes of his stand-up days seemed to have deserted him. "One of the shocking things to me is how few people remember how big I was. It's more curiosity than ego trip."

Reiner still loves the film dearly. Martin, on the other hand, remains chilly when the subject comes up. As funny as it is, its reception that June seems to have left a scar. "I view *The Jerk* as successful, but I don't view *The Man with Two Brains* as successful," he says. "I don't look at it and think, 'Wow, that's really funny.' I know it had a little cult following. I don't think it was received very well. But I had a really good time making it, working with Carl."

As 1984 began, the future had never seemed so uncertain. His fifth film, *The Lonely Guy*, flew in and out of theaters, leaving dust in its trail. Playing a despair-ridden greeting-card salesman, it turned out, wasn't the panacea for his ails. Steve Martin, a keen student of Picasso, was experiencing his own Blue Period. And all he could do was keep on trucking.

"I'm like a loaded gun—I'm ready to kill," he declared that September. "I really feel enthused. I know that eventually there will be a hit. Eventually."

WHILE STEVE MARTIN was floundering, up north in Canada an admirer of his was having more success than he had ever thought possible. His name was Rick Moranis, and despite being slight, unassuming, and adorned with geeky spectacles, his career was going stratospheric.

Nobody found it harder to believe than Moranis himself. He and comedy partner Dave Thomas arrived in Regina in 1981 for their first public appearance since becoming a phenomenon with *SCTV* characters the McKenzie Brothers, having been invited by the notoriously hard-partying Saskatchewan Roughrider Cheerleaders to have drinks with them. But when their plane landed, they found the airport besieged by 1,500 cheering fans. "I mean, it was craziness," says Moranis. "There were thousands of screaming people chasing us. The closest thing to it was what I saw watching the movie *A Hard Day's Night*. The amount of celebrity was unlike anything I had ever encountered."

As they finally escaped, driving to a hotel to meet the cheerleaders, their car went under an overpass. The graffiti on it read TAKE OFF, EH—the catchphrase Moranis and Thomas had made famous. "We were kinda awed by that," Thomas says. "Graffiti in Canada is very rare. And specific graffiti that is related to something you're doing, which you can actually be blamed for, is even more rare."

The people Moranis had grown up with had all become doctors, lawyers, or accountants. He himself had initially dreamed of being in a band, before falling into a job at a radio station. In his free time he tried stand-up comedy in Toronto, but never came offstage feeling euphoric. "It didn't satisfy me," he says. "I found that if a joke was funny on Monday, I didn't know why I was doing it on Tuesday. Maybe the reason I never hooked into it was that I didn't have a persona. I didn't do monologues; I did non-sequential odds and ends, some characters, and some stuff with my guitar."

Still, the cerebral Ontarian was capable of spinning comedy gold out of the unlikeliest of subjects. While working in radio he learned about Canadian content regulations: it was mandated by the government that 30 percent of music played on the station had to be homegrown. Thinking the idea was idiotic, Moranis began parodying it in his stand-up material. Then, after he got a job at *SCTV* in 1980, just as John Candy left, the subject came up again, with government-funded station CBC demanding that two minutes of each episode be "Canadian."

Moranis exploded. "I went ballistic because every single thing we were doing was Canadian. We were all Canadian. We were in Canada. We could be doing a parody of *War and Peace* and it would be Canadian." He proposed that as an act of rebellion he and Thomas could be filmed doing the most stereotypical things imaginable: sitting in front of a map of the country, wearing parkas and tuques, frying up back bacon, chugging beer, and adding "Eh?" to the end of every sentence. To his amazement, the show's bosses shrugged and agreed. The duo stayed behind at the end of the day, with a skeleton crew consisting of one cameraman, one soundman, and a guy in the audio booth, cracked open a six-pack, and shot over a dozen two-minute clips, one for each show of the season.

What everyone expected to be filler—and its creators considered an extended act of sarcasm—blew up into a phenomenon. The dim-witted McKenzie Brothers (Moranis as Bob, Thomas as Doug) suddenly became the most popular part of the comedy show. Rick Moranis being Rick Moranis, his first response was acute embarrassment. "I felt bad that all this other work we were putting so much effort into with makeup and hair and wardrobe and writing and editing and long days of shooting was taking a backseat to this little improvised two-minute thing," he says. "And it wasn't fair to the other cast members that we were being disproportionately praised. I remember *Rolling Stone* giving us a cover line that said, '*SCTV*'s Best Joke.' That bothered me. *SCTV* didn't have a best joke: it was full of all these dynamic, interesting, colorful, unusual sketches."

Despite his discomfort, the McKenzies kept getting bigger and bigger. When Thomas and Moranis were asked to record a comedy album, *The Great White North* shot to number one on the Canadian charts and stayed there for eight weeks.

"The record changed everything," says Thomas. "I remember going Christmas shopping and getting mobbed. I had to stop shopping.

That was a new and actually fairly unpleasant experience. Because the McKenzie Brothers appealed to a heavy-metal, beer-drinking crowd. We went from people coming up to us saying, 'Excuse me, big fan of *SCTV*. Really enjoyed your parody of Bob Hope' to people raising their fists in the air and going, 'EEEUURRGGHH!' It was kind of scary, because our fans went from being smart people to violent morons."

Inevitably, Moranis and Thomas were asked to make a movie with the characters, just as Aykroyd and Belushi had with the Blues Brothers. The result was 1983's *Strange Brew*, a peculiar Hamlet-inspired concoction that pitted the backwoodsmen against a madman, played by Max Von Sydow, bent on drugging Canada's beer supply. The stars had hoped to be fairly hands-off, given that they were burned out enough by doing their ninety-minute weekly TV show, but they ended up not only rewriting the script but directing the film themselves. "It was insane: we'd never directed; we didn't even want to direct!" says Thomas. "We were sort of reluctantly scrambling to salvage it as something we recognized as true to the characters."

Costing nearly $4 million, the movie made just over double its budget, decent enough but proof that the McKenzie magic was starting to fade. Moranis, who had had less input into the film than the record, was anxious to move on. He had begun to infiltrate Hollywood circles, rubbing shoulders with his American counterparts. At a party one night in Thomas's L.A. house, he met Dan Aykroyd, who enthused about the McKenzie Brothers and suggested writing them into *Never Say Mountie*, a movie he envisioned for himself and Belushi that never came to fruition.

Another relationship was forged out of the oddest of circumstances. One of Moranis's most popular characters on *SCTV* was Larry Siegel, a thinly veiled send-up of macho, blustering Hollywood producer Joel Silver. The skit was a hit not just in Canada but in L.A., where Universal Studios president Sean Daniel had fifty copies of it put onto VHS tapes and sent all around town. Martin Scorsese loved it but mistakenly thought he was the one being lampooned, cornering Moranis at a dinner party one night and saying, "That's me, right? No, no, no, that's me. That's me." As for Silver himself, he was approached in the bathroom of an L.A. hotel by a man who asked if he was Larry Siegel from *SCTV*.

Fortunately, he saw the funny side. One morning Moranis got a phone call out of the blue from the producer, asking why he had worn a tiny gold necklace in one of the skits, since Silver never wore jewelry himself. The two became unlikely friends.

IT WAS SILVER who approached Moranis with a pitch in early 1983. The film was called *Streets of Fire*, and it was to be Walter Hill's follow-up to *48 Hrs*.

"I want you to do in this what Eddie did in that," said Silver.

"Well, what is it?" asked Moranis.

Silver replied, "Don't worry about the script. There was no script on *48 Hrs.*—they made it all up, they made the whole thing up. You gotta do this movie. You should do this movie."

The offer looked pretty sweet. Moranis says he was told that Bruce Springsteen and Daryl Hannah were in talks to play the leads, in what was to be a rock-opera action flick about a soldier of fortune trying to rescue a beautiful singer from an evil biker gang. Moranis was to play the singer's nebbish manager/boyfriend, Billy Fish.

"It was a Hollywood movie, which I had never experienced," he says. "And *Strange Brew* was in post-production. If I didn't do this, I was gonna be sitting there with Dave in the editing room. So I signed the deal. Next thing I know, Bruce Springsteen is not in the movie. And Daryl Hannah is not in the movie: She's taking a movie called *Splash*. Suddenly it was shifting into something else. And as I recall every idea I came up with that might have remotely attempted to come close to something comical was rejected."

Hill denies that Springsteen was ever sought after. "I've never even met him," he says. "We did try to get the Springsteen song 'Streets of Fire' at one point; Jimmy Iovine, who came onto the movie and was close to Springsteen, felt he could get it. But those negotiations broke down. Now, Daryl Hannah, we did meet with her and the studio very much wanted her. Then all of a sudden she took the mermaid movie."

Diane Lane was signed instead. As for the male lead, Moranis's new sparring partner was Michael Paré, an intense New Yorker. The two did not get along. "Rick Moranis drove me out of my mind," said Paré in 2011. "What I wanted to do was just hit him once and let him go through the whole movie like Jack Nicholson in *Chinatown*." Recalls Hill: "I certainly don't think Rick and Michael were on the same wavelength. Michael had his own personal problems, I think, on the film. I have to say that if I were Rick I would have watched my step around him. If they had rather violently disagreed I know who I'd have bet on. Mercifully for Rick, they did not come to blows."

The shoot stretched from April to August 1983. After shooting exteriors around Chicago and L.A., the production camped down under a huge tent on the Universal back lot; despite being set entirely at night, they couldn't shoot nights without the motorcycle noise and gunfire disturbing nearby residents. Deprived of sunshine and falling fifteen days behind schedule because of light leaking in through holes in the tent, cast and crew found it a rough haul. "It was not a particularly enjoyable experience," says Moranis, who was stuck playing an uncharacteristically unlikable character. "Except I had a lot of fun with Joel." When he introduced Silver to Don Rickles's comedy album *Hello Dummy*, the producer became addicted to it, cruising around L.A. in his Mercedes-Benz sedan, the insult comic's burns blasting out of the speakers.

One day Moranis got a call from Silver, saying, "I've had an idea—you gotta write a movie for Rickles." So he did. Titled *Killer Charlie 5* and inspired by the *Death Wish* franchise, it was about a tough, taciturn actor who only makes revenge movies. "It opened with the trailer for *Killer Charlie 4* and was all about how he doesn't want to make *Killer Charlie 5*—he wants to do a pet project instead," recalls Moranis. "It was an inside show business movie, about sequels and action pictures and all that kind of stuff. I wanted to direct it too."

He and Silver flew to Vegas to pitch it, arriving at Rickles's hotel suite to find the door opened by a man wearing only a bathrobe. It was Rickles's manager, Joe Scandori, who proceeded to show them the neck-to-navel scar he had from open-heart surgery, before explaining that they'd be sleeping in the suite, Moranis on the floor and Silver on the sofa. "It was so weird. Walking down to dinner with Rickles, we were trying to figure out what to do," Moranis says. "We couldn't get a flight, so were we going to rent a car and drive home through the night? We weren't going to stay in Joe Scandori's room."

Fortunately, they were recognized by the hotel manager and comped the Presidential Suite. Moranis had his balls busted repeatedly at dinner by Rickles, who had found out that the young comedian impersonated him on *SCTV* too. But *Killer Charlie 5* never came to pass: Universal head Tom Pollock decided Moranis wasn't a big enough commercial draw.

Moranis didn't have time to mope. As *Streets of Fire* continued to film, another offer came in: a small role in a big movie that sounded very interesting indeed. "Rick and I didn't really get to know each other well during the shoot," says Walter Hill. "But as I recall, *Ghostbusters* was pressing on his mind."

CROSSING THE STREAMS

JOHN BELUSHI'S FUNERAL was held on March 9, 1982, at Abel's Hill Cemetery on Martha's Vineyard—the only part of the world, Belushi had told Dan Aykroyd, where he could get a good night's sleep. Wearing a black leather jacket and black jeans, Aykroyd led the funeral procession on his motorcycle. He helped carry his fellow Blues Brother's casket to the grave site, where the headstone read HERE LIES BURIED THE BODY OF JOHN BELUSHI. "I MAY BE GONE, BUT ROCK AND ROLL LIVES ON."

He and his fellow pallbearers listened to James Taylor sing "That Lonesome Road" as snowflakes gently fell. Then, two days later, in New York's Cathedral of Saint John the Divine, he played the Ventures' "The 2,000 Pound Bee," a hard-charging, thoroughly cathedral-inappropriate rock song, to a thousand mourners, keeping a promise he'd made to his departed pal.

Never one to betray his emotions, he looked like he was holding up fine. But inside he was in agony. "What's blue and sings alone?" went a joke he started telling people. "Dan Aykroyd."

He'd lost the friend he had been able to call at any time of day or night, the man he regarded as his platonic soul mate. "When I saw him come into a room, I got the jump you get when you see a beautiful girl," Aykroyd said after Belushi's funeral. "Being with him was electric, really electric."

He was also thirty-one and still single, having broken up with Carrie Fisher, with whom he'd fallen in love on the set of *The Blues Brothers*. "While in Chicago we obtained blood tests for compatibility from an East Indian female doctor," he was to remember of that relationship. "Contemplating marriage, I gave Carrie a sapphire ring and subsequently in the romance she gave me a Donald Roller Wilson oil painting of a monkey in a blue dress next to a tiny floating pencil." The romance was brief but intense. One weekend they flew up to Reno, took acid, and spent three days weeping to Christmas songs. "Certainly one of the planet's greatest occasions where LSD was a factor," Aykroyd reported. But it ended when Fisher left him for Paul Simon.

Even his health was looking rocky. He'd never taken much care of himself, prompting his government-official dad to tell him, shortly after Belushi's funeral, that he'd been prepared for years to get a call saying, "Your son is in a box." After an impromptu checkup, his doctor looked at the results of the blood test and advised him to quit drinking. He reluctantly agreed.

Aykroyd's future suddenly seemed incredibly uncertain. Not least because *Ghost Smashers*, the screenplay at which he had been slowly chipping away, had been intended as another vehicle for him and John. Now he wasn't in much of a mood to continue work on the script, which was already weirdly dark and depressing. "It was pretty grim," Aykroyd admits. "There wasn't much fun in it. You know, the energy could take you down if you weren't careful, that type of thing. It was much more of a horror than a comedy."

Ghost Smashers was a heady blend of many of Aykroyd's passions: ghosts, cars, complex machinery, even more complex terminology, New York. He was a lifelong fan of the supernatural-comedy subgenre, cherishing such films as *Spook Busters*, *Hold That Ghost*, and the Bob Hope vehicle *The Ghost Breakers*, which was remade as *Scared Stiff* with Dean Martin and Jerry Lewis. Moreover, fascination with phantasms had long been a family trait. His great-grandfather Dr. Sam Aykroyd had exchanged letters with fellow spiritualist Sir Arthur Conan Doyle, while his grandfather once commissioned a sketch of a high-vibrating crystal he believed would be able to cut through to the fifth, sixth, and seventh dimensions.

As a boy, Dan would spend vacations in the family's summer cottage in Kingston, Ontario; there he would spy on séances and rifle through parapsychology journals. He recalls, "As an eight-year-old I had access to my great-grandfather's entire library. The impressive thing was that all these people writing, from Albert Durrant Watson to Conan Doyle, were serious inquirers." Their dizzying notions of what came after death became lodged permanently in his mind. Early in life he became, quite literally, a card-carrying member of the American Society for Psychical Research.

Turning this material into a blockbuster script, however, was proving a fearsome challenge. For one thing, the story he had concocted was mind-bogglingly vast. "It was set in the future and on another planet," remembers *Stripes* director Ivan Reitman, to whom Aykroyd showed his efforts. "There were many teams of characters battling stuff and there were monsters on every page. It would have cost hundreds of millions of dollars to make."

The central premise was that catching specters is a blue-collar job, like collecting garbage or putting out fires. But anyone without a scientific degree would have struggled to understand the reams of exposition about "nutrona wands" and "interdimensional interceptors." Besides, there was now a huge, Belushi-shaped hole at the heart of the project.

Aykroyd reluctantly put away the eighty pages he'd completed. He decided to concentrate on other things.

FIRST UP WAS *DOCTOR DETROIT*. After the fiasco of *Neighbors*, Bernie Brillstein had advised his clients Belushi and Aykroyd to work separately for a while. It was probably sound advice. Unfortunately, the first solo project he thrust at Aykroyd turned out to be a dud of titanic proportions.

The idea had originated with novelist, playwright, and part-time Hollywood player Bruce Jay Friedman—also involved to various degrees in the Gene Wilder–Richard Pryor vehicle *Stir Crazy*, the Steve Martin flop *The Lonely Guy*, and *Splash*. Friedman saw *Doctor Detroit*, an adaptation for Universal of his own short story *Detroit Abe*, as potentially a sophisticated, highbrow comedy. Its hero was stuffy college professor Clifford Skridlow, who lectures on Lancelot's chivalric code in his comparative literature class. When a desperate crime boss fingers him as a nonexistent pimp called "Doctor Detroit," he is drawn into the seedy Chicago underworld and forced to create an intimidating persona in order to protect a stable of prostitutes.

Then Dan Aykroyd signed on. A few things about the project appealed to him. First, the idea of shooting again in Chicago, the city that he and Belushi had ruled while making *The Blues Brothers*. Second, the opportunity to build up a dual role from scratch, with minimal interference. The studio was even willing to let him inject his own ideas, like a live performance at the end of the movie from *Blues Brothers* guest star James Brown.

Meeting with screenwriter Robert Boris and director Michael Pressman at the latter's house, Aykroyd acted out scenes, cranking up the comedic volume as if he was overcompensating for the absence of Belushi. In particular he relished the professor's felonious alter ego. With candy-colored clothing, blond fright wig, bizarre metal hand, permanent sneer, and accent that sounded like Paul Williams with severe nasal congestion, Doctor Detroit became a character as full-strength as any Aykroyd had played on *Saturday Night Live*.

This wasn't exactly what the writers had originally had in mind. "I really wanted to do it as if it was Cary Grant and Katharine Hepburn in *Bringing Up Baby*, and the film ended up as a low-rent Marx Brothers comedy," lamented Boris. Sure enough, as production proceeded over the summer of 1982, it became difficult to describe anything about *Doctor Detroit* as sophisticated or highbrow. New wave band Devo was hired to create a thundering electro theme tune; the climax was retooled as a bizarre synchronized dance, in which Doctor

Detroit leads a chorus line of prostitutes, grinding and swinging his metal arm.

"Danny made a lot of bizarre character choices and there was nobody to rein him in," says Carl Gottlieb, who after doing a patch-up for Universal on the script for *Jaws 2* was flown into Chicago by the studio to try to salvage *Doctor Detroit*. "The producer, Bob Weiss, was in the business of protecting his stars and giving them whatever they wanted. So if Danny wanted to wear a bizarre costume, 'OK!' He was going through a period of intense grief because of what happened with Belushi. Occasionally he would go out to a blues bar in Chicago and toast John's ghost, as it were."

Fortunately for Aykroyd, there was a silver lining to this gloomy cloud. Donna Dixon, a willowy blond beauty who was playing one of the film's many prostitutes, had taken a shine to him, even though she was already involved with KISS rocker Paul Stanley. And her feelings were returned. Watching her perform one day from off-camera, Aykroyd remarked to anybody within earshot, "She's really getting to me. She's really getting to me. . . ."

Two days before the picture wrapped, Dixon was urged by co-star Fran Drescher to go into Aykroyd's office, kiss him on the lips, then walk away. "I can't do that!" protested Dixon. "You can if you're Lauren Bacall, honey," Drescher encouraged.

Aykroyd, sitting alone and clad in Doctor Detroit's lime-green polyester suit and wig, was startled to see Dixon march in. "I did just what Franny said," she recalled decades later. "And as I was walking away he grabbed my hand and we kissed again. And this time it was fireworks."

Dixon quickly ended her relationship with Stanley. But wanting to make sure this was real, Aykroyd proposed an experiment: they would spend seventy-two hours together on the road, then see whether they wanted to marry or kill each other. Dixon agreed, and they drove to Canada, a freeway quest just like the ones he used to take with Belushi. "I showed her the single-wide trailer, the mud, the gray trees, no leaves, the shack that my ancestors grew up in," Aykroyd remembered.

"I said, 'This is it. This is what we got. Now, would you consider maybe becoming part of our family?' It was March, a drizzly, gray day, and basically I formalized it there."

The star had been adjusting to life as a loner on-screen and off, remarking to Gene Siskel, "You come on this planet, you're born and you die alone. It's a solo journey. Sure, you can give love and take love, but basically life is a solo trip." But suddenly he felt differently. He and his new bride bought a house together, a spooky-looking twenty-room pile in the Hollywood Hills, covered in overgrown vines. They called it the Witch House.

JOHN LANDIS TOUCHED DOWN in New York on a mission. Now thirty-two but still as intensely energetic as he had been shooting *Animal House*, he hailed a taxi and headed to 30 Rock. It was another in a long series of visits to the home of *Saturday Night Live*, but this time was different. His buddies Aykroyd and Belushi were gone; in fact, Landis hadn't been able to bring himself to watch the show since John's death. In their place were a bunch of young comedians he'd never heard of, plus somebody he had heard of—Eddie Murphy.

It was early winter of 1982, and *48 Hrs.* had not yet come out. But the buzz from preview audiences had swept through Paramount's Hollywood lot. Jeffrey Katzenberg, the president of the studio, took note of the high enthusiasm for Murphy's performance and gave Landis a call about something they'd once discussed in passing. "Hey, you know that dead movie we had for Pryor?" he said. "It could be right for this kid."

The dead movie was *Black and White*, a clever fiscal farce in the vein of Frank Capra or Preston Sturges. It had been written for Richard Pryor, but in 1980, after freebasing cocaine for several successive days, Pryor suffered self-inflicted burns after pouring cognac over his head and lighting it. "Richard unfortunately set himself on fire," Landis says, "and the movie stalled out. But when I saw the script I got very excited, because it was very old-fashioned in its structure. Essentially it's a '30s comedy. It's classic screwball."

Before taking his flight to New York, Landis had studied clips of Murphy on *Saturday Night Live*. He was relieved to discover that the genuine article was every bit as charismatic. "I was very pleased with Eddie," he says. "He was terrific. He was nineteen or something, just full of beans. At that time in his life, he was just bursting with energy."

Murphy eagerly signed up to play homeless street hustler Billy Ray Valentine, whose life is transformed when two rich old men, for a bet, arrange for him to switch places with snooty success story Louis Winthorpe III. Casting the latter role seemed like a no-brainer: Landis immediately thought of Dan Aykroyd. But Paramount fiercely resisted the idea, aware of the stench drifting from across town at Universal, courtesy of *Doctor Detroit*.

"The conventional wisdom was that Aykroyd without Belushi didn't mean anything," Landis says. "It was kinda similar to when Jerry Lewis and Dean Martin broke up. People went, 'Oh, poor Dean Martin. What'll happen?' So the studio was very upset with me." Still, they finally conceded, on the condition that Aykroyd accept a smaller-than-usual salary. Landis also won a separate battle being waged over Jamie Lee Curtis's casting as gold-hearted hooker Ophelia. "Why are you casting has-beens and crap actresses?" exasperated executive Barry Diller asked the director one day.

As Christmas approached, Aykroyd, Murphy, Curtis, and Denholm Elliott (playing Winthorpe's butler; Landis's first choice, Ronnie Barker, refused to work more than seven miles from his London home) headed to Philadelphia to start work on the movie, newly retitled *Trading Places*. It was bitterly cold. "Fuckin' freezing!" Landis laughs. "The wind was always whipping around. Oh man, it was cold. And we only had five or six hours of light each day." Like Belushi on *Animal House*, Murphy was still appearing on *Saturday Night Live*, so he had to commute back and forth between Philly and New York, a two-hour train ride. By anyone's standards, it was a grueling slog.

Murphy, however, couldn't stop smiling. His first movie had been a rough ride; this time he was going to enjoy himself. On one particularly arctic morning, with the whole crew decked out in Michelin Man parkas, he sat in a giant black Rolls-Royce with octogenarian co-stars

Don Ameche and Ralph Bellamy, competing for the hot air blasting out of a space heater. "You know, this is my forty-ninth motion picture," noted Ameche. "Well, it's my forty-ninth motion picture too," retorted Bellamy. After a beat, Murphy exclaimed, "Hey, between the three of us we've made a hundred films!"

There are curious similarities between *Doctor Detroit* and *Trading Places*. Both cast Aykroyd as a highfalutin' fellow who is brought low, ultimately for his own good, through a series of misunderstandings. And both feature friendly prostitutes. The two films were, however, to meet very different fates. *Doctor Detroit* came out on May 6, 1983, and flopped hard, making just $10 million from an $8 million budget. While Roger Ebert and Vincent Canby found kind things to say, critic Vern Perry pushed on what must have been a sensitive area for Aykroyd. "The question has to be asked—how does Aykroyd fare without his friend and cohort, the late John Belushi? Aykroyd certainly has enough talent of his own that he does not need a partner. But you can't help but wonder if Belushi were still alive . . . would *Doctor Detroit* have been much improved?"

Just a month later, as that film quietly left theaters, *Trading Places* roared in. Its inspirations may have been old-fashioned, but its sharp wit and raunchy humor made it a movie of the moment, drawing people back again and again. By the end of 1983, it had made $90.4 million in the United States, making it the fourth-biggest earner at the domestic box office, behind only *Return of the Jedi*, *Flashdance*, and *Terms of Endearment*. Even the ebullient Murphy could surely not have dreamed that his smash-hit debut would be followed by the most successful comedy of the year.

"It makes Eddie Murphy a force to be reckoned with," said Richard Schickel in *Time*. "It takes nothing away from Aykroyd's perfect prissiness as Winthorpe . . . but Murphy, using his Tyrone Green character as a sketch for a full-scale portrait, demonstrates the powers of invention that signal the arrival of a major comic actor, and possibly a great star. He makes *Trading Places* something more than a good-hearted comedy. He turns it into an event."

Aykroyd got his fair share of raves too. Most effusive was Rex Reed, who had savaged *Neighbors* but who in his *New York Post* review of June 8 wrote: "I expected another trashy Dan Aykroyd farce. Instead I got a film with real wit and imagination . . . featuring the most consistently sustained piece of acting Aykroyd has yet managed in feature film. He is splendid."

The two stars were suddenly more red-hot than ever. And crucially for Aykroyd and, it would turn out, several of his old friends, *Ghost Smashers* was back from the dead.

NOBODY REMEMBERS now whether the idea to transplant the story to New York came from Aykroyd or Ivan Reitman. But everyone agrees that it saved the movie. "Suddenly the idea of those blue-collar guys hunting a panoply of spooks, goblins, and other things made sense," says Reitman. "They were pest control, or sanitation men. It was a relatable idea." Reenergized by the change of milieu, Aykroyd brought in not only Reitman but Harold Ramis to help him with the project. The trio tweaked the title, turning it into *Ghostbusters*, bulked up the number of heroes from three to four, and got to work.

"For that first draft, I went to a quarry and got a big fucking hunk of pink Italian granite," says Aykroyd. "It was everything you could get out of the concept. Then we went in and sculpted it."

Wherever the three of them could get together, they did: Canada, Los Angeles, New York. At Aykroyd's house in Martha's Vineyard they hunkered down for two weeks of solid writing. "The house is up on a hill, with a 272-degree view of the ocean," says Aykroyd. "But we sat in the basement, like Ian Fleming, who wrote the Bond books at GoldenEye in Jamaica facing a corner, so he wouldn't get distracted. We just buried ourselves in there, getting takeout from the local lobster place. For eight hours a day we just stayed down there in the hole, coming out blinking like moles."

For a while the Ghostbusters drove a refrigerator-repair truck; it became a 1959 Cadillac Miller-Meteor. The darker edges of the original draft were pared away, replaced by silly riffs like a librarian ghost who hasn't let death stop her from doing her duties. The movie's third act remained a vague sketch, but they were convinced they'd found the right tone. To their relief, Columbia agreed, green-lighting the movie with a $25 million budget.

The casting process began. And as with *The Blues Brothers* and *Caddyshack*, the search was on for a male-heavy ensemble. The Ghost-busters had a female secretary, but they were all guys—there was no space for, say, Aykroyd's *SNL* cast mate Gilda Radner, or Goldie Hawn, or Carrie Fisher. "I think it started with who was doing stand-up and sketch comedy," says Reitman. "And really through the '70s and '80s the ratio was five to one in terms of men and women. In general there was a reluctance to do movies that starred women, in all of Hollywood. It was partially about what would work outside of America, in the international market. And the comedies that ended up working were the more action-based or physical ones, which were more male-oriented. It's only literally in the last five years or so that it's starting to go the other way."

Aykroyd and Ramis would take two of the three lead roles in *Ghostbusters* themselves. Eddie Murphy had read an early draft but declined, saying he wanted to focus on his upcoming stand-up show. Another near miss was John Candy, to whom Aykroyd offered the small but flashy role of Louis Tully, next-door neighbor to the main female character, Dana Barrett. One story goes that Candy insisted on playing Tully as an overbearing German man with a pack of big dogs. Another, the one given by Candy in subsequent interviews, is that he didn't want to take a pay cut from the $350,000 fee he'd got-ten for *Splash*, causing Reitman to balk. Whatever the reason, the role ended up going to Candy's former *SCTV* cast mate Rick Moranis, who turned Louis into an overenthusiastic brainiac accountant.

"I don't know why John didn't wind up in it," says Moranis, who knew enough about tax accounting to write his own dialogue for a party scene where Louis reels off mind-numbingly boring jargon. "I think it might have been a deal he couldn't make. They were all at the same agency, CAA—Ivan and Danny and Harold—and John wasn't. Whatever the reason, he would have been fantastic. But I wound up getting it. I think what worked was that I was so out-there, so broadly drawn, that if you believed a guy like that could exist, maybe you could believe that ghosts could exist too."

After casting Sigourney Weaver as Dana—the actress inspired the movie's possession plot strand, after getting down on all fours and barking like a dog during her audition in Reitman's office—the team had only one major part left to fill. And it was perhaps the most important. Peter Venkman, the most skeptical and potentially funniest Ghostbuster, was originally written for John Belushi. In Aykroyd's mind, there was only one choice to play the new iteration of the wise-acre spirit-breaker: Bill Murray.

The problem was, Murray was looking to go straight. *Where the Buffalo Roam* had turned out to be his only big-screen failure, but it had done little to dent his resolve to prove himself as a serious actor. He had taken an uncredited role as Dustin Hoffman's roommate in *Tootsie*, but the idea of starring in another comedy held little appeal. Instead, he was trying desperately to convince a studio to make *The Razor's Edge*, an adaptation of W. Somerset Maugham's book about a young American World War I veteran on a spiritual quest, with him in the lead role. So invested in the project was he that he had cowritten the script with director John Byrum, working together in the noisiest bars they could find, since Murray believed all good things came from difficult conditions.

It was a conundrum. But after several phone conversations with Murray, Aykroyd thought he saw a way forward. Murray had admitted to him that seeing the old gang at Belushi's funeral had made him realize he missed them. The sense of community he'd felt doing the National Lampoon comedy show and *SNL* had been replaced by careerism and days spent in trailers. Part of him yearned for the kind of ensemble experience that *Ghostbusters* represented. Aykroyd cleverly suggested a compromise: tell the studio he'd star in their big comedy if they green-lit his passion project. Murray picked up the phone, dialed an executive at Columbia, and said, "I'm going to do *The Razor's Edge* or there'll be no more Biggie-Goes-to-College movies."

It worked. *The Razor's Edge* shot over the summer of 1983, in England, Paris, India, and the Himalayas. Murray spent his thirty-third

birthday on a charter plane from Delhi to Srinagar, literally screaming with excitement. "It's a beautiful place, on a mountain lake. The
architecture is straight out of *Arabian Nights*," he recounted. "The local
production guys had gotten us cars to drive us to the locations. They
were old things that looked sort of like Ramblers. There was one that
said 'Director,' another that said 'Producer,' and my car said, 'Hero.'
And all the kids would run after, going, 'Hero! Hero! Hero!'"

Back in America, everyone awaited Murray's return, some patiently,
others less so. "The nervous anticipation and the breath-holding came
in wondering, 'Will he show up?'" says Aykroyd. Throughout September, however remote the location, Columbia found a way to get
messages to the *Razor's Edge* set, missives that read, "Is Bill finished?
He's supposed to be doing *Ghostbusters* on the 25th." One day Murray
called his agent from the Taj Mahal, to be told, "You gotta get right
back." Instead, as soon as the shoot wrapped, he headed to Delhi and
holed up in a hotel room for four days straight, sleeping and reading.
Then, upon finding out that a rough cut of *The Razor's Edge* was ready
to view, he flew to London to watch it.

One day later, he was on a Concorde, heading to New York to play
Peter Venkman in *Ghostbusters*. Fittingly, he felt half-dead himself.

ON OCTOBER 18, 1983, the delayed production finally began, with
four weeks of on-location shooting in New York. Aykroyd and Ramis
were already in their costumes, bland beige jumpsuits with devices
resembling vacuum cleaners strapped to their backs. Ivan Reitman was
checking the cameras, trying not to think too much about the effects-
heavy sequences coming up in the schedule. Then a limo pulled up. A
bleary Bill Murray emerged.

"Murray never read the script before we started shooting," says
Reitman. "He read it for the first time on the limousine ride into Manhattan. We got into two vans, with Ramis, Murray, and Aykroyd in
the front one in their outfits, and when they jumped out it was the first
time I saw them together in their costumes. I saw them walking toward me down Madison Avenue to walk into the shot, and it just sent

a shiver down my back. The three of them in those costumes against the backdrop of Manhattan—I thought, 'We have something pretty special here.'"

One of the stars was from Canada, the other two from Chicago. But the Big Apple embraced them like sons. "We owned New York," says Aykroyd. "Watching the people in the city react when we drove about in *Ecto-1*, or strutting about with the packs and the traps, it was a great time." Though they also made at least one enemy: science-fiction novelist Isaac Asimov, whom Aykroyd worshipped, accosted the star angrily after his car was caught in a *Ghostbusters*-derived traffic snarl-up near Central Park West.

For the first couple of weeks, Murray found the whole thing a struggle. Severely jetlagged, he'd limp back to his trailer during camera setups and crash. "They'd send three sets of people to knock on the door and say, 'They really want you,'" he remembered shortly after the shoot. "I'd stumble out and do something and then go back to sleep. I kept thinking to myself, 'Ten days ago I was up there working with the high lamas in a gompa, and here I am removing ghosts from drugstores and painting slime on my body.'"

But gradually he got into the spirit of things, starting to suggest gags and action beats. His inner comedian began to awaken. Whenever he and Aykroyd were asked for autographs, they'd sign each other's names. After one New Yorker took a look at their tech-enhanced costumes and said, "Hey, the *wrong* stuff!," riffing on astronaut picture *The Right Stuff*, Murray started using the line himself.

In the evenings, the principals would retire to JP's, on Eighty-Second Street and Second Avenue, for drinks and reflection. All agreed that the combination of epic phantasmagorical set pieces and laid-back interplay seemed to be working well. Murray's Venkman delivered the acid punch lines, Aykroyd's Ray Stantz was the movie's heart, Ramis's Egon Spengler brought the brains, and Ernie Hudson's Winston Zeddemore, a second-act addition to the team, was the Everyman audience proxy. Weaver, following up *Deal of the Century* with this far goofier comedy, fit right in. And Aykroyd was particularly pleased with what Moranis was doing, a hyper-committed riff on an old *SCTV* character.

"Any of his scenes are my favorite," he says. "If I were to watch a clip on my videophone—who the fuck has time to do that?—I would have all of Moranis's scenes from *Ghostbusters* on loop."

By the time they got to L.A. for the soundstage portion of the script, Murray had fallen in love with the film. "This is the only movie I've ever had lines in that were good enough to say," he raved of the script to movie critic Roger Ebert during an interview in the executive dining room at Burbank Studios. In his downtime he liked to wander onto the gigantic stage, where the top of a Manhattan skyscraper had been created for the movie's climax, wrapped around by a vast skyline diorama. "If you look very carefully," he revealed to Ebert, "you will notice that some of the buildings have illuminated windows, and in 14 of those windows you can see very small figures engaged in intimate practices. The painters put them in to amuse themselves. We've all had a lot of fun trying to find them."

Aykroyd, meanwhile, enjoyed wandering across the street to Universal to see Steven Spielberg, who was editing *Indiana Jones and the Temple of Doom*, a film he would shoot a quick cameo for. "One day I borrowed a bike from Spielberg's office, and it turned out to be the bicycle from *E.T.*," he says. "I didn't find out until later; I thought it was just a messenger's bike. So all through shooting *Ghostbusters* I was riding the *E.T.* bike around. And the basket was broken so I fixed it. If you want a psychometric touchstone, me riding that bike might have helped us with the movie. Anywhere you can get near Spielberg, I think a little gold dust will fall off."

A SPECIAL-EFFECTS COMEDY of this scale had never been attempted before. By the time the fast-paced shoot was nearing its end, the budget had swollen to $33 million. Aykroyd was, frankly, terrified. But one day at lunch, as he picked at his food glumly, he was surprised to hear Murray begin to laugh. Aykroyd recalls: "He looked at me and just said, 'Pal, you've written one of the biggest comedies of all time. Relax.'"

Murray's optimism started to spread, particularly after a test screening of the film, with no visual effects, was a triumph, eliciting cheers from the audience. Effects wizards Richard Edlund and Boss Film Studios were yet to add the various ghouls—the bile-green Slimer, the 112-foot-tall Stay Puft marshmallow man, the movie-opening library ghost—but already the movie's air of scruffy fun was infectious. A theme song was hastily commissioned, written, and recorded in a matter of days by R&B artist Ray Parker Jr. And a music video was taped, with the cast dance-walking down a New York street in costume, then calling in friends to mug for the camera. Among them was John Candy, whom Reitman visited on the set of *Brewster's Millions* with a boombox and cassette tape of the song. And the video ends with Chevy Chase, flipping a cigarette around with his mouth. It's easy to imagine him in another dimension—possibly one reached via an interdimensional interceptor—playing Peter Venkman.

Ghostbusters was released on June 8, 1984. In its first week it scared up nearly $23 million, smashing Columbia's previous one-week record, $17 million for *Tootsie*. It would reign at the top of the chart for seven further weeks, making two comebacks after being knocked out by the Prince vehicle *Purple Rain* and the Clint Eastwood thriller *Tightrope*, and even more amazingly became a giant hit overseas, a rarity for a comedy.

"It was like hitting a gusher in the oil business," says Aykroyd. "That kind of hit is good for a lot of people. It was good for everyone who worked on *Ghostbusters*, it was good for the agents, it was good for the studio and the lenders, it was good for shareholders. Roberto Goizueta, the brilliant Cuban entrepreneur who became president and CEO of Coke, saw the movie and hated it. He thought, 'Why did we buy this?' And then of course three weeks later Coca-Cola stock was climbing on the basis of the box-office returns for Columbia. So he had us to thank for an uptake in Coke stock."

Reitman was staggered by the movie's success. "I was pretty cocky by then, because I'd had this run of *Animal House*, *Meatballs*, *Stripes*, all in a five-year period," he says. "All of them were not just hits, but had a kind of cultural heat to them. But nothing was like *Ghostbusters*. It really exploded all over the world and became central to the culture for a year." Murray, Aykroyd, Ramis, and Moranis, the two guys from *SNL* and the two from *SCTV*, were not just famous, but megastars. Moranis got fan mail from an unlikely source: "I heard from many accountants, who were pleased by the little bits of inside info." Aykroyd fled L.A. for Canada. "That summer was great," he says. "I just went home to the farm and hid out. And believe me, in my hometown people don't really care."

The movie's final worldwide tally was $295 million. It was huge; in fact, it was the number-one movie of the year. Or so it appeared. Unbelievably, its crown would be taken from it in the dying moments of 1984. Another comedy phenomenon was coming—and this one had a badge.

10

MURPHY'S LAW

IN THE FIRST week of June 1983, Eddie Murphy signed a five-picture deal with Paramount. Netting him $15 million, plus a $4 million bonus, it was the kind of Old Hollywood deal not seen since the days of Marilyn Monroe. "If you had asked me a year ago if I would ever have made such an arrangement, I would have said, 'Never!'" Paramount president Michael Eisner told the press. "But when we saw the results of *48 Hrs.* and the rushes on his next film, *Trading Places*, we said, 'Wouldn't it be great to have him exclusive?' Now anyone who wants to make a picture with Eddie Murphy has to come to Paramount and make their movie here."

The studio threw a lavish welcome party for him in August, drawing the likes of Michael Jackson, Prince, Sylvester Stallone, Richard Pryor, and Burt Reynolds. Their spectacular show of confidence in Murphy cemented his status as Hollywood's hottest new property. He calibrated his lifestyle accordingly. As the box office for *Trading Places* kept shooting up, the twenty-two-year-old went on a shopping spree, spending his new cash on mountains of jewelry, racks of designer clothes, and two sports cars: a Porsche 928 (red) and a Jaguar

XJS (black-on-black). Then he purchased a new house in a rarefied area of New Jersey, where his neighbors included Stevie Wonder and the Isley Brothers. An edifice of gleaming glass and polished white marble, its walls were decorated with blown-up magazine covers of himself, prompting him to joke to a visiting reporter, "I gotta get some pictures of my family." In the den, a four-foot-wide Mitsubishi TV frequently aired repeats of his talk-show appearances, helping him hone his anecdotes.

One morning, as Murphy stepped out of the Porsche in New York, his foot came down into a curl of dog crap. But even this couldn't break his stride. Gingerly taking off his expensive, now-besmirched Italian shoes, he left them on the street and walked on. Another pair was hurriedly couriered direct to his feet.

It was just the latest acquisition for Murphy, whose life was rapidly swelling, both with objects and people. "I love it that despite all his success, Eddie acts like he's 22 years old," said his *Trading Places* co-star Jamie Lee Curtis. "His life is cars and girls, girls and cars. More cars. More girls."

His collecting extended, of course, to celebrity friends. Besides Wonder, Murphy had gotten to know Prince and Rick James. But the most exciting new acquaintance was his childhood hero, and the man he'd replaced on *Trading Places*: Richard Pryor. In the family basement as a kid, Murphy had listened over and over to Pryor's *That Nigger's Crazy* LP, finally performing a compilation of his favorite bits to friends. He loved the comedy legend's rawness and willingness to charge headlong into the most sensitive of subjects. So when he happened to be on the same plane as Pryor in 1982, he didn't hesitate to approach him. The two hit it off and stayed in touch, with Pryor offering so much advice that Murphy started calling him Yoda.

As a child he had followed in the path of his edgy elder, and he continued to do so now. His Paramount deal in fact was signed just one month after Pryor entered into a similar arrangement with Columbia, promising his exclusive service for five years in a $40 million production deal. And Murphy's next move would also follow the Pryor playbook. The year 1982 had seen the release of *Richard Pryor: Live on the Sunset Strip*, a hugely successful concert film in which the comic discussed his drug meltdown two years earlier and painful recovery. Murphy's idea was to hit the stand-up stage again for his own taped show.

But this wouldn't be a one-night affair. Instead, it would be a turbo-charged tour of America, hurtling him from one giant arena to another via private jet. Aptly titled *Delirious*, it would involve thirty-five gigs in eighteen cities throughout the summer of 1983, culminating in an HBO special to be aired nationwide. That and a videocassette released by Paramount would alone earn him $1 million.

It was money well spent. From the get-go, Murphymania broke out at every venue, with female fans screaming and crowds lined up outside, holding up signs that said EDDIE MURPHY FOR PRESIDENT. His five sold-out concerts at the Westbury Music Fair in Long Island, New York, were recorded for an album, CBS's *Eddie Murphy: Comedian*. His August 17 show at Constitution Hall in Washington, DC, mean-while, was the one selected for the HBO taping. That day saw a happy accident occur. The outfit Murphy had picked to wear couldn't be found, so he and his crew headed to a nearby mall to find new threads. In a store there he laid eyes on a skintight leather suit, resplendent in fire-engine red. Murphy laughed, then considered, then bought it.

That evening, he strutted onstage in the outrageous suit, jacket unzipped to the navel, a chunky medallion around his neck with the initials "EM" spelled out in glittering diamonds. The 3,700-strong crowd went berserk. His opening salvo doubled down on the shock factor, taking the form of some homophobic rhetoric that has not aged well: "I got some rules when I throw down. When I do my stand-up, I got rules and shit. Faggots aren't allowed to look at my ass while I'm onstage. That's why I keep moving while I'm up here."

It turned out to be apt that the stage at Constitution Hall was blue; over the next seventy minutes, Murphy unleashed a blisteringly outra-geous set, with filthy language (the word "shit" shot from his mouth 171 times; "fuck" 230 times), riffs on herpes ("You keep that shit for-ever, like luggage"), and a moment where he asked for a camera from an audience member, then snapped a shot of his crotch. Like Pryor, he was explosively R-rated. But he swaggered like a comedian had never swaggered before. "This is the business to be in if you want pussy," he bragged while on the subject of sex. "Too *much* pussy. Pussy be falling out my pockets and shit."

In a moment of reflection near the end, Murphy pointed out that decades earlier African American singer Marian Anderson had been barred from performing in that very auditorium because of the color of her skin. But his material was geared more toward attacking his fellow entertainers than honoring them. With a series of impressions, he savaged the likes of Michael Jackson, Mick Jagger, and even his boyhood hero, Elvis Presley. At one point he imitated the *A-Team* star Mr. T having anal sex.

On HBO, the stand-up set was preceded by a warning that "the following program contains frank and explicit language." But that caution didn't prevent a noisy backlash. A group calling itself the "Eddie Murphy's Disease Foundation," or EMDF, sent in letters to newspapers, complaining about the homophobic material and urging people to write to HBO and CBS. Howard Rosenberg, critic for the *Los Angeles Times*, attacked Murphy for claiming AIDS could be spread through kissing. The comedian would apologize for his words, but not until 1996, when he was still being picketed by AIDS activists and finally released a statement: "I think it's unfair to take the words of a misinformed twenty-one-year-old and apply them to an informed thirty-five-year-old. . . . I know AIDS isn't funny . . . I deeply regret any pain all this has caused." He signed it, "Peace, love and condoms, Eddie Murphy."

Back in 1983, however, he remained bullish in interviews. "They're wasting their money," he said of the EMDF's campaign. "They blew it all out of proportion, and if they want to, I don't give a fuck. Do all the ads you want to. Kiss my ass." As for the celebrity takedowns, he told *Ebony* magazine: "There are no icons. You can't say that Michael Jackson and Mr. T shouldn't be touched." In fact, he heard that Jackson, whose high-pitched voice he'd targeted, had watched the HBO special with his mother and laughed all the way through. Michael's brother Jermaine, on the other hand, approached Murphy at a party and hissed, "I don't like the jokes you do about my brother."

Murphy never heard from Mr. T.

EDDIE MURPHY: DELIRIOUS was a game changer, not just for the star but for comedy itself. It inspired a generation of young black men, from Chris Rock to Martin Lawrence, to follow in his steps. And it showed that stand-up could be a multimillion-dollar industry. For Murphy himself, it was a liberating experience, setting him loose from the restrictions of TV and turning him into the first true rock-star comedian.

No wonder the prospect of returning to *SNL* didn't appeal. At 30 Rockefeller Plaza, he was no longer commanding the stage, but part of a troupe, subject to the whims of producer Dick Ebersol, with whom Murphy had a fractious relationship. He was a movie star, stuck in a TV world, and it chafed. After griping that the small screen was too restricting, putting limits on what he could say or do, he made the decision that this would be his last year on the show. His final live appearance would be on February 25, 1984.

The second half of 1983 trudged by, with Murphy frequently cooped up in his shabby white *SNL* dressing room, up on 30 Rock's eighth floor. He took less interest in the material these days, giving it a polish but not getting involved in the writers' room. In mid-November, with Jerry Lewis in town to host, he declined an invitation to rehearse with the comedy legend, kicking off a small storm of inside politics. Lewis complained to Ebersol, who responded, "Jerry, do you think you could talk to Eddie? Because I don't think he's handling his fame well." At least, that's the report that made its way back to Murphy; it further deteriorated his relationship with the *SNL* show runner.

Finally, February 25 arrived. The thought of taking a final bow on the show hadn't softened his attitude: that night he told a *Rolling Stone* reporter, "I can't wait to leave. I don't like the show. I don't think the show is funny. I hate it." It was fitting, he informed anyone in earshot backstage, that musical guests Kool and the Gang were playing their hit "Celebration," because he was in the mood to celebrate himself. Still, he delivered a solid performance, or rather several solid performances, reprising his famous James Brown impression, channeling Jesse Jackson in a soul ballad apologizing for anti-Semitic comments in the *Washington Post*, and performing in a final skit called "A Nickel," with he and Joe Piscopo as old codgers reminiscing about days gone by.

And then, with a final flub—he misread "stove" on a cue card as "stone"—he was done. The show that had turned him into a star, and which he had turned back into a sensation, was behind him. He was now a full-time movie actor, with five Paramount credits to cash in.

Unfortunately, the first one of those would be his first flop. *Best Defense*, a Dudley Moore vehicle about a sex-mad military contractor, had been turned down by director Robert Altman, before being taken over by the writers of *Indiana Jones and the Temple of Doom*, husband-and-wife team Willard Hyuck and Gloria Willard. They cast *Doom*'s lead actress, Kate Capshaw, in the major female role, but if anyone was expecting the thrills of *Indiana Jones* to be replicated, they were to be sorely disappointed. Clumsily paced and confusingly plotted, the action comedy, locked in for a July 1984 release, tanked with preview audiences. Desperate, Paramount executives huddled. Then one of them had an epiphany: why not parachute in their golden boy, Eddie Murphy? A handful of scenes could be shot with him as a tank commander in the Middle East, then spliced into the movie. Murphy's legions of fans would surely turn up in droves, chanting, "EDD-IE! EDD-IE!"

Paramount dangled a hell of a carrot in front of the star: $1 million for one week's work. Murphy was suspicious, but it *was* a lot of money. Against his better instincts, he flew to Israel to shoot scenes in a tank, essentially disconnected bits of shtick, shouting lines such as, "How do you say 'Get the fuck out the way in Arabic?'" and "You know, I'm sick and tired of this *Lawrence of Arabia* shit!" He shared no scenes with Moore, whose footage was set and shot in America, and received the unusual billing of "Strategic Guest Star."

The gambit bombed. Murphy's fans, or at least those who showed up in July, were furious when they found out he was on-screen for only twelve minutes. Exhibitors felt equally duped, with several threatening to sue Paramount for false advertising. Critic Roger Ebert moaned, "You see more of Murphy in the average *Saturday Night Live*." As for the star himself, he almost immediately threw the movie under the bus. "*Best Defense* turned out to be the worst movie ever done in the history of anything," he said in his opening monologue on *SNL*, when he returned as guest host in late 1984. "All of a sudden I wasn't that hot no more. So I called up the producer of *Saturday Night Live* and I go, 'Um . . . you still got my dressing room?'"

It was a rare bit of self-deprecation from Murphy, and of course it wasn't true. Before *Best Defense* had even come out he was deep in production on his next movie, and everything about this one screamed hit. He had played a crook, a bum, and a soldier. His latest assignment: cop.

BEVERLY HILLS COP may be the only movie in Hollywood history to be inspired by a traffic ticket. As the legend goes, one morning in 1975 Michael Eisner drove across L.A. for his first day as Paramount president. He was on the freeway when a well-groomed and over-officious police officer pulled over his vehicle, a battered station wagon he'd brought from New York, for driving five miles an hour over the speed limit. When Eisner finally arrived at work, he announced, "We gotta do a movie about the Beverly Hills cops."

Producer Don Simpson was to later claim it was his idea, although his pitch had been about a rough-and-ready Hispanic officer who is transferred from East L.A. to Hollywood. Whoever was responsible, the project slowly coalesced under the auspices of Simpson and producing partner Jerry Bruckheimer. Writer Danilo Bach turned in a draft called *Beverly Drive*, about a Pittsburgh cop called Elly Axel. Another writer, Dan Petrie Jr., was brought in, changing the hero's name to Axel Elly and making the character's home city Detroit to avoid similarities to the Pittsburgh-set Simpson-Bruckheimer movie *Flashdance*. With more screenwriters adding their spin to it, including

Vincent Patrick and Bill Wittliff, the project went through seventeen drafts. The title was tweaked to *Beverly Hills Cops*, before becoming singular. "Nobody knows how it became *Beverly Hills Cop*—it may have been a typo somewhere along the way, and it just stuck," director Martin Brest was to explain.

The movie was always intended to showcase the peculiarities inherent in policing a population of the rich and famous. But *Beverly Hills Cop* was originally conceived not as a comedy but a dark drama. When original star Mickey Rourke bailed to make *The Pope of Greenwich Village*, Al Pacino, Dennis Quaid, James Caan, and Jack Nicholson were all considered. Then somebody realized that, due to a quirk of studio politics, the project had to be offered to Sylvester Stallone before anyone else. "He had an overall deal on the lot, and it was considered common courtesy that every leading-man role for a movie Paramount had just green-lit would be offered first to Stallone," says Petrie. "It was an absolute article of faith that he would pass. And they were stunned when he said that he'd like to do it."

By this point, Petrie's work on the script had made it drift in a considerably lighter direction than the version pitched to Rourke. "I was working in a small cubbyhole office at the corner of Santa Monica and Rodeo Drive, in the dead center of Beverly Hills," he remembers. "The air-conditioning was broken and so the window was always open, and I would witness all this funny stuff happening outside. I would hear a screech of brakes and see a Mercedes entangled with a Rolls and a poodle escaping and women tearing their wigs off. I would pass art galleries and my jaw would just drop: 'Someone is going to purchase this and put it in their home and live with this hideous monstrosity?'"

His incredulous reactions to the area's chichi, overpriced madness informed Axel's own personality. *Beverly Hills Cop* started becoming funny, something that didn't necessarily gel with Stallone's screen image. "I thought they'd sent it to the wrong house," the star later said of the screenplay. "Somehow, me trying to comically terrorize Beverly Hills is not the stuff that great yuk-festivals are made from."

Stallone's reaction was to amp up the action. After attempting to

Chevy Chase (left) and John Belushi take a break in the hectic hallways of 30 Rock in 1976. The *Saturday Night Live* co-stars would become bitter rivals as their movie careers took off, with Belushi labeling Chase a "brick."
(Michael Tighe/Donaldson Collection/Getty Images)

Steve Martin entertains a dog on *The Carol Burnett Show*. The set, promising "no canned barks," was typical of Martin's goofy, groundbreaking brand of comedy.
(CBS Photo Archive/ Getty Images)

A few months after departing *SNL*, Chevy Chase huddles with then wife Jacqueline Carlin (the reason, he claimed, that he'd left the show) and Jack Nicholson at rehearsals for President Jimmy Carter's 1977 Inaugural Gala. Dan Aykroyd and Chase would play Carter and exiting President Gerald Ford in front of an audience packed with stars, including Paul Newman, Bette Davis, and John Wayne. *(Ron Galella/WireImage)*

Chase, returning to *SNL* as guest host in February 1978, poses with Jane Curtin, Bill Murray, Gilda Radner (the only female star to get the kind of opportunities in Hollywood that the men did), and Laraine Newman. Behind the smiles was tension: two days later, Chase and Murray would get into a fistfight backstage. *(AP Photo/Marty Lederhandler)*

A jokey press conference to herald the start of production on *Oh! Heavenly Dog*, Chase's 1980 comedy. Like many of his early movies, it was a lightweight affair that bombed at the box office. *(AP Photo/Nick Ut)*

Murray moved in a more serious, less commercial direction, going Method to play Hunter S. Thompson in *Where the Buffalo Roam*. His in character antics alarmed some of his friends and *SNL* colleagues. *(Everett Collection Inc/Alamy Stock Photo)*

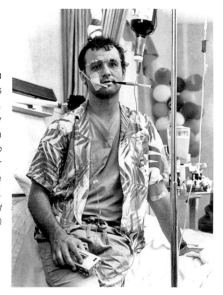

Martin tap-dancing his way through 1981's *Pennies from Heaven*. After the high of *The Jerk*, the star tried a number of innovative experiments in an attempt to get back on top. *(MGM/courtesy Everett Collection)*

Elwood and Jake Blues, aka the Blues Brothers, started life on *SNL* as a wheeze for Aykroyd and Belushi, then became a bona fide phenomenon, with sold-out concerts, a double-platinum album, and a highly successful movie. The latter established the pair as the first viable leading men to come out of *SNL*. *(Michael Ochs Archives/Getty Images)*

Murray and Chase light a peace pipe (more precisely, a peace doobie) on the set of cult hit *Caddyshack*. Onlookers feared they would come to blows; as one crew member said, "There was a sense that anything could happen." *(Moviestore Collection Ltd/ Alamy Stock Photo)*

Eddie Murphy poses with Eddie Murphy in November 1983. The ultra-confident comedian had just wowed crowds with his live show *Delirious,* and would soon be shooting megahit *Beverly Hills Cop.* *(The LIFE Picture Collection/ Getty Images)*

The gentle, gregarious John Candy, a Canadian described by Pauline Kael as a "mountainous lollipop of a man." Rising to fame through *SCTV*, he charmed everyone he encountered. *(Keith Beaty/Toronto Star via Getty Images)*

Rick Moranis made for an unlikely A-lister, with his geeky looks and meek manners. But like his fellow Ontarian Candy, he exploded in the early '80s: after landing in Regina with *SCTV* comedy partner Dave Thomas for their first public appearance, he was chased down the street by a large mob of fans. *(Trinity Mirror/Mirrorpix/Alamy Stock Photo)*

Director John Landis confers with Murphy and Aykroyd on the set of the 1983 hit *Trading Places*. Landis and Murphy would make two more movies together, despite coming to blows on their next one, *Coming to America*. *(Stanley Bielecki Movie Collection/Getty Images)*

Aykroyd, Harold Ramis, and Murray share a joke on the set of *Ghostbusters*. Its phenomenal success would catapult Murray into the upper echelons of the A-list, and give Aykroyd freedom to make pet projects like *Dragnet*. As for Ramis, he'd focus on directing, reuniting with (and falling out with) Murray on *Groundhog Day* nearly a decade later. *(AF archive/Alamy Stock Photo)*

The Three Amigos at their premiere in December 1986. The trio played tricks on one another constantly, and initially Martin and Chase planned to turn up at the event in suits, leaving Martin Short alone in his flamboyant costume. *(The LIFE Picture Collection/Getty Images)*

Like many of his fellow comedy superstars, Martin struggled with the side effects of fame. In the early 1990s he started handing out a comedy autograph card to avoid protracted fan encounters. *(The LIFE Picture Collection/Getty Images)*

Chase tried his hand at talk-show hosting in 1993, with *The Chevy Chase Show.* Despite a starry roster of guests and a highly publicized launch, it was hastily pulled off the air. *(Everett Collection Inc./ Alamy Stock Photo)*

Axel Foley dancing with cartoon animals in *Beverly Hills Cop III* (1994)—further proof that Murphy's killer instincts had started to fail. The man once dubbed Mr. Box Office was suddenly having trouble picking winners. *(Moviestore Collection Ltd/Alamy Stock Photo)*

Combining big laughs and philosophical subtext, *Groundhog Day* was a perfect storm for Murray. Out of all the comedy stars of his era, he proved the most durable, going on to make a series of acclaimed dramas with talented directors. *(Pictorial Press Ltd/ Alamy Stock Photo)*

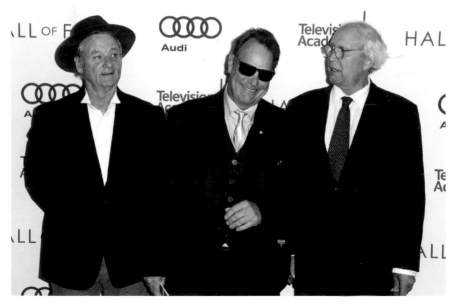

Murray, Aykroyd, and Chase reunite in November 2017 at the Television Academy's 24th Hall of Fame Ceremony in North Hollywood. They've survived to see themselves become legends, their films be hailed as classics, and their casually uttered zingers become part of the zeitgeist. *(Frederick M. Brown/Getty Images)*

convince Martin Scorsese to direct it, without success, he spent two weeks feeding script notes to Petrie. When the new draft was submitted to Simpson and Bruckheimer, just a couple of weeks before the shoot was ready to commence, the super-producers' faces went white. Instead of just nipping and tucking the dialogue, Stallone had transformed the entire script, stacking it with huge action set pieces.

The all-new finale saw the hero (whom Stallone had renamed Axel Cobretti) in a stolen sports car, playing chicken with an oncoming freight train. "There's a wing on a Lamborghini," notes Petrie, "that your stunt guy could hold on to. You could do a version of the Indiana Jones thing but on top of a Lamborghini. I also wrote a shootout in the middle of the Neiman Marcus store in Beverly Hills. There was this gigantic modern chandelier in there that was just begging for someone to destroy it."

It was, essentially, *Rambo Goes to Hollywood*, with exploding buildings, Rolls-Royces flying through storefronts, and other assorted budget-blowing spectacles. An emergency meeting was called and a deal offered to Stallone: he could either shoot the original draft, the one he had radically altered, or take his new material to a different studio and make another movie from that. He chose the latter, ultimately making *Cobra*, about grim cop Marion Cobretti, at Warner Bros.

Beverly Hills Cop was now starless. Scrapping it was not an option—Paramount had invested eight years and $2 million in the project. But they needed a new leading man, and fast. Simpson, who had taken a few general meetings with Eddie Murphy and even discussed *Beverly Hills Cop* with him, dropped his name into the conversation. The room went quiet. Then Paramount chairman Barry Diller took his cigar out of his mouth. "I love it," he announced. A copy of the script was rushed via taxicab to Murphy's offices in New York. Within two days he had committed.

The heat was on.

New sets and costumes were hurriedly assembled. New York–born director Brest, himself skittish about directing a big action movie for the first time, got to work with Murphy and Petrie, figuring out the whys and wherefores of the lead character, now at last called Axel

Foley. Rather than the buffed-up, hardboiled guy he had become in recent drafts, they turned Axel into a scruffy wiseass, always flying by the seat of his pants. "We wanted Eddie to look like a kid," said Simpson. Though a law-enforcement officer, Foley was to be an underdog perpetually snapping at the heels of his affluent enemies. And despite the fact the script had been written with white stars in mind, Murphy's skin color only sharpened the him-against-them dynamic.

Murphy himself rejected the initial outfit that Brest, Simpson, and Bruckheimer picked out: it was, he told them, "too slick." Instead, he opted for a pair of squeaky sneakers, a faded T-shirt marked MUMFORD PHYS. ED. DEPT., and a shabby sweatshirt; the garments would match the character's car, a blue Chevy Nova that was dented and covered in rust. "Everything he had was the cheapest, most lowdown possible," said Brest. "The only thing he had going for himself was his wits." Rather than keeping his gun in a holster, Axel would tuck it into his jeans—something Brest saw being done by real detective Gilbert Hill (whom he'd cast in the film as Foley's foulmouthed superior, Inspector Todd) during a research recce to a Detroit cop shop.

In spring 1983, production began, with final changes to the script completed that very morning. Murphy's first scene was a tense exchange about hijacked cigarettes in the back of a truck, with dialogue inspired by a Harvey Keitel–Robert De Niro interaction in *Mean Streets*. Brest's nerves quickly melted away as he realized Murphy was capable of fizzing up even the most generic of lines. "Every time, he came up with something that knocked me to the floor," he said. "He's a director's dream. He magnifies every bit of work you do by a thousandfold." The director kept a VHS tape of *48 Hrs.* on hand on-set, so he could watch snippets of it for inspiration. But his star consistently delivered footage funnier than he'd imagined. One day Murphy, who never touched coffee, drank a strong cappuccino before improvising a monologue. The resulting caffeine-fueled riffs made Brest laugh so much he had to retreat to a nearby room and listen through headphones, covering himself with blankets to soundproof his giggles.

Foley and Murphy were a perfect fit: both were imbued with superhuman chutzpah, waltzing through Hollywood, listening to no one, making jokes out of everyone. "Of all the characters I've played, Axel is the most like me," the star acknowledged. "He walks like me, he talks like me, he reacts to situations the same way that I do." Backed up by the Laurel and Hardy double-act of John Ashton and Judge Reinhold, as well-meaning but dozy cops Taggart and Rosewood, he made the most out of every gag he got. Not least a memorable bit of business with a banana (replacing the original script's potato), which Foley stuffs up the tailpipe of a pursuing villain's car. Like *Trading Places*, *Beverly Hills Cop* was ultimately a movie about class, the blue-collar hero cutting a path through a procession of straight men, from a snooty maître d' to dead-eyed, art-gallery-dwelling villain Victor Maitland (Steven Berkoff).

What was new for Murphy was the action. On *48 Hrs.*, he'd been content to wave a gun around and channel Bruce Lee, but here he got to do some bona fide stunts, albeit not the steroidal ones Stallone had had in mind. The movie's opening sequence, in which Foley battles henchmen in the back of a speeding truck, was shot in downtown L.A., with the vehicles running through red lights as a police escort led the way. It was the most dangerous day of shooting Brest had ever been involved in; he sat in a pursuing car, gripping a megaphone with a white-knuckled hand, bellowing at Murphy before each turn so he could hold on tighter. The climactic shootout, meanwhile, was filmed at a stately mansion once owned by gangster Bugsy Siegel.

Murphy arrived each morning in a stretch limousine, filled with friends and hangers-on. It was his first time shooting a movie in California and he partied nonstop, paying frequent visits to a discotheque called Carlos 'n Charlie's and on one occasion getting into a fight there that ended up as a wrestling match on the dance floor. But despite the late nights, his co-stars were impressed by his focus. Berkoff marveled, "He is the perfect Brechtian. He stands outside his character and works it like a puppeteer. . . . When you do a scene with Murphy, he really listens to you, like he's studying you . . . as if he was absorbing you, sucking your molecules." Berkoff was even more impressed when the comedian caught him studying the stretch limo one afternoon, then let him have it for his journey back to his hotel.

Long before the picture wrapped, it had become evident that *Beverly Hills Cop* would not be another *Best Defense*. When rough footage was screened to a test audience, it elicited such rapturous reactions that Murphy, sitting at the back with Brest, exclaimed, "It's hot!" And that was before the ludicrously catchy theme tune, a synth number recorded by Harold Faltermeyer on a Roland JX-3P and Yamaha DX-7, had even been added. So confident were Paramount that they decided to open it on Wednesday, December 5, rather than the planned Friday, December 7, and wider than usual. They also front-loaded their advertising campaign, splashing out $5 million pre-release rather than the standard $3 million.

The result was delirium for the studio and calamity for their rivals. "This is the year the Grinch stole Christmas," lamented 20th Century Fox's president of distribution, Tom Sherak, as he watched *Beverly Hills Cop* stick bananas up the tailpipes of its expensive competitors, the likes of the Clint Eastwood–Burt Reynolds team-up *City Heat*, the sci-fi epic *Dune*, and the well-reviewed *Starman*. A staggering one in three ticket buyers was opting to see the comedy; half of those polled coming out of it said they wanted to see it again. It became the first Eddie Murphy film to do gangbusters not just in cities, but in America's heartland and across the globe. Having cost just $15 million, its receipts soared up and up and up, eventually surpassing $316 million worldwide, about $20 million more than *Ghostbusters* had made.

Unlike that film, it had zero in the way of visual effects. Unless you counted Eddie Murphy's grin, a huge, infectious thing the *Washington Post* described as a "Studebaker-grille smile." It helped make *Beverly Hills Cop* that rarest of things: a fun movie about a cop. "In most films the cop wakes up alone in a shitty apartment, has a cup of horrible coffee, then gets served divorce papers by his wife," says Petrie. "But in this one you can see the enjoyment pouring out of Eddie all the time. Even though he's at odds with all the people around him, he charms them all."

That charm wafted off the screen like a love spell, intoxicating all who took a sniff. "Everybody seems to love it. Old folks, young folks, men, women. I imagine that even cops in Beverly Hills love it," wrote newspaper columnist DL Stewart. "When it first came out, friends used to call me in the middle of the night to urge me to go and see it. Strangers stopped me on the street to tell me how great it is."

Fans kept going back and back and back. "Me and my friend Fred Barton, we saw *Beverly Hills Cop* three times the first day it came out," says Chris Rock, who would make his movie debut in the sequel. "We just wouldn't leave. Doing a movie twice was normal. We did *48 Hrs.* twice, we did *Trading Places* twice, but this one we did three times. It was like, 'Whoa!'"

Faltermeyer's theme became a number-three hit on the Billboard chart. Even Axel Foley's shabby sweatshirt became must-buy merchandise. Samuel C. Mumford High School, picked as the source of Foley's signature garment because producer Bruckheimer was a graduate, got a flood of phone calls, asking where the sweatshirt could be bought. The school eventually commissioned Kansas company Artex Manufacturing to make up twenty-four thousand, sold for $10 a pop.

The promotional tour was intense; for the first time Murphy was the sole front man, deployed not just to *Saturday Night Live* but all over the country. The day after the movie opened, he drove alone to the shopping mall in his hometown of Englewood Cliffs, New Jersey, utterly exhausted. Instead of exiting the car, an unremarkable older model instead of the Porsche or the Jaguar, he turned around so his face was pressed against the seat, and took a nap. He was woken by the sound of a group of people walking past the vehicle, yelling, "Bum!" and "Get a job!" He stayed there facedown, just listening.

Two days later, he returned to the same mall. This time, people in the parking lot, immediately recognizing him, greeted him with high-fives and shouts of "Hey, brother!"

"Both days," Murphy reflected of the dissonant experiences, "were really cold for me."

BESIDES HIS SMOOTH TRANSITION to bona fide leading man, there were two major changes for Murphy as 1984 concluded. First, his personal life was transformed when, in a shocking move, the legendary ladies' man decided to settle down.

"I'm in my sexual prime. I fuck," he'd bragged onstage during *Delirious*. As *48 Hrs.* director Walter Hill succinctly put it, "Eddie can hear the rustle of nylon stockings at fifty yards." Murphy was famous for hitting clubs and leaving within an hour with the most beautiful woman in the room, plus sometimes the second and third most beautiful women too. But all that changed when he met Lisa Figueroa. A biology major at Adelphi University, she was a studious Puerto Rican who still lived with her parents. But she was feisty enough to challenge Murphy, and to make him rethink his ultra-promiscuous lifestyle. "We're gonna have spicy black children," he declared. "And she's got a straight-A average." By the summer of 1985, they were engaged.

Second, there was Bubble Hill, his new home. Murphy had considered moving to L.A. before deciding to stay in New Jersey. Partly he was sick and tired of being bugged by people wherever he went. Partly he was fearful of becoming a showbiz phony. Instead, he'd bring Hollywood glamour to the Garden State, with a five-acre residence as flashy as anything in Malibu. Paying $3.5 million for the hilltop mansion, located in Englewood Cliffs, he set about turning it into the palace of his dreams, his own private Xanadu. One of his first moves: ordering the driveway to be extended into the shape of a 9, his lucky number.

Then the gates swung shut. Murphy wouldn't be seen again on-screen until the end of 1986. It was time to take a break, to celebrate his stupendous, unbelievable, insane success. After all, Bubble Hill had been significantly named. In the slang used by Murphy and his friends, "bubble" meant "party."

EUROPEAN VACATIONS

BILL MURRAY HAD a routine. Every morning, wearing a battered pair of Converse tennis shoes, he strolled into Paris's 5th arrondissement, passing such landmarks as the majestic Val-de-Grâce church and the tropical Jardin des plantes. Arriving at Sorbonne University, he climbed a steep spiral staircase. At his destination, a hushed classroom overlooking the Eiffel Tower, he sat at a desk for the day's lessons. When they were over, he headed back down, smoked a cigarette hand-rolled with Gitanes tobacco, bought lunch, and popped into his favorite chocolatier for 150 grams of candy. Then he treated himself to a silent movie at the Cinémathèque. Often it was something by Buster Keaton. He worked his way through the canon of D.W. Griffiths: he loved *A Romance of Happy Valley*, and once sat through *The Birth of a Nation*, nibbling on chocolate, not caring that the intertitles were in Russian and impossible to understand.

If Murray had had a publicist, they would doubtless have been frantically trying to reach him, asking why he was content to let big-money offer after big-money offer slide past. With the smash success of *Ghostbusters*, he had rocketed right to the top of the A-list. But rather than capitalize on it, Murray would take four years off, including a six-month sojourn at the Sorbonne, studying philosophy and history. By the standards of Hollywood, or anywhere else for that matter, it was an insane decision. But to him it made perfect sense.

For one thing, the public's response to *Ghostbusters* had been everything he'd feared when hesitating over *Meatballs* in 1978. Peter Venkman inspired Peter Venkmania, and everywhere Murray went, people wanted a piece of him. "They scream your name like they're being raped or killed," he said of hysterical fans after the film's release. "Things got really weird this summer."

There were perks to fame, like the time he met his idol. "I went to dinner with my agent—I was a movie star, a big shot in my mind—and there across the restaurant was Cary Grant," Murray recalls. "I was gobsmacked. It was everything I could do to not get up and walk over to his table. But I didn't. I just held it together. And as he left the restaurant, he gave me a look that said, 'That was cool. I know what you were doing. I know what you felt. And you sat there and didn't do it. And that was cool.'"

But others did not afford him the same courtesy. From mid-1984 on, he could no longer dine, visit a store, or even walk down the street without getting mobbed. He grew his hair long and turned his stubble into a beard in an attempt to elude recognition, but it didn't work. One morning he woke up at five, feeling panicky, headed to the airport, and flew to Montreal to meet Dan Aykroyd. They got in a car and just started driving, ending up in Wisconsin, where Murray had relatives.

Word quickly got out that two Ghostbusters were in town. Recalled Murray: "We'd go out to some bar one night and the next night it would be packed with thousands of people. . . . After a few days I'd lie awake in bed in the middle of the night, and it was like there were carloads of people out there, driving out in the dark looking for me."

Even when he was safely ensconced inside his brand-new New York apartment, the phone rang constantly, with producers and executives offering him weak parts in expensive films. He felt deeply disillusioned, saying, "I get the same number of lousy ideas. . . . They don't make movies. They make deals." Or maybe his appetite for work had just gone completely. He hemmed and hawed when his brother Brian and Harold Ramis approached him about a film they were writing called *Club Sandwich*, about a tacky holiday resort. Even when Aykroyd dreamed up a vehicle for the two of them called *Law of the Yukon*, which they would film in Alaska, he couldn't be pinned down.

At the same time as Murray was struggling with the consequences of massive success, he was trying to come to grips with one of the most painful failures of his life. He had poured his heart into *The Razor's Edge*, seeing the coming-of-age tale as a parallel to his own journey from the Chicago suburbs. At the film's junket in a Beverly Hills hotel in October 1984, Murray asked the manager to mix him up a Champa Tampa, the orange-juice-and-Champagne combo he'd enjoyed back in his *National Lampoon* days, and looked out of the fourth-floor window, pondering the future. "There are no dancing gophers or marshmallow men in this thing," he said, trying to prepare audiences for his first true serious role. "I know I'll probably jump off the ledge if it doesn't open big."

It didn't. In fact, it opened to a big universal shrug, making $6.6 million, less than half of what *Ghostbusters* pulled in on its opening weekend. The critics were as apathetic as everyone else. "India looks fine. Paris looks fine. *The Razor's Edge* looks awful and Bill Murray looks stoned," wrote William E. Sarmento. "This performance is one-dimensional from start to finish." He went on to call the film "Somerset Mauled."

Dejected, Murray agreed to a few public appearances, including a ceremony at Harvard University to pick up a gold pudding pot as Hasty Pudding Man of the Year 1985. "I consider myself the luckiest man on the face of the Earth," he told the audience, in a speech that was followed by thunderous applause and the *Ghostbusters* theme tune. But he felt anything but. After some deliberation with his wife, Mickey, he took action.

First he turned down an offer from *Time* magazine to appear on their next cover. He set up a voicemail account linked to an 800 number, so people could leave him job offers without him having to talk to them. And then, like his tormented *Razor's Edge* character Larry Darrell, he headed to France—although Murray at least had company, given he was taking Mickey and his two young sons, Homer and Luke.

In fact, it was far from a hermitlike existence. "He knew the local butcher and the local grocer and the bistros near him," says Ivan Reitman, who visited Murray in Paris a couple of times. "He was on first-name terms with everybody and they protected him. You know, he was both really serious about what he was doing and at the same time had an odd, goofy sense of humor about it. But it was legitimate. He was doing what he needed to do to survive."

Murray would remain there for six months. But he wouldn't appear in a substantial role on the big screen again until 1988. "I'm famous enough," he said. "Being more famous isn't going to do anything but cause me more problems."

At the peak of his success, Bill Murray was pulling the ripcord.

CHEVY CHASE, as it happened, was also on an extended sojourn in Europe. Unlike Murray, however, he had no time for luxury chocolates or afternoons at the picturehouse. He had plunged into a breakneck schedule: three film shoots in one year, with barely enough time for a massage between them.

Although he often pointed out that only three of his movies (*Deal of the Century*, *Oh! Heavenly Dog*, and *Under the Rainbow*) had actually lost money, Chase was fretting that he had lost his way in Hollywood. He had tried playing it straight, as an arms dealer in 1983's *Deal of the Century*, directed by William Friedkin, the man behind *The Exorcist* and *The French Connection*. Friedkin had considered Bill Murray and Dan Aykroyd for the role too—despite the serious subject matter, he saw it as a dark comedy—but was blown away by Chase's chops. "I had a special fondness for Chevy; I thought he was terrific in the film," says

Friedkin now. "I never thought of anyone else. He had the perfect balance of sincerity but with an underlying comic presentation. The guy is extremely intelligent and naturally sardonic."

But Chase wouldn't repeat the experiment; as he put it, "I just know what I am. People ask me if I want to do something besides comedy, but what else is there except tragedy? I don't want to do *King Lear*." Besides, he had suffered enough darkness in his personal life not to want to dwell on it in work hours: "I've been doing *Ordinary People* at home all my life." Instead, his plan was to get back to basics, making comedies that would remind people why he was Chevy Chase and they weren't.

First up was a thing called *Fletch*. The tale of an investigative reporter named Irwin "Fletch" Fletcher, the project had bounced around at Universal since the late '70s, surviving three changes in regime. Burt Reynolds had come close to starring at one point; so, weirdly, did Mick Jagger. The latter was personally nixed by the character's creator, novelist Gregory Mcdonald, who told the execs, "I admire Mick Jagger, but he is not my idea of a young American male." Mcdonald did, however, like the sound of Chevy Chase. Though arguably not so young anymore—Chase was in his early forties when he bagged the role in 1984—he received a telegram from the mystery writer, enthusing, "I am delighted to abdicate the role of Fletch to you."

Star and character were a smooth fit. Part journalist, part private eye, Fletch is a laidback rebel who glides his way through one tricky situation after another. He's charming but goofy, a suave klutz who employs such unconvincing aliases as "Harry S. Truman," "Dr. Rosenpenis," and "Frieda's boss" ("Who's Frieda?" "My secretary"). Sizing up the role, Chase knew he was onto something special. "He's a very wiseacre kind of guy, and he's cheeky, glib," he considered. "He's the kind of guy it's easy for me to play, because he's almost like me."

For *Fletch*, he stayed in the States, shooting in Los Angeles and Utah (the noirish plot involves a real-estate deal in Provo, the state's third-largest city). Chase got along well with the director, Michael Ritchie, veteran of *The Candidate* and *The Bad News Bears*, since Ritchie gave him near-unlimited freedom to improvise. He didn't get along nearly so well with screenwriter Andrew Bergman, for much the same reason. "Andrew Bergman didn't write *Fletch*. I wrote *Fletch*," Chase would say later on the publicity trail. "I don't take screenwriting credit because I don't need it. People who know me recognize my lines."

No matter who came up with it, *Fletch* is stuffed with great dialogue, much of it tossed away like candy wrappers by its star. "You'll be wearing rubber gloves. Do you own rubber gloves?" asks the villain (Tim Matheson), asking Fletch to murder him for money. "I rent 'em," quips Fletch. "I have a lease with an option to buy." Chase also gets to adopt thirteen different disguises over the movie's ninety-six-minute run time, from drug addict to tennis instructor. Most important, he's given the boost of an actual, polished story, far from the sheer nonsense of *Modern Problems* or *Under the Rainbow*. It was the most likable he had been on-screen for years.

Perhaps because of his back catalog, however, or the fact he was playing so close to his own persona, critics were sniffy. "He projects such an inflexible mask of cool detachment, of ironic running commentary, that we're prevented from identifying with him," said Roger Ebert. The *Daily Herald* called his performance "embarrassing." But Chase didn't care. The film had performed well, making $7 million in its opening weekend (doing particularly well in coastal cities; Chase lacked Eddie Murphy's ability to charm the US heartland) and taking second place at the box office after *Rambo: First Blood Part 2*. Suddenly the idea of more *Fletch* films was on the table at Universal—and with fourteen Mcdonald books and counting in stores, there were plenty of cases to choose from. But before getting into that, Chase was off to make a different sequel, his first ever.

DESPITE HIS STABLE FAMILY LIFE—he and Jayni had one child with another on the way—the truth was that Chase had been battling a drug habit since the late '60s. He first tried pot as a fledgling writer in New York; the coke came later, at *Saturday Night Live*, where he frequently pulled Friday all-nighters to work on his jokes for "Weekend Update."

As he recalls in his memoir, he was flying particularly high on May 17, 1976, the night he won an Emmy for his work on the show. "I gave my speech," he wrote, "came offstage out of view of the camera, and Redd Foxx shoved a spoonful of cocaine up my nose in a congratulatory way."

Given that he'd performed a particularly histrionic pratfall on the way to the podium, the bump probably doubled as a pain reliever. Chase's determination to do his own stunts took its toll over the years, causing him severe backaches, which he self-medicated with painkillers, prescribed by one of his numerous doctors. By the mid-'80s, Jayni was seriously worried, particularly about her husband's cocaine habit: Chevy was experiencing an agonizing throb in the inside of his nose and making regular visits to an ENT specialist.

Rather than slow down and face the problem, in September 1984 Chase boarded a flight to Europe. Ahead lay a $17 million adventure, his first major trip to the Continent. *National Lampoon's European Vacation* (which was for a brief period titled *Vacation 2 Europe*) would be a whirlwind three-month tour, taking in London, Paris, Rome, and the Italian Alps, under the guidance of Amy Heckerling, a thirty-one-year-old who had previously directed the well-received *Fast Times at Ridgemont High* but was struggling with her latest film, *Johnny Dangerously*. "It was not scoring very well," Heckerling remembers. "I had worked really hard to get where I was, and I kinda had the feeling that a woman could not have a failure and continue. If *Johnny Dangerously* tanked, my career would be over. So to stay in the game I signed up for this sequel to a successful movie. When I read it I thought it could work, if the funny stuff was found."

Her comedy credentials were impressive, but Chase, a decade her senior and with triple the credits, wasn't impressed when he met her. He had wanted Harold Ramis to return, but Ramis was busy shooting *Ghostbusters* in New York, and in his opinion this strong-minded young woman from the Bronx was no substitute. As the production advanced, their relationship failed to improve. In Austria, the crew trekked up the same Salzburg hill where Julie Andrews had crooned for *The Sound Of Music*, for a quick skit lampooning the 1965 musical;

as he trudged through the meadow, Chase thought to himself, "Why am I doing this?" He thought the project was being rushed (a theory lent credence by the fact the lead characters' surname is misspelled as "Griswald" in the opening credits), that Heckerling didn't know how to shoot comedy, that it was devoid of the original's wit and warmth, despite being again written by John Hughes. He was concerned by its crasser aspects, like the pedophile game-show host in the prologue, or a wife-swap riff. And both he and Beverly D'Angelo, returning as Clark's wife, Ellen, felt wary of how the Griswalds/Griswolds interacted with the foreigners they met, fretting that they came off as racist.

Chase and D'Angelo (the only other returning cast member, since both children were replaced, something that would become a series trope) had a brother-and-sister connection. D'Angelo called Chase "Sparky," a pet name that made its way into the film. That friendship, along with occasional visits from Chase's family, including a trip up the Eiffel Tower with his two-year-old daughter, Cydney, got him through a shoot that was otherwise miserable. He felt homesick, desperate to get home for his second child's birth in January. Rain seemed to follow them wherever they went. And he had a sinking feeling that the movie would not turn out well.

In that, he wasn't alone. "I was of course very nervous because I really needed this to not fail," says Heckerling. "But everything just sucked. We were at the Spanish Steps in Rome and I thought, 'Steps? Chevy Chase? Shouldn't he trip up and fall down them and go on and on and on?' But by the time we got to Italy everything had gone to hell and we couldn't do it. We were being steered toward rewriting scenes that weren't going to be as good. I was assigned certain actors that when I met them didn't look the way they did in the photos, or did not speak English well or at all. And there were times when Chevy didn't show up or whatever. Sometimes he'd say he was in a lot of pain; I remember one meeting where he showed us his X-rays, the places where he'd messed up his back. He was not a happy camper. And neither was I."

The director, in fact, kept a plane ticket to New York on her person at all times during the shoot, so she knew if needed she could make a rapid escape. When Heckerling got back to America, she couldn't stop herself from telling a journalist that the experience had been "almost unbearable." And a decade on she would write a telling line of dialogue for her 1995 rom-com *Clueless*: "Searching for a boy in high school is as useless as searching for meaning in a Chevy Chase movie." It was changed at the last moment, when Paramount head Sherry Lansing, a friend of the actor's, intervened, resulting in a name-check for Pauly Shore instead. "I'm a Taurus; I hold a grudge," Heckerling says with a laugh now. "I apologized to Pauly Shore later. I have nothing personal against him. He seems like a very sweet guy."

"I can't say Amy and Chevy were pals," says Matty Simmons, who returned as producer and maintains that *European Vacation* is his favorite of the series. "I don't imagine Chevy has even spoken to Amy since they finished that picture. But I never saw any open hostility."

Excitingly for Chase, given that his big break had come in a line for a Monty Python movie, he had gotten to not only perform some slapstick shtick in the film with Eric Idle, but sing at a party with Idle and Keith Richards. Over beers in London, he and Idle discussed the possibilities of a *Vacation* film that visited Australia, scribbling down a few set pieces involving sharks and snakes. Ultimately, though, the notes were abandoned; Chase lacked enthusiasm to come back for a third. "The first was enjoyable, the second was hard and there was a different chemistry," he would say a year after *European Vacation* wrapped. "I won't do another. It would be a waste of time."

Six months on, reviews were lousy. One, bearing the subheading "Too Much Chevy Chase," called Heckerling "Hollywood's latest crashed meteor." It made number one at the box office on its first weekend, then collapsed, earning a total of $49 million domestically, roughly $12 million less than the first film's business. Not a disaster, but yet another perceived failure for the onetime golden boy of comedy.

Chase did limited press for the film, over the phone. He was back in Europe, with a new daughter, Caley, and a new movie in production,

Spies Like Us. Uncharacteristically for him, ever the lone wolf or the ladies' man, he was working in a double-act with another male comedian. Asked why, he offered an answer straight from the heart: "It's a lot easier to work with somebody else whom you can flop with."

SAID "SOMEBODY" WAS DAN AYKROYD, Chase's old cohort from *Saturday Night Live*. The two had always been cordial, despite the tension between Chase and John Belushi, and the distaste that Aykroyd, ever the team player, occasionally felt for Chase's limelight-hogging. "He likes to focus attention on himself," said the Canadian, many years on from *SNL*. "It was the arrogance of the New Yorker. When you live in Manhattan, you kind of have a view of the world that's superior." As they threw themselves into their respective movie careers, they lost touch with each other. Chase's cameo in the *Ghostbusters* music video was as close as they'd come to a collaboration. Still, they were destined to reunite.

Like *Ghostbusters*, *Spies Like Us* had originally been written by Aykroyd in the early '80s as a vehicle for him and Belushi. A riff on the Bob Hope–Bing Crosby *Road to . . .* movies Aykroyd had loved as a child, it was another wish-fulfillment fantasy: instead of spook zappers, the two heroes were a pair of spies, albeit colossally bumbling ones, who accidentally get embroiled in Cold War intrigue. When Belushi died, Aykroyd slipped it into a drawer, only to pull it out again when *Ghostbusters* became a go project, restoring his Hollywood clout.

He headed to Jamaica with his friend Dave Thomas for a writing stint, visiting the GoldenEye Plantation and sitting at the desk where Ian Fleming typed his James Bond novels. Belushi's character, an oafish Armenian named Karmissian, disappeared; the lead characters became Austin Millbarge and Emmett Fitz-Hume (very Aykroydian names). Then he teamed with *Splash* writers Lowell Ganz and Babaloo Mandel, refining the plot and trimming down the amount of impenetrable espionage jargon. Aykroyd's wife, Donna, who referred to *Spies Like Us* as one of Dan's "little-boy fantasies," signed up to play a physician love interest. Bob Hope himself agreed to do a walk-on cameo.

The stew was finally cooking, but Aykroyd still needed a director and a co-star. For the former, his instincts told him to go after John Landis, the man who had steered *The Blues Brothers* and *Trading Places* to glory. But Landis was in the middle of a personal nightmare. While shooting his segment of *Twilight Zone: The Movie* in July 1982, an on-set accident involving a helicopter had resulted in star Vic Morrow and two young Vietnamese children being decapitated by rotor blades. Landis had been away from the set that night—it was a second-unit stunt—but still became the subject of a civil and criminal lawsuit that would last nearly a decade.

"It's a horror story," Landis remembers now. "Warner Bros., who made *Twilight Zone*, were acting despicably. And while that was going on they sent me Danny's script for *Spies Like Us*. I was thinking, 'Warner Bros.? Fuck them.'" Landis's attorney, however, argued that he should take the movie: if the studio was willing to trust him with another big-budget project, their case that he was irresponsible would be weakened. "I mean, they'd be obviously lying!" Landis says. "So that was what happened. I was sort of reluctant. Then I read the script, and it was silly, but it was an opportunity to do a road picture."

As for Aykroyd's comedic foil, the search took a little longer. For a while, Warner Bros. was in talks with new *Saturday Night Live* star Joe Piscopo, a close friend of Eddie Murphy's and purveyor of an accomplished Sinatra impression. That fell apart. Then Aykroyd ran into Chase at a party, and the two got to reminiscing about old times, those golden 30 Rock days. What if, Chase suggested, they got back together? *Spies Like Us* finally had someone to play Emmett Fitz-Hume.

The bulk of the picture was shot in the UK, partly at Twickenham Studios, where a replica Stonehenge had recently been toppled for *National Lampoon's European Vacation*. With Chase and Aykroyd sharing the top billing rather than having to carry the movie on their own, they felt like they were shooting a super-long sketch. "In this movie, Chevy brought me back to the real kernel of comedy," Aykroyd enthused. "The nut, the heart, the funny faces and weird voices that we did on *SNL*."

Still, those days were gone, and the realities of global stardom applied. At Twickenham Studios, everybody seemed to know Aykroyd: *The Blues Brothers*, *Trading Places*, and *Ghostbusters* had all been hits in the UK. Chase, on the other hand, rarely got a second glance. "It sort of drove Chevy crazy," says Landis. "He became particularly obnoxious for a while. There was no awkwardness between he and I because of *Animal House*—he didn't know I didn't want him in the movie! But he can be a strange guy. There's a direct connection between his id and his mouth."

The gentle rivalry between the two stars continued as the production went on the road. Not only was Chase romancing Aykroyd's wife, Donna, on-screen, but there were practical jokes behind the scenes. *Spies Like Us* shot for one day in California's Palm Desert, two days in Washington, DC, then flew to Morocco (doubling for Afghanistan and Pakistan) and Norway (doubling for Russia). One day, as the two stars drove a Jeep through the sweltering Sahara Desert after shooting in Ouarzazate, a town two hundred miles from Marrakech, they spotted a squadron of local troops. Aykroyd took a photo; the soldiers took offense, and started chasing them in a truck. The pursuit ended when, as Chase tells it, he and Aykroyd reached their hotel and hid in a Volkswagen bus. "We could see, through the curtains, soldiers coming out with the guns," he recalled. "Like they didn't want us to take their picture!"

The next morning, Chase arrived back on-set, to be told Aykroyd had been captured and put in a Marrakech prison. Stunned, he sat alone in his trailer, until the door opened and Aykroyd walked in, laughing. He couldn't believe his prank had worked.

ANOTHER CLOSE CALL was to go down in Norway. After a succession of night shoots in freezing weather, the schedule called for a week's filming atop a mountain near Sognefjord, doubling for the Tajik Soviet Socialist Republic. Each day, Aykroyd and Chase hiked to the summit, clad in fur-lined parkas, and performed parts of a pivotal action sequence involving a Soviet SS-20 rocket. Until, that is, the production office received telephone calls from the US Department of Defense and the Norwegian government. It turned out that the rocket had been spotted by an American satellite and reported to the relevant authorities. After some explanation by one of the film's producers, a military invasion of the set was averted.

Spies Like Us brought the two *SNL* stars full-circle. On TV, current affairs had regularly been grist for their mill, whether it was Aykroyd impersonating Presidents Nixon and Carter, or Chase announcing from behind the "Weekend Update" desk that "Generalissimo Francisco Franco is still dead." Now, after years of creating purely escapist movies, populated with dancing gophers and ghosts, they were making something grounded in the real world.

"The interesting thing about that movie is the politics," says Landis. "The Soviet Union was really in Afghanistan at that point. It deals with Reagan's Star Wars defense. And you know who's in that picture? The Mujahideen. Those are the people who were fighting the Russians in Afghanistan, and we and the British armed them. They of course became Al Qaeda. The politics are fascinating."

Still, despite the hot-button backdrop, it was chock-full of daffiness: cameos from Landis's director pals (Joel and Ethan Coen, Sam Raimi, Terry Gilliam); silly gags ("What's a dickfer?" "For peeing"); and Three Stooges–esque riffs (a scene of absurd length in which a roomful of doctors greet one another with the word "Doctor"). And the daffiest part was yet to be added. In September 1985, as he locked the edit, comfortably ahead of the film's December release date, Landis received a call from Mark Canton, an executive at Warner Bros.

"John, guess what?" Canton all but yelled down the phone. "Paul McCartney is going to write the title song for *Spies Like Us*!"

Trying to process this information, to figure out if it was good news or bad, Landis quickly replayed the opening of the movie in his head. It was a long tracking shot through a Washington, DC, market, totally unsuited to a chipper pop song. "But it's finished," he told Canton. "We have the answer print. It's done."

"No, no, John, you don't understand," Canton fired back. "Paul McCartney is going to write the title song for *Spies Like Us*."

The director was told the truth: the Beatle, a huge fan of Landis's music video for Michael Jackson's "Thriller," had contacted Warner Bros. on his own and offered to do a song for free. The studio head had agreed. There was no backing out now, without the bruising of giant egos. An hour later, Landis received another call, this time from McCartney himself, saying, "Hey, mate. I'm so excited to be doing this song for you. . . ." The director, a serious Beatles fan who had seen the band play the Hollywood Bowl when he was fifteen, folded like a lawn chair. Then, with the phone back on the cradle, he thought to himself, "What the fuck am I going to do with this song?"

His solution was to put it at the end of the film, not the start, and kick off with the only part of the song he liked: the chorus. "The regular part wouldn't begin until most people had left the theater," he says with a laugh. But that wasn't the end of it. Landis got another call from Canton telling him to get on a plane to London the next day, where he would shoot a music video at Abbey Road. McCartney had dreamed up a wacky concept in which he, Chase, and Aykroyd would play together as a band, switching constantly between instruments.

Landis, heavily jetlagged throughout its shoot, is not particularly proud of the results. "I was thrilled to meet Paul and Linda," he says, "but I only had a day to prep. We also had to deal with weird UK union rules, which dictated you can't pretend to play an instrument if you don't actually play it on the record. That limited what we could do with Danny and Chevy; it really was a very odd situation. Funnily enough, the song became a big hit in the UK. But not anywhere else that I know of."

As for *Spies Like Us* itself, it got a mixed reaction, with more than one critic lambasting it for wasteful spending, despite the fact it had been brought home for about $20 million, a whole $10 million less than *Ghostbusters*. A newspaper ran its review under the banner, "*Spies* funnymen fail as team." But Chase and Aykroyd, who had tossed each other cigarettes throughout the press tour, survived as friends and would collaborate again. The movie, which did a solid $60 million in business, would inspire some viewers like the Hope-Crosby movies had inspired Aykroyd.

"I know for a fact that there are young people in the intelligence service that went in after seeing that movie," he says. "In the same way there are people playing in bands because of *The Blues Brothers*. You know what? I've created jobs."

12
GOING WEST

STEVE MARTIN'S BANK balance was expanding, and so was his art collection. On the stark-white walls of his Beverly Hills home, a one-story, L-shaped building without front windows that he shared with partner Victoria Tennant, hung works by Picasso, Hopper, Lichtenstein, Hockney, O'Keeffe. The bookshelves were neatly and alphabetically stacked with volumes on painters: Martin owned twenty about Whistler alone. Perfectly suited to the serene, museumlike mood of the Bedford Drive abode, two pet cats, a calico called Betty and a white Persian called Mary, padded around, rarely disturbing their master.

Once a casual hobby for Martin, the art collection had become a psychological refuge. "This art is so different from what I do that it's an escape for me," he said. "Sometimes I feel so lucky to own them. It's like, 'Good grief, these things are so beautiful—how did this happen?'"

When they were working, Martin and Tennant sat beside each other tapping away at identical Hewlett-Packard Vectra word processors; when they weren't, they would occasionally sit and look at a particular painting together. With Tennant just as intensely private as he was, it wasn't a place for parties so much as a silent fortress. In fact, Martin had a nickname for the residence: "The House That Says Go Away."

The mid-1980s was a time of deep reflection for Martin. Or rather, even deeper reflection than usual. The biggest comedy star of the '70s was, it was clear to all, far from the biggest comedy star of the '80s. While Eddie Murphy and Bill Murray were exploding, Martin was struggling in vain to repeat the success of *The Jerk*. That film had made $40 million domestically; his next five movies hadn't even made that combined.

Pennies from Heaven and *Dead Men Don't Wear Plaid* were daring experiments that tanked, at least commercially; *The Man with Two Brains* had gone back to zany basics but died; his most recent two, *The Lonely Guy* and *All of Me*, had also failed to ignite. The latter, in particular, was a disappointment for Martin, who had pulled off some spectacular physical comedy as a man with an additional person (an eccentric millionaire played by Lily Tomlin) stuffed inside him, vying for control of his limbs.

So he became an actual lonely guy, secluding himself away for most of 1984, trying to deep-think his way through the problem. Just as he had meticulously analyzed stand-up comedy in his early days, Martin now attempted to calculate why certain things in films were funny, and others not. He became fixated with the way Meryl Streep mispronounced "seersucker" in *Sophie's Choice*, a small detail in an otherwise solemn film that reduced him to tears of laughter.

And slowly, his mojo started to return. "My mind's been rejuvenated," he said in September that year. "Really, all it takes is one hit movie and you're back in the business. With a hit movie, all is forgiven."

MARTIN HOPED that hit could come from a story outline that had languished in his filing cabinet since the late 1970s. Where *Spies Like Us* had been conceived as a two-hander for Aykroyd and Belushi, *¡Three Amigos!* had been intended as a vehicle for those two, plus Martin. Perhaps inspired by the comedian's youthful stint at Disneyland's Fron-tierland, it was a western, a silly riff on *The Magnificent Seven* in which a trio of idiotic 1930s movie stars think they have been paid to put on a show for a south-of-the-border village, but are actually facing a gang of authentically brutal bandits. There would be songs, slapstick, saddles, and sombreros. Martin called it a "Mexican-Western fiesta musical with a million gags."

The cast reshuffled in 1981: there was now talk of Robin Wil-liams and Bill Murray joining Martin, to be directed by Steven Spiel-berg. But Spielberg got immersed in *E.T.: The Extraterrestrial*; besides, given his experience with *1941* two years earlier, he was gun-shy about jumping into another comedy starring *SNL* alumni.

In any case, *¡Three Amigos!* was a long way from being ready. "I hired two writers to turn it into a screenplay, and that didn't work," says Martin. "It was just very different. Very based on puns."

A few years later, Martin was visiting *SNL* boss Lorne Michaels at his holiday home in St. Barts. When he showed him the failed *¡Three Amigos!* script, Michaels said, "I think we should throw this away and write a new one together." Martin agreed, then rang up another friend, songwriter Randy Newman, and got him on board too. These three amigos got to work on *¡Three Amigos!*, meeting on and off for seven months at Martin's house. "We had a blast writing it," Martin remem-bers. "Lorne would come into town, stay at a Beverly Hills hotel, and walk over to my house. Every day at two, as I recall."

The star, who sat at the word processor and did the typing, more often than not had the final word when it came to jokes. A singing bush, an idea that had tickled Martin for half a decade, was shoe-horned into the plot, as was an invisible swordsman, a ludicrously com-plicated salute, and a campfire sing-along with a menagerie of desert critters. "It's a strange script, but a very smart one," says John Landis, who joined the project as director. "Like *Animal House*—the movies are so silly and outrageous, I don't know if people are aware of how sophisticated they are."

Martin himself would play the preening Lucky Day. For the first of the remaining Amigos, he had to look no further than the poker games he took part in on Wednesday nights, as a member of the ultra-exclusive "Hollywood Gourmet Poker Club." Other celebrities in the group included Johnny Carson, Carl Reiner, Neil Simon, and Chevy Chase: the careful Martin was the most consistent winner, while Chase was no amateur himself, distracting his rival players with incessant patter. As Simon, a perpetual Wednesday-night loser, phrased it, "Chevy hid everything behind the humor." Martin offered him the role of Dusty Bottoms, a cocky but vacuous matinee idol who, when invited by a Mexican beauty to kiss her on the veranda, replies, "Lips would be fine."

For the last of the three key roles, diminutive dimwit Ned "Little Neddy" Nederlander, Landis and Martin decided to take a shot on a fresh-faced *SCTV* star who had never before appeared in a movie: Martin Short. "I was the Carrot Top Amigo," says Short, a chipper Ontarian. "It was my very first film and it couldn't have been a more luxurious way to start."

Short's first proper meeting with Martin took place at the latter's house on May 4, 1985, as the film was deep into pre-production. A *Jerk* fanatic but not one to get star-struck, Short entered the vast domicile, gazed in wonder at the original Picassos hung on the walls, and whistled.

"How did you get so rich?" he asked his host. "Because I've *seen* your work."

Martin burst into laughter. He'd just made a friend for life.

STARTING IN FEBRUARY 1986, the *¡Three Amigos!* shoot proved a rejuvenating experience for its two veteran stars. "I remember what a tremendous amount of fun it was to make," says Steve Martin. "We were in Tucson and the Mojave Desert, on location, having the time of our lives."

Each morning he would clamber into his ridiculous Amigo threads—a black flared bolero jacket and enormous matching sombrero, designed by Landis's wife, Deborah—and head to the set for the day's designated tomfoolery. Between camera setups there were epic

Scrabble games. And at the slightest prompt, the cheeky Short would launch into his full-force Katharine Hepburn impression: "Where's my *bicycle*? I wish I had my *bicycle*. We could go *picking blueberries*. . . . It's such a *beautiful* day!"

Chevy Chase, meanwhile, was happy to be in a triple-act for the first time in his movie career. For one thing, it meant he had other comics to spar with. "What was fun—for me anyway—was watching the three of them constantly one-upping each other," remembers Landis. "They'd sit there making cruel and cutting remarks that were truly funny." The ribaldry extended beyond words: on his first day, Short entered his trailer to find that someone had taken a gigantic dump in the toilet and not flushed. He suspected Chase, who in 2018 seemed to confirm his guilt by admitting to playing the same trick on Martin.

Less funny, for Landis at least, was the day Chase forgot he was wearing a mike. The three stars were standing on a cliffside, waiting for a shot to be lit, when Chase made an off-color joke, to the effect that the director should be more careful with his actors after the *Twilight Zone* tragedy. He and Landis, whom Chase had already been needling about what he considered to be bad editing on *Spies Like Us*, nearly came to blows. It would be the last time the two worked together.

Back in L.A., *¡Three Amigos!* stormed Universal Studios for a few days to shoot a silent-movie sequence on its oldest exterior set, built for a Tom Mix movie. "The tourist trams go through it every ten minutes and the boys would shoot their six-guns and dance for them," says Landis. Short and Chase started car-pooling from their homes in the Pacific Palisades; one morning, Short looked across to see his co-star apparently asleep, head resting on the steering wheel. It was, of course, a vintage Chevy Chase prank.

For the Amigos, the jollity continued even after the movie wrapped, with them continuing to meet up for a never-ending succession of restaurant outings. During one, Martin found a tooth in his salad and complained, only to realize it was one of his own. Landis, on the other hand, struggled through a tough post-production period, forced to edit only at night because of the *Twilight Zone* trial. When he handed over his cut, the executives at Orion found it lacking and removed several scenes Landis considered crucial, including an elaborate opening tracking shot through an Old Hollywood studio, featuring Fran Drescher, and a cameo from subversive stand-up comic Sam Kinison as an ax-wielding maniac.

Though still hilarious, the version that hit theaters had a limited impact on the box office, making more money abroad than it did in America. Even so, it had its champions, including critic Brian Hutton, who wrote, "What makes this film so funny is that the three comedians have blended their talents so well, forsaking their individual comic trademarks. None of the three has ever appeared together in a feature film, but they perform as a team in a screenplay that gets the most out of each."

Martin had mixed emotions: he was disappointed with the numbers, but satisfied that they'd pulled off his mad idea as well as it could have been. "It's a funny, silly comedy," he says now. "It just works. That scene where we all sleep together in the same bed: it's so Laurel and Hardy."

CHASE WAS LESS FOCUSED on the film's performance; he had other things to worry about. During the shoot his back pain had intensified and he had found himself unable to perform physical slapstick. It didn't go away after the movie wrapped. In fact, taking more and more painkillers, largely Percoset, and snorting so much cocaine that his nose began to hurt, he was struggling to make it through the day, sweating heavily and having panic attacks.

One afternoon, his wife and doctors made an intervention. "Chev, we think you've got a problem," Jayni told him, "and there's only one way to get out of it." He agreed to go to the Betty Ford Center, out in the desert in Rancho Mirage, for a stint of rehab, snorting the last of his cocaine in the car on the way there.

He wasn't going quietly, though. "I was a little like Jack Nicholson in *One Flew Over the Cuckoo's Nest*. I didn't care for the scare tactics there," he told *Playboy* in 1988. "You'll never see me back in one of those places again. Never. You could put one of those pills in front of me right now, and I'll say, 'No, I don't want it.'" Beat. "You don't, by any chance, have any on you, do you?"

Chase appreciated the irony of his ending up at a clinic founded by the wife of Gerald Ford, the president whom he had not only famously lampooned on *Saturday Night Live* but derided with the words, "Looking into his eyes is like looking into fifteen milligrams of Valium." The Fords were gracious enough to visit their former victimizer during his stay. Less gracious were his *¡Three Amigos!* co-stars, who couldn't resist making fun of their beleaguered friend.

First it had been Martin and Chase plotting against Short, planning to trick him into coming to the premiere in full Amigo costume, while they turned up in normal clothes. They abandoned that at the last minute—"We laughed so hard at the thought of us turning up in suits and him standing there with the big hat on," says Martin—but an offer for the trio to host *SNL* just before the film's release, and a matter of weeks after Chase's release from rehab, provided another opportunity for mischief. Midway through the monologue, Short and Martin struck. "They just started throwing pills at me," recalls Chase. "'You want some pills, Chevy? Here!' To make fun of the fact I had gone to Betty Ford for pills."

"Well," considers Short decades on, with mock compassion, "that was *wrong*."

RICK MORANIS had been as taken aback by the seismic success of *Ghostbusters* as most of his co-stars. As he'd worked on it, he'd had no idea what the final product would look like, or whether it would work. "It felt like we were just shopping for ingredients, and maybe Ivan knew what was for dinner," he says. "But I certainly didn't have a handle on it. They were nice people and it was a fun character to do. But it wasn't the same kind of fun as *SCTV*, where you're doing volumes of material in a day. It wasn't the fun of a Mel Brooks movie, where everybody's so broad. It was its own kind of thing."

By 1986, the year that animated spin-off *The Real Ghostbusters* de-buted on TV, a wave of tie-in toys had started hitting stores. Along with a pizza-chomping Slimer, a haunted toilet ("Fearsome Flusher"), and an *Ecto-2* helicopter, a five-inch version of Moranis was available for kids to buy. Louis Tully came with green slime you could coat him with, plus a "four-eyed ghost." The character could also be purchased in monster-dog form.

All of this was great for the comedian's profile, but he was having a tough time keeping the momentum going. He took a small part in 1984's *The Wild Life*, directed by Art Linson from a Cameron Crowe script, as the wild-haired manager of a clothing store. He spent a cou-ple of days on the set of *Brewster's Millions*, shooting with Richard Pryor and old *SCTV* buddy John Candy, the man from whom he had inherited his *Ghostbusters* role. And he was asked by John Hughes, whom he had met through their mutual friend Joel Silver, if he wanted to play the janitor in *The Breakfast Club*. Moranis said yes.

It turned out to be a bad experience. Up in Toronto in early 1984 to supervise the renovation of his house, Moranis started working up a character based on one of the builders, a burly Russian with a beard. He grew out his own facial hair, developed a silly accent. But he couldn't reach Hughes on the phone, to make sure the director was OK with the decision. Neither was he able to get hold of a copy of the script.

Finally, he flew down to Des Plaines, Illinois, for the start of prin-cipal photography. The first day seemed to go smoothly enough. But the next morning Hughes approached him, looking tense, and said, "You know, the editor looked at the dailies, and doesn't think the char-acter is right for the movie."

Moranis was unhappy. "You know, John, there's a wonderful thing in show business called casting," he said. "And I suggest you do some casting for this part. Because I've been trying to get you on the phone and I don't know what you want here. So why don't you find somebody else to do this?"

The two parted ways, not so amicably, and Canadian actor John Kapelos was brought in to play the part instead.

The year 1985 didn't prove to be a much better one for Moranis. He played another minor role in the Judge Reinhold vehicle *Head Office*, then went to the West Indies to make *Club Paradise*, the Harold Ramis comedy that Bill Murray turned down. He got to spar with Robin Williams (Murray's replacement), meet Peter O'Toole, and hang out with *SCTV* friends such as Joe Flaherty and Eugene Levy. He even got a tan. But the movie, a muddled resort farce, was lousy, and his performance as a nerdy tourist a wan retread of what he'd done in *Ghostbusters*.

Then, out of nowhere, came his first leading role. He happened to be friendly with Hollywood mogul David Geffen, who was producer of a strange off-Broadway show and attempting to get a film version off the ground. The show was *Little Shop of Horrors*, about a carnivorous plant, a kind of cross between a Venus flytrap and Bela Lugosi, which resides in a dilapidated New York flower store. Fed human blood and eventually human meat by its master, browbeaten shopkeeper Seymour Krelborn, Audrey II becomes ever bigger and ever more famous, boosting the fortunes of Seymour as it does.

A musical that would require elaborate special effects, it was, thought Geffen, a perfect fit for Muppets behind-the-scenes wizard Frank Oz, whom he offered the directing job. Oz took some convincing. "It had fourteen songs, it had guest stars, it had a plant that goes from fifty pounds to a ton," he remembers. "I read it and said, 'No!' David said, 'Nobody says no to me.' But I wasn't trying to be obstreperous—I just didn't know how to do it. Only when the pressure was off and I was in Toronto shooting commercials or something did it occur to me how I could do it. I rewrote it in such a way that it became a 360-degree experience. A cinematic sensibility, rather than a proscenium." He also thought he'd found the perfect leading man: Moranis, whom he'd sized up over a cup of coffee.

The project turned out to be even more monstrous than Oz had feared. The stage version had actually been inspired by a schlocky Roger Corman film from 1960, which was rehearsed over three days, shot over two, and so low-budget, costing just $20,000, that the entire cast had to share a single script. By comparison, the 1986 Warner Bros. version would require $30 million (the official number; some reports have it at $40 million) and take over the whole of Pinewood Studios in the UK. A Skid Row street set with vast skyline transparency was erected inside the 007 stage, while the final iteration of the puppet plant required fifty-five technicians to operate it.

For Moranis, the challenge was almost as great. Besides belting out a series of big musical numbers, he had to climb onto an elevated set each day and act opposite a piece of vampiric vegetation, ignoring the many puppeteers below. And for some shots featuring both him and the swollen, sassy Audrey II, he had to do everything in slow-motion, so that the footage (shot at sixteen frames per second) could be speeded up later, making the plant look lifelike. "I remember thinking, 'How could an actor sing, perform, and move at half speed?'" says Neal Scanlan, the film's animatronics supervisor. "They had a morning's practice and when we saw it in rushes it was like, 'Are you kidding me? They've really nailed it.'"

"It was tough to get right," says Moranis. "But I figured out that the trick was not to tighten your butt when you walk. Funnily enough, on another stage at Pinewood was Sigourney Weaver, operating at sixteen frames with the big monster on *Aliens*. So we would get together and move at sixteen frames together. 'How you doing?' 'Pretty good. How are you?'"

Intended as a three-month shoot, *Little Shop of Horrors* turned out to take almost a year. It was complicated, often maddeningly so. But Moranis, who was staying in a lavish Belgravia flat, was having a blast. "I was pinching myself daily," he says. "Nothing like it had ever been done before at that scale. It was a roll of a dice. But it was one of the best experiences I ever had."

One winter morning, during a snowstorm, Oz had to rush off to the hospital, where his wife was about to give birth. Instead of calling off the day's work, he left Moranis in charge of the shoot. "And when I came back, he'd got through about nine setups, which is more than I usually did, directing himself and everything else," says Oz. "It annoyed the hell out of me. He's a very smart guy."

LITTLE SHOP OF HORRORS was a landmark movie for another reason, one that had nothing to do with its floral fiend. It saw Bill Murray break his four-year self-enforced hiatus, returning to a set to shoot an electrifying scene. His partner for the scene: Steve Martin.

After Paris, Murray had returned with wife Mickey, toddler Homer, and new son Luke to the Hudson River valley, where the family settled down in a remote farmhouse with a wooded backyard. There Murray had continued his period of deep contemplation, retiring to a small office to read Irish novels. When he was spotted out in the world, it was mostly on the New York subway, headed to Yankee Stadium with his brother Brian for a weekend game. But these sightings were few and far between, and fans continued to ask, "Where the heck is Bill Murray?"

They weren't alone; the studios were missing him too. Warner Bros. pursued him for the male lead in _The Witches of Eastwick_. Disney wanted him for _Who Framed Roger Rabbit_. He and Eddie Murphy were considered the world's two biggest box-office draws, and the money being offered to him kept going up and up each year, despite the fact he wasn't working—or perhaps because of it. By the second half of the 1980s, he was being offered as much as $5 million to make a comeback picture. Each time he said no.

One of the reasons was the ailing health of his mother, Lucille, who had retired from a lifetime of clerical work around the time _Ghostbusters_ came out. Instead of being able to finally kick back, she was diagnosed with lymphatic cancer and underwent massive chemotherapy. The news was a body blow to her son. "The idea of her being gravely ill really threw me hard," Murray said in 1988, the year she passed away. "She'd always been a massive influence on me. She's so animated, I even used to tape phone conversations with her in order to steal material."

With two young kids to look after (one of whom, Luke, had gotten hooked on the _Real Ghostbusters_ cartoon series) and a parent to care for, work didn't appeal. But one person did manage to lure him back onto a movie set: Frank Oz, with whom Murray occasionally played basketball. One day, Oz offered him the small but plum role of a pain-loving dental patient, played in the 1960 version of *Little Shop of Horrors* by Jack Nicholson. It was an in-and-out, smash-and-bash gig that would take just two days.

"Do I have to do the script?" Murray asked Oz, when the director caught him on the phone.

"No, I don't care if you know the words or not," said Oz. "The important thing is you have to be the masochist and Steve has to be the sadist. He'll be the constant, you're the variable."

The result was a powerhouse, movie-stealing dance between two comedians at the peak of their powers. Steve Martin had already filmed a funky song introducing his sadistic, Elvis-esque dentist, a man so depraved that he punches a nurse and twists the head off a child's doll. "I was there for a couple of setups and couldn't believe what I was seeing," marvels Moranis, who met Martin for the first time on the movie. "I had no idea Frank was planning that." The loopy musical number—"I thrill when I drill a bicuspid!"—featured such virtuoso visual riffs as a motorbike that behaves like a horse and a shot of Martin's Orin Scrivello, DDS, from inside a patient's mouth, as if the camera is nestling just behind the tonsils. By the time he faced Murray, Martin had the character down. As he wielded terrifying-looking implements and huffed down nitrous oxide, Murray went giddily off-script, chanting, "Candy bar! Candy bar! Candy bar!"

Unlike the duo's scene in *The Jerk* seven years earlier, this one would survive the cutting room. Lasting four and a half minutes and ending with Scrivello disgustedly kicking out his patient with the words "Goddamn sicko!" it tore the roof down at the film's first test screening, in San Jose. Listening to the fevered applause from the back of the auditorium, Oz grinned. But his smile faded when the film reached its demented climax—a huge, expensive set piece in which Audrey II goes on a rampage, eating everyone, including Seymour and love interest Audrey (Ellen Greene)—and the audience started to boo. Moranis, it turned out, was *too* likable. Although he was uncomfortable with changing the story to give it a happy ending, seeing as it was intended as a riff on Faust, Oz reshot a whole new conclusion in which the hero survives.

A decent earner on release and a smash hit on VHS, *Little Shop of Horrors* won over viewers with its commitment to silliness and brilliantly executed set pieces. One review posited that it was "one of the year's freshest, fastest, funniest, most stylish cinematic assaults—and a movie that certainly beats out the dismal likes of *Annie* and *Xanadu* as the best Hollywood-made musical of the '80s."

There was Oscar buzz for Martin, although only composer Alan Menken and the effects team ended up getting nominations. Moranis had been transformed into a leading man. And Murray had made a triumphant return to the screen, getting a complimentary dental examination in the bargain.

13

EDDIE MURPHY RAW

YEARS BEFORE MIMICKING his hairdo and hip wiggle for *Little Shop of Horrors*, Steve Martin met the real Elvis Presley. It was 1972 and Martin was in Vegas to do a warm-up act for actress-singer Ann-Margret, a close friend and rumored lover of the Jailhouse Rocker. Backstage after the show, Presley swept down the hallway, clad all in white with a diamond buckle, spotted Martin, and drawled, "Son, you have an *ob-leek* sense of humor." Then he was gone.

Eddie Murphy never got to meet Presley. But in the mid-'80s, the King of Hollywood was becoming increasingly obsessed with the King of Rock 'n' Roll. Upstairs at Bubble Hill was a themed wing, walls bedecked with framed memorabilia. Murphy owned Elvis gold records, Elvis street signs, Elvis biographies. . . . He often slipped into an impression of his hero: *"Thankyou . . . thankyouverymuch!"* Sometimes he liked to pop a Presley tape into a VHS machine, hooked up so the film would play on every TV in the house. "So that everywhere you walk," he explained, "there's Elvis playing."

It wasn't Presley's music he admired, or the lifestyle. He turned his nose up at the legend's latter-day drug-taking, weight gain, and eccentricity. Instead, he was fascinated by the man's *presence*. As Murphy put it, "There was something about him that made you have to look at him, even if you didn't give a fuck about him." Still, as Murphy retreated behind the towering gates of Bubble Hill, his very own Graceland, and surrounded himself with an equivalent of Presley's Memphis Mafia—a group of ever-present buddies he called the Black Pack—rumors began to swirl.

Eddie Murphy is secretly gay. Eddie Murphy smokes crack. Eddie Murphy hosts orgies that would make Caligula blush.

It's not difficult to deduce the source of that last bit of scuttlebutt. Murphy's ever-swelling entourage was exclusively male: cousin Ray-Ray, valet Federoff, high-school buddy Kenneth "Fruitie" Frith Jr., fellow comedians Arsenio Hall and Keenan Ivory Wayans, guys with names like Fed and Rough House. But when it came time to party, in poured the women, torrents of them. The female-to-male ratio at Murphy's Bubble Hill parties tended to be three-to-one. Limos jammed the 9-shaped driveway, dispensing models, actresses, and party girls. A rain machine moistened the dance floor; comely guests were encouraged to strip down and jump into the indoor pool. At one of the revels, a toast went, "To health. Wealth. Success. And women."

By 1985, the workaholic Murphy already had success, more than he had ever imagined—and he had imagined quite a lot. Over the next few years he would concentrate on the "women" part. As Arsenio Hall explained, "While I was playing, Eddie was in clubs working. Now he's a millionaire and he wants to play." Murphy was happy to discuss the literal ins and outs of his sex life with whoever was in earshot; he would even reveal to one journalist that his penis was unusually crooked. "I figured someone would call me Hook Dick," he mused. "But women act like they never notice it."

Still, he insisted he wasn't the wild sex freak that some made him out to be. Some nights, while a party was raging, he would slip quietly upstairs and retire alone. The truth was that Bubble Hill was becoming an actual bubble, insulating him from reality. Women acted differently with him now he was gigantically famous—some aloof, some obsequious. He needed bodyguards whenever he left the house, and those trips outside tended to involve shaking a hundred clammy hands; already a moderate germophobe, Murphy started taking four showers a day and washing his hands as many as fifteen times. Some fan encounters were even more stressful, like the time a boat filled with frenzied admirers crashed into his own vessel in the Bahamas. The collision resulted in a painful tear in his jaw muscle.

Occasionally he felt the urge to be completely alone. Then he would grab the keys to one of his many cars, the blue Rolls-Royce or his new Porsche, and cruise through New Jersey, heading for the most run-down part of town. "I like to see the hookers, the drug addicts, the bums, street fights, people getting arrested and shit," he said. "I do that a lot."

IF HE WAS LONELY, even when surrounded by bodyguards and friends, it was most likely because he had broken up with the woman he had considered the love of his life, Lisa Figueroa. After years of casual flings, this relationship had felt serious, with Murphy sometimes waking up with an urge to ask Lisa to marry him. But in early 1985, on a sojourn to London, he ended it. Although he was happy to talk about almost anything in public, even the shape of his penis, he would never give a specific reason why, usually just quietly stating that they had outgrown each other. He claimed he was able to forget people completely as soon as they were out of his life. But the breakup pitched him into a dark mood, which would persist for a long while to come. "Love is no punk, boy," he told *Rolling Stone* in 1989. "Love will whip your ass."

Murphy began to throw himself once more into his work. Music studios were installed in his two homes, Bubble Hill and the one in Beverly Hills, so he could spend long nights making what he called "hard funk." He began developing movie projects of his own, hoping to use his clout to make something interesting that didn't involve waving a gun around. *Soul, Soul, Soul* was a *This Is Spinal Tap*–style mockumentary, set in the soul world and spanning decades. *America 1990* was about a group of Vietnam veterans who try to take over a National Guard base, an idea that had occurred to Murphy while he was stuck in the tank in Israel for *Best Defense*. After picking up an un-likely paperback—Dante Alighieri's *Inferno*, a work of epic fourteenth-century poetry more often seen in the hands of professors of literature than Hollywood funnymen—he scribbled down an outline for a modern retelling titled *Satan's Key*. He tried, and failed, to get the rights to remake Charlie Chaplin's *The Kid*.

None of these projects came off, but it's debatable just how serious Murphy was about making them anyway. He spoke about his admiration for Bill Murray and his pursuit of profound material: "All the flak he got for *The Razor's Edge* is still no reason not to do serious shit. Bill's a good actor. He's the most versatile actor of us all." Still, more than anything else Murphy wanted hits—giant, record-smashing hits—and he knew that popcorn movies were the way to get them.

In early 1986, he had serious conversations with Paramount about starring in *Star Trek IV: The Voyage Home*. With Leonard Nimoy directing, it would see the crew of the USS *Enterprise* visit Earth in the present day, on a mission to find whales, and the studio thought Murphy would be the perfect star to give it a jolt of energy. As it happened, he was a lifelong Trekkie, who had riffed on the show in *Eddie Murphy: Delirious*: "I like Captain Kirk, 'cause Captain Kirk will fuck *anybody*."

Writers Steve Meerson and Peter Krikes were charged with tailoring the *Voyage Home* story around Murphy's persona. "We didn't have meetings with him, but we had input from his people," says Meerson. "He was going to play a big thread in the tapestry—a professor of astrophysics at Berkeley. Let your mind run with that one!"

In fact, Murphy's character would have been an alien-obsessed academic bent on proving that extraterrestrial life exists. "There was a scene in that first draft where the *Enterprise* uncloaked as it flew over the Super Bowl," says Krikes. "Eddie was the only one who didn't think it was part of the half-time show. Everyone thinks he's a nut, but he's redeemed when he tracks the crew to Monterey Aquarium."

Ultimately, though, Murphy dropped out. A different project had caught his eye, not sci-fi but fantasy. And way-out-there fantasy at that. *The Golden Child* was a story that had been dreamed up by professional photographer Dennis Feldman, a man with only one previous Hollywood credit to his name. It was a bizarre blend of detective noir and mysticism, in which a Los Angeles social worker encounters astral projection, Tibetan monks, and a three-hundred-year-old woman who is half snake. But Murphy liked it, seeing it as a possible launch for an Indiana Jones–style franchise. And he was proving so picky that Paramount was desperate just to get him into something—anything.

"This is the first script Eddie has liked from beginning to end," said David Kirkpatrick, the studio's executive vice president in charge of production, who had coined the phrase "M-E-G-O"—"my eyes glaze over"—to describe the meetings in which he sat in restaurants with Murphy, rapidly pitching ideas as the star's focus began to drift. The star had been offered *Uriah*, about a witch doctor who becomes America's hottest new singing sensation; *Sob Sisters*, which would require him to dress as a woman; and *Black Sheep*, a CIA thriller. He nixed them all.

"Eddie and John Hughes were Paramount's cash cows," says Feldman. "And John Hughes was working all the time and Eddie wasn't working at all. One plane was on the ground and one plane was in the air. It was very important for Frank Mancuso, the head of the studio, to get him activated." So, willing to do anything to get their prize asset working again, the studio entered into a bidding war on his behalf, wresting *The Golden Child* from competitors by putting down $330,000. Locations were scouted in Nepal. And the tone of the movie was recalibrated to give it more of an Eddie Murphy flavor. "Heartbroken, I was made to edit out twenty pages of the script," Feldman recalls. "There was a very sinister supernatural character with a rat's head and a human body, who smoked. He went. As soon as Eddie was signed onto it, in the minds of the producers it had to be a comedy. I thought it would have been a much better idea to have him play it straight as an action hero."

Sure enough, lead character Chandler Jarrell went from a moody Mel Gibson type to a cocksure firecracker in a kufi cap. Approaches to some exciting A-list directors, meanwhile, came to naught. "George Miller was sent to talk to Eddie, but Eddie thought he was a weird guy, something like that," says Feldman. "Eddie had a small list: he wanted Spielberg, Clint Eastwood, a couple of others. Martin Scorsese actually wanted to do it for twenty-four hours, maybe because of the Tibet setting." In the end, *The Golden Child* was shot by *Fletch* director Michael Ritchie, who was happy enough for the movie to morph into a campy *Beverly Hills Cop* clone, giving Jarrell a maroon Mercedes that surely no social worker could afford.

Delighted to have Murphy back after a two-year break, hardcore fans flooded into theaters to see it. But its $80 million gross was a long way from the $316 million of *Beverly Hills Cop*. *The Golden Child* wasn't the pop-culture phenomenon, or franchise-launcher, Paramount had hoped for. Critics sniped at the visual effects and Murphy's apparent narcissism, the fact he'd cast himself as a world-saving Chosen One. Murphy bristled at complaints about its fantastical elements, wondering aloud why the Indiana Jones films got away with similar mumbo-jumbo.

"He rides on the outside of a submarine across the world?" he grumbled to *Interview*, referring to a scene near the end of *Raiders of the Lost Ark*. "I don't remember any critics making a big deal of it, and *that* was some stupid shit."

As Chandler Jarrell, Murphy faced down a snooty British villain (albeit one with teleporting powers), packed a .38 revolver (rather inexplicably, given his job), and broke into motor-mouth shtick to sneak a magical dagger through customs. He may have ridden a yak, but the character was, unmistakably, a diluted Axel Foley. Murphy's next step, he decided, would be to bring back the actual Axel, uncut. Paramount couldn't agree fast enough. In early 1987, the studio announced that work had begun on *Beverly Hills Cop II*.

From the get-go, the sequel had a very different vibe from the original. Where that had been shaggy and loose, the new movie was Bugatti-slick: storyboarded, lit, and lensed to within an inch of its life. High-gloss director Tony Scott was personally picked by Murphy, who in an early edict told him, "Make me look as good as Tom Cruise in the volleyball game in *Top Gun*." No longer did the priority seem to be to make a funny movie, so much as to make its star look consistently fantastic. The opening credits set the pace: wearing only a pair of black briefs, the words "EDDIE MURPHY PRODUCTIONS" hovering in huge letters over his crotch, he shows off his toned body. Then he blows himself a kiss in a mirror before breaking into laughter for no apparent reason. It's an unusual sight: a man high on being himself.

"The whole joke of the first movie was that Axel mocks people like that," says Dan Petrie Jr., the original's writer. "He's wearing a sweatshirt, driving a beat-up car, and thinks all this shit is really pretentious. But you'll notice that in *Beverly Hills Cop II* miraculously they found reasons to get him into an Armani suit. I worked with Eddie some years later doing a production rewrite and he was always so nice to me, but to see this enormously talented man kind of isolate himself from the world—the world he was so smart and quick about observing—it was a big contrast."

With a plot inspired by, of all things, Agatha Christie's *The ABC Murders*, *Beverly Hills Cop II* brought back Judge Reinhold's Rosewood, John Ashton's Taggart, and Foley's unique brand of japery (at one point he pretends to be "Johnny Wishbone, psychic extraordinaire"). But it's a considerably more thunderous, swaggering work. Driving a $67,000 hot-red Ferrari Testarossa and clad in Porsche Carrera sunglasses, Foley is no longer the hungry, scrappy underdog, more a well-fed elite breed. There's also an odd undercurrent of anger to the character, who repeatedly refers to the female villain played by Brigitte Nielsen (over six feet tall in heels) as a "big bitch."

Nielsen, it turned out, would be the source of a personal problem for Murphy. He claimed later that he had hired her only to do his friend Sylvester Stallone, Nielsen's husband and the guy who had walked away from the original *Beverly Hills Cop*, a favor. But one day he got a call from Stallone, who growled, "You fucked my wife!"

"Down, brother!" Murphy retorted. "I didn't fuck your wife!"

But the damage was done. Believing the rumors, Stallone stopped socializing with Murphy, even leaving one party early when he saw him arrive. The two had worked up a pitch for a third *Godfather* film

starring them and Al Pacino, and had talked about doing pictures together called *Soldiers of Misfortune* and *Boys*, but all that evaporated.
The A-list friendship was over.

"A noisy, numbing, unimaginative, heartless remake of the original
film," said *Variety* of *Beverly Hills Cop II*. Opening against the only two
films that dared face it, *Ernest Goes to Camp* and *The Chipmunk Adventure*, the sequel made plenty of money, $300 million, but less than the
original. And Murphy certainly wasn't in a hurry to defend it. *"Beverly
Hills Cop II* was probably the most successful mediocre picture in history," he told *Rolling Stone*. "It was a half-assed movie. *Cop II* was basically a rehash of *Cop I*, but it wasn't as spontaneous and funny." In the
same interview, he went on to call *The Golden Child* "a piece of shit."

The one silver lining was that he still wielded power, enough to
change the direction he was going. "My pictures," he said, "make their
money back."

ON APRIL 11, 1988, Eddie Murphy got into a limo and rode to L.A.'s
Shrine Auditorium for the 60th Academy Awards. Though none of
his films were in contention, it was to be a big night for him: he had
been asked to present the Best Picture Oscar at the climax of the evening. But only a few people knew that Murphy was on a mission. In his
pocket was a speech railing against what he perceived as Hollywood's
inherent racism.

Robin Williams, one of the handful of friends Murphy had told
about his plans, had cautioned him against it, saying, "I don't know,
man. It might start some shit." But Murphy felt strongly about the
subject. He had refused to attend a *LIFE* photo shoot to celebrate Paramount's seventy-fifth anniversary, a group photo featuring the likes
of Tom Cruise, Robert De Niro, and Charlton Heston, after hearing
that he would be the only black person there (in fact, Lou Gossett Jr.
was in the fourth row). And he even suspected that many white critics
had lambasted *The Golden Child* for racial reasons: "You had a black
man that was not only a realistic sexual presence but who saved the

world. . . . I really feel, on some level, white critics had a hard time dealing with that."

And so, as the ceremony passed the three-hour mark, Murphy strode onto the stage, wearing tails and a gold medallion, faced the assembled Hollywood elite, and let loose. "Black people will not ride the caboose of society, and we will not bring up the rear anymore," he declared. He told the audience, and the millions of TV viewers, that he had considered not turning up at all, because of the dearth of black Oscar-winners. Then he reflected, "I'll probably never win an Oscar for saying this, but what the hell, I've got to say it."

It was pretty far from the yuk-fest the Academy had expected when they asked him to wrap up their big night, and many there were outraged. After the show, Warren Beatty approached him and told him it wasn't the time or the place for that kind of outburst. Murphy, who had been under attack from director Spike Lee for not doing *enough* to help black people in show business, was unrepentant.

The speech caused shock waves around the industry, but in fact this wasn't Murphy's most controversial onstage appearance of the past six months. Not by a long shot. He had considered doing a follow-up to 1983's *Delirious* for some time, the idea of escaping from the sluggish rigors of blockbuster moviemaking more appealing than ever. So *Eddie Murphy Raw* was born. Filmed at New York's Felt Forum and released at the end of 1987, the stand-up set was another stupendous hit for the star, but also a revealing insight into his headspace at the time.

The look, again, was figure-hugging leather. While not as retina-singeing as his red *Delirious* outfit—which had become damaged after Murphy bet Keenan Ivory Wayans he wouldn't wear it for a night on the town—the new costume was a purple-patterned one-piece, accessorized with dark scarf, racing gloves, and a chunky gold ring. The night's two big themes: fame and women. Murphy seems fixated with celebrity, both his own (the film begins with fans naming their favorite of his films; one guy blurts out, "I like *Best Defense!*") and other people's. Once again he attacks Michael Jackson, bringing up the time Jackson took Brooke Shields to the Grammys and saying that if he had done the same, "Y'all would lose your mind. Because y'all know Brooke would get fucked that night." He rags on Bill Cosby for a while. And he takes an extended swipe at Stallone, seemingly still raw about the Brigitte Nielsen fall-out. "Stallone have all you white people pumped," Murphy says, then does an impression of a Rocky-loving Italian-American who gets beaten up by the black guy he starts a fight with.

His main preoccupation, though, is with the opposite sex. For more than a third of the film's run time Murphy waxes on about expensive custody battles ("No pussy is worth $150 million!") and the manipulative games women play. Lisa Figueroa's name doesn't come up, but he declares that he nearly got suckered into walking up the aisle himself before wising up: "I said, 'Fuck this. I'm getting out.'"

He's in astonishing, virtuoso form throughout, switching effortlessly between voices as he transforms into family members, Richard Pryor, and goofy white guys. But there's a strain of bitterness, paranoia, and misogyny that runs through the whole show. Midway through, he tells the crowd that there's only one way he'll ever tie the knot. "If I ever get married, I have to go off to the woods of Africa and find me some crazy naked zebra bitch that knows nothing about money. She's gonna need to be butt naked on a zebra with a bone in her nose and a big plate lip and a big fucked-up afro."

He didn't know it at the time, but these angry words were to be the seed of his next movie.

AS CHAOTIC AND PAINFUL as his personal life could sometimes feel, Eddie Murphy was still on top of the world as the '80s rolled on. He had his own table at Spago, Hollywood's most exclusive restaurant. There was talk of a Hanna-Barbara cartoon in which an animated Eddie Murphy would go on adventures, presumably more sanitized than his real ones. Other movie stars looked at his hit-rate with awe. "He's instinctual, like a shark who knows where the blood is," marveled Robin Williams in 1988. "He knows what his area is and what he does. That's why he's on top of the script food chain." *Forbes* estimated that in 1987 alone Murphy made $27 million.

At Paramount, where he was still under contract, he was treated like a living god. In his office, which he shared with uber-producers Don Simpson and Jerry Bruckheimer, his personal filing cabinet bore a label reading "MONEY." This was, in fact, his nickname around the lot. He had made the studio so much cash—over $1.5 billion from his first seven movies—that a special trophy was created, depicting Murphy holding up the Paramount logo, and given to him as a gift. He could often be seen driving around in a customized golf cart with Rolls-Royce grille, getting executives' attention by yelling, "Hey, suits!"

His was the kind of fame where you could get a movie green-lit from a scribble in a notebook. Which is exactly what he did. While on the tour bus for *Raw* he had vented his anguish about his breakup with Lisa on paper, in a book belonging to his cousin Ray Murphy Jr., expanding his "zebra bitch" riff into a story about a superwealthy African prince who decides the only way he can find true love is to travel to America and pretend to be poor. The parallels between the pampered Prince Akeem and Murphy himself are clear, although only one of them literally has their ass wiped for them. Paramount allotted $40 million to the project, titled *The Quest*, then retitled *Coming to America*.

To direct it, Murphy handpicked an old collaborator: John Landis. "Out of all the movies I did, Landis was the director I enjoyed the most," he said. "On *Trading Places*, I didn't want to leave at night. A lot of the films, like *Cop II*, I just wanted to finish."

Landis signed up enthusiastically. "When Eddie first told me about the story and characters, I came home and said to Deborah, my wife, 'What do you think about this?'" he says. "What she got right away was that it's a fairy tale, a Maurice Chevalier–Jeanette MacDonald movie. What was really exciting was that up until that point, in every film that starred people of color, their color was a plot point. Eddie is the 'black guy' in *48 Hrs.* Sidney Poitier was always the 'black guy.' And in *Coming to America*, the color of their skin has fuck-all to do with the story. They're just people in it, this silly little romantic movie."

Unfortunately, this second collaboration between director and star was to sour, in dramatic fashion.

Coming to America was a challenging shoot as it was, with a disgusting Brooklyn tenement set built on Stage 5 at Paramount, complete with stopped-up toilet and genuine cockroaches; a stint in Brooklyn so cold that fake rain froze on a street sign; problems with elephants and zebras during scenes set in the fake African kingdom of Zamunda; and a schedule too short for what Landis wanted to achieve. A sequence that would have featured Michael Jackson, Prince, and Murphy having a dance-off on a New York street was scrapped. Murphy got increasingly irritated that Landis wouldn't let him watch dailies, a blanket rule the director applied to cast and crew. And Landis, who had been upset when Murphy didn't testify for him during the *Twilight Zone* trial, chafed at what he saw as a new attitude from the star.

"Eddie was such a monster star now, and it was different," the director says. "The biggest difference was that he had lost the sparkle. He could summon it forth and still be incredibly creative and brilliant, but he was dark on that movie. I don't know what his issues were. It's difficult when you're nineteen and an instant superstar. You're suddenly the golden goose and you don't know who to trust. And so very often performers will get their friends from school, or their family, around them. As soon as your friends and family members basically become your employees, they have a vested interest in not telling you the truth."

Landis became specifically irked with Murphy's "posse," the entourage that constantly surrounded him on-set. Shooting at Madison Square Garden one day, he broke into laughter at the sight of Murphy and a dozen burly companions tiptoeing along a slim plank across the ice; Murphy caught his eye, unamused.

On another occasion, when Mike Tyson visited, Murphy felt that Landis treated the boxer in a derogatory fashion. With Murphy hearing rumors that both the director and his wife were bad-mouthing him behind his back, the atmosphere was turning poisonous. It felt like the two men, whose power dynamic had changed drastically since their last collaboration, were heading toward an almighty clash. And they were.

One day, as Murphy told it, he heard that Landis was talking derisively in front of the crew about Murphy's financial dealings. So he walked up behind the director, grabbed him around the throat in a strong-arm grip, and said to his hulking friend Fruitie, "What happens when people put my business in the street?" Fruitie replied, "They get fucked up." Not realizing yet how serious Murphy was, Landis play-fought back, aiming toward Murphy's groin. Murphy responded by putting pressure on his windpipe, choking the director.

"There was one moment where he exploded and I still don't know why," says Landis. "I never found out what inspired it."

After the two men had been separated, Murphy headed back to his house with Arsenio Hall, still fuming. When Hall suggested that some alcohol might calm him down, he knocked back an entire quart of Absolut vodka, until he was drunk as a skunk and bent over a toilet, puking. The final stretch of the *Coming to America* shoot was about as tense as any shoot has ever been. "The motherfucker was on his fucking toes for the rest of the show and didn't fuck with me for the whole rest of the picture," Murphy told *Playboy* in 1990, still red-hot about the confrontation.

Creatively, at least, *Coming to America* saw Murphy at the top of his game, playing not just the guileless Akeem—a departure for him from his usual smart-ass leads—but three other characters, donning extensive Rick Baker makeup to become a soul singer, a barber-shop manager, and an old Jewish man. It would be the first of several times in his movie career that Murphy would play multiple roles in the same scene, with him reprising the trick in *Bowfinger* and *The Nutty Professor* films. Before their rift, Landis had been inspired to consider a project in which Murphy and Robin Williams would play fifteen roles each, at one point portraying the entire staff of a Chinese restaurant. "The makeup freed him up in a way," the director says. "He started relying on it too much, I think. But it worked wonderfully in *Coming to America*."

But the film's travails would continue even into its release. Despite being Paramount's biggest grosser of 1988 and the third biggest film overall, beaten only by *Rain Man* and *Who Framed Roger Rabbit*, reviews were generally negative. "Murphy's colossal comedic gifts and Landis' countercultural sensibilities are largely wasted, never pushed to the floor in this idling, curbed comedy," read the critique in the *Hollywood Reporter*.

What's more, the star's "story by" credit came under assault, with a lawsuit filed by writer Art Buchwald and producer Alain Bernheim, alleging that *Coming to America* was a work of plagiarism. Buchwald had sold a script outline to Paramount in 1983 about an African king who comes to Washington, is overthrown, and becomes a bum in the ghetto. After seeing Landis's film, he became furious and took it to court. Murphy, Landis, Arsenio Hall, Paramount Pictures chairman Frank Mancuso—all were questioned extensively, although Murphy declined to appear in court. Newspapers and magazines followed the case closely. And finally the judge decided that there was enough evidence to rule in Buchwald's favor. Paramount settled for $900,000.

The highly publicized trial not only called into question Murphy's honesty but revealed financial arrangements that he would have preferred remain secret: the cost of a twenty-four-hour limousine, the price of his luxury trailer, even a $235.33 receipt for a lunch at McDonald's. Murphy maintained that *Coming to America* was all his—"I know what I wrote and I know what I did," he said to a journalist—but the case had put another dent in his once-undentable confidence.

"I feel old, real old," he lamented after his *Coming to America* experience. "If you see me naked, my balls hang down to my knees and there's gray hair on my balls. That's when you know you're not young anymore."

PARTNERS IN CRIME

POST-*SPLASH*, JOHN CANDY took a trip to the ocean in Santa Monica. But it wasn't a recreational visit: there was to be no lounging in deckchairs, lathered in sunscreen. Instead, Candy checked into the Pritikin Longevity Center, an establishment that sounded like it belonged in a sci-fi B-movie, on a mission to get himself in shape.

He was thirty-three, just a little younger than his dad, Sidney, had been when he'd died of a heart attack. And as he looked forward to the possibilities ahead of him, he formed a new resolve to drop his rum-and-Coke, shake-and-fries lifestyle. "The family history was not a good one," says director Carl Reiner, who was working with Candy on rehearsals for *Summer Rental* at the time. "He was one of the dearest men in the world, such a hale fellow well met. But he knew he was going—that was the terrible thing. He was always overeating. So I said, 'John, you have to come out to the Pritikin Institute, where my wife and I go. You learn to eat vegetables and chicken, rather than steak.'"

Agreeing, Candy signed up for a month of austere discipline: five miles of cycling a day, no alcohol, no red meat, no cigarettes. Each morning he ate a big bowl of bran flakes, then walked along the seafront. A freshly minted movie star, he was living the life of a monk.

Toward the end of his stay, he received a phone call. It was director Walter Hill, offering him a role opposite Richard Pryor in the forthcoming comedy *Brewster's Millions*. Happy to have something to take his mind off his rumbling stomach, Candy accepted and asked for the script. The comedy, about a minor-league baseball pitcher (Pryor) who has to spend $30 million in thirty days with the help of his catcher buddy (Candy), was destined to be a classic, although on-set there was friction between the two stars, whose personalities were oil and water.

"John would walk through the stage doors and start entertaining the grips or electricians, getting lots of laughs with low jokes," Hill recalls. "Richard would come through the stage doors and find the most obscure seat over in the darkest corner and sit there. He was friendly with John, but wary—John could see that there was some bridge he wasn't going to get across there. And one time Richard got mad at me, saying he wished I'd treat him with the same respect that I treated John. It was bullshit. I probably laughed too much at John's jokes."

Brewster's Millions was to be the first of a flurry of films Candy made in quick succession. Making up for the lack of partying, he plowed his energy into his work, as well as into taking care of his second child, Christopher, who was born in the second half of 1984.

The scripts he picked, however, were not great. For *Volunteers*, a CIA farce set in Thailand, he flew to Mexico and reunited with his *Splash* pal Tom Hanks, but didn't get much to do, spending day after day moping around his cockroach-infested hotel room. *Armed and Dangerous*, which had been designed as a Belushi-Aykroyd film, then a Ramis-Aykroyd film, then an Aykroyd-Candy film, ended up as a two-hander for Candy and Eugene Levy, in which John played a kind of binge-eating Dirty Harry. It limped in and out of theaters without making anyone's day.

There were incredible experiences, such as working with the Sesame Street puppets in *Follow That Bird* and collaborating with his comedy hero, Mel Brooks, on *Spaceballs*, in which Candy played a dog-man, Barf, that he based on his yellow Labrador, Keema. The cash was flowing in too. In the summer of 1986, the comedian bought a $2 million, eleven-room mansion just north of Sunset Boulevard in L.A., moving his family down from Toronto. His new vehicle of choice was a big black Mercedes, which he took for spins through the palm trees. And in 1985 he was named one of the ten sexiest men alive by *Playgirl*, who gushed, "The shaggy moptop, dimpled cheeks, physical grace—nobody is sexier than this giant of comedy who turns us on with good humor." The article was exquisite ammunition for Candy's *SCTV* buddies, who gave him endless shit about it.

On the down side, his healthy-living routine hadn't lasted long. On the set of *Summer Rental*, where Reiner had even hired a Pritikin cook to make lunches, the director soon found Candy going off the rails: "He stayed on it for a while. Then soon after I walked in and he's got mountains of fried shrimp he's nibbling on. He was a bad boy, that way."

The perfect role, meanwhile, the one that would allow him to unleash his full comedic power, eluded him. Until one day in late 1986. A package arrived in the mail, from his old buddy John Hughes, with an untitled, 145-page script inside. Candy sat back, started reading. His giant frame was quickly shaking with mirth. "I just cried with laughter," he recalled. "It's like it was written for me."

AS A YOUNG COPYWRITER in the advertising world, John Hughes had once been dispatched for a one-day business trip from Chicago to New York. It should have been simple. But five days later, he staggered into his house, almost destroyed by a snafu-packed odyssey that had seen him diverted to Phoenix. Hughes turned the trip over in his mind for years, embellishing it and making it even more hellish, finally setting the tale down on paper (with the route reversed) as *Planes, Trains and Automobiles*.

The story wasn't just a procession of mishaps, though. It was a touching portrayal of a friendship slowly gestating between two polar opposites: control-freak executive Neal (Hughes's avatar) and a slobbish, jolly, but deep-down-sad salesman of shower-curtain rings called Del.

Although surprised by the thickness of the script—comedies usually clock in at around ninety pages—Steve Martin jumped at the chance to play Neal. "At that point in my career, that was the direction I was headed for—more emotional roles," he later said. "So this was a real breakthrough for me." And Candy saw a poignancy in Del to which he could relate. He and Martin had both done small, crazy cameos in *Little Shop of Horrors*, but here they had a chance to forge a powerful double-act, like Laurel and Hardy in reverse, with the thin one angry, the portly one guileless. When they met there was instant comic chemistry. "We'd look into each other's eyes and it felt good together," said Martin. "We had great timing."

Planes, Trains and Automobiles was, aptly, a giant road trip of a production, shooting in New York, Chicago, L.A., and all over the Midwest from February to May 1987. Also aptly, it was a race against time. Just as in the story Neal and Del are speeding across the country to get home for Thanksgiving, so, with a release date of November 25, the production was racing to get into theaters for actual Thanksgiving. Not helping matters was Hughes's insistence on shooting every detail of his mammoth screenplay (of an extra in the back of a shot holding a shoebox with white mice in it, the director said, "I thought it'd be funny, maybe you're watching it for the third or fourth time on cable somewhere, your mind wanders away from the main activity in the scene, and . . . 'Are those mice?'") and the fact that they had to keep relocating to find fresh snow. One actor, cast as a truck driver with a single line of dialogue, was kept on standby for so many days because of the weather that he was able to make the down payment on a house.

Martin and Candy, clad in a topcoat and parka, respectively, were freezing their butts off. But they knew they were making gold. Between takes, Candy would crack up Martin by pretending to act out a cheesy gladiator movie, moving his lips in a way that made it sound like he was dubbed. And Martin was particularly impressed by one bit of improv by his co-star: during the scene where Del reveals that his wife has died and explains that's why he attaches himself to people, Candy added the line, "But this time I couldn't let go." Long after Candy's death, Martin would get a tear in his eye remembering it.

As for the funny stuff, there was an ample amount: a driving scene where Candy gets his arms trapped and sets fire to the car; an open-air ride on the back of a truck with a half-frozen, furious dog; a Martin meltdown with so much swearing that it singlehandedly got the film slapped with an R-rating. But however silly it gets, it never loses its empathy for its two heroes, culminating in a tear-jerking ending where Neal invites Del into his home. It was an ideal showcase for its two stars: Martin got to zanily flip his lid *and* be a solid straight man; Candy got to be a clown while revealing a raw emotional core.

In November, after Hughes finished wrestling the movie down from four and a half hours to a more commercial ninety-two minutes, a *Planes, Trains and Automobiles* press conference was held on the Paramount back lot. With Candy an hour late, trekking in from a shoot in Fresno, Martin did an impromptu stand-up set to entertain the crowd of three hundred journalists, riffing on the roast-turkey banquet laid on by the studio: "We already had some of that very same turkey while we were making the movie—and we shot the film a year ago."

Once Candy arrived, the grilling began. Martin was quizzed on his use of the word "fuck" in the film, responding, deadpan, "I only used it nineteen times." Candy was told that he looked like a sumo wrestler by a tactless Japanese reporter, who then added, "We admire big people because we are a nation of small people. . . . Do you plan to diet?"

Candy, who had had multiple pieces of exercise equipment moved into his hotel suite during the shoot but never used them, embarrassedly admitted, "I do eat a lot of junk food, and I think about [dieting] for health reasons." Martin jumped in with a joke. "At one point during filming, John went down to 110 pounds, which I thought was a little excessive . . ."

Aside from the awkward lines of questioning at publicity events, *Planes, Trains and Automobiles* was a moment of glory for Candy, certainly his finest hour since *Splash*. He was deluged with offers, including one from Monty Python's Graham Chapman, who flew over from England to discuss a movie he wanted to write for Candy called *Ditto*, about a man who falls into a photocopier and somehow duplicates himself. Chapman would die of cancer before that could come to fruition, but it was a sign of Candy's growing international stature. Wherever he went in the world, people wanted to give him a hug.

SOME PEOPLE COLLECT baseball cards. Others collect antiques. Dan Aykroyd collected police badges. By 1986, he had amassed an impressive haul, including a handpainted badge from Kenosha County in Wisconsin, one from New Orleans, one from Joliet, and one from Tijuana, a present from John Landis, for which the director had had to barter with a Mexican cop. Aykroyd's enthusiasm for law enforcement was such that he had even been made an honorary member of the Long Beach Police Officers Association. He liked to tell people he was following in Elvis Presley's footsteps, saying, "Apparently a couple of times in Memphis he'd pull up and go, 'You just went through that red light there, brother. I'm gonna give you a warning right now. . . . '"

Despite all of this, Aykroyd had more often than not been on the wrong side of the law on-screen. In *The Blues Brothers* he'd been chased across Illinois by a veritable blue army; he'd been jailed in not only that movie but *Ghostbusters* and *Trading Places* as well. He had been considered for the role of comic-book detective Dick Tracy in the early 1980s, for a film adaptation directed by John Landis, but that project fell through.

His third movie as writer and seventh as leading man, however, promised to finally put him in uniform. In fact, *Dragnet* felt like destiny.

Way back in October 1976, in an episode of *Saturday Night Live* guest-hosted by Eric Idle, a skit spoofing the classic 1950s police serial had aired, featuring Aykroyd and Idle. "It was a perfectly ordinary

Sunday," Aykroyd had deadpanned. "My name's Friday. My partner's name is Saturday Morning. We only worked weekends." The routine had been his idea: as a kid in Ottawa, he had watched *Dragnet* on TV from the age of three, eventually honing an impression of star Jack Webb. He lost the *Dragnet* police badge he'd sent off for, one of his first pieces of memorabilia, but never lost his affection for the series, a hard-boiled procedural in which Sgt. Joe Friday (Webb) and a roster of partners trawled the streets of Los Angeles, solving crimes and doling out their catchphrase—"Just the facts, ma'am"—to the accompaniment of a booming four-note theme tune.

The idea of adapting the show into a 1980s blockbuster in fact came from producer David Permut. But as soon as Aykroyd heard about it, his brain started churning with possibilities. *Law of the Yukon*, the film he'd hoped to make with Bill Murray in Alaska, had stalled out. And the thought of returning to the role of Friday, this time not in a no-budget TV skit but in a lavish action-comedy spectacular, was immensely appealing. It was clearly a part he was built for: a hilariously emotionless, crime-solving machine; a man with a computer for a brain. It would allow him to disappear into a role, chameleon-style, just as he had back on *SNL*. And dropping Friday (actually, the nephew of the TV detective) into the amoral chaos of modern-day L.A. promised to be the makings of a wild comedy.

The writing process saw Aykroyd's Scriptatron GL-9000 go into overdrive. Just as he had before with *The Blues Brothers* and *Ghostbusters*, he whipped up page after page after page, delivering a first draft that was three hundred sheets thick, or five hours of screen time. The story pitted Friday and partner Pep Streebek against a diabolical cult called PAGAN (People Against Goodness And Normalcy), taking them to a pornographer's mansion and a ritualistic gathering at which they have to grapple with a giant snake. Co-writer Alan Zweibel, the *SNL* writer who had helped John Belushi create his legendary Samurai character, watched with amazement as Aykroyd frequently slipped into his Jack Webb impression for extended periods: "We were role-playing while we wrote one draft at Danny's home on Martha's Vineyard. I really felt I was living with Joe Friday." The director picked for the project, Tom

Mankiewicz, was equally impressed, noting, "Aykroyd's voice has the same timbre and frequency as Webb's. It's almost eerie."

The role of Streebek would go not to an *SNL* or *SCTV* alumnus (although John Candy was considered), but Tom Hanks, who had recently had a rough time at the box office, with *Volunteers*, *The Money Pit*, and *The Man with One Red Shoe* all underperforming. Unlike Aykroyd, Hanks couldn't care less about the original *Dragnet*. But the script's car chases and wanton mayhem was something new he wanted to try. "I went up to the black tower on the Universal lot," he explained to *Premiere*, "and said to the executives, 'Hi, guys. Here's why I would like to do *Dragnet*. See, I want to wear a gun and a badge and have some muscle on my arms.'" Streebek was also an appealingly scuzzy character, the chaotic ying to Friday's orderly yang. For the scene in which they infiltrate the PAGAN gathering, Hanks worked up a grubby costume he dubbed the "El Cholo," referring to a famously down-and-dirty L.A. Mexican eatery.

Pre-production took up most of 1986, with endless script revisions as Mankiewicz, Aykroyd, and Zweibel tried to catch the right balance between homage and send-up. "One of the biggest problems was avoiding making the story wacky, zany and all those bad words," said the director. At last, in October, the show got on the road.

For fifty-six days, including seventeen straight nights, *Dragnet* filmed in thirty-five locations around L.A. Aykroyd carried around a Walkman, loading it with cassettes of Jack Webb dialogue to which he'd listen whenever he was off-camera. He wanted to be true to his boyhood hero, channeling Webb's staccato, stentorian tones in monologues such as this one to Streebek: "I don't care what undercover rock you crawled out from. There's a dress code for detectives in Robbery-Homicide. Section 3-605. 10. 20. 22. 24. 26. 50. 70. 80. It specifies: clean shirt, short hair, tie, pressed trousers, sports jacket or suit, and leather shoes, preferably with a high shine on them." Such moments—and the script was full of them—were pure Aykroyd: delicious, Sahara-dry, delivered faster than a Nolan Ryan pitch.

By the time *Dragnet* wrapped in early January 1987, Mankiewicz had shot a staggering thirty thousand feet of film, so much that he dubbed the film "Lawrence of Dragnet." Universal was nervous, not least that the budget had swelled to $20 million, rather than the agreed-upon $18 million, but the studio hoped it had a *Ghostbusters*-sized hit. They commissioned an electro remix of the TV show's famous theme, and green-lit a music video to help promote the film. Titled "City of Crime," the truly bizarre song took the form of a rap performed by Hanks and Aykroyd, with lyrics by Dan's brother Peter.

"It was choreographed by Paula Abdul, believe it or not," recalls Hanks, who in the video dances around in tight shorts and cavorts inside a cage. "That was back when all those things were like marketing ploys. You'd make a video, put it on late at night, and hope it'd help you sell your film. It was fun, though. We shot it in two days." Aykroyd claims that it did the trick and then some: "Universal Pictures credits that video with helping *Dragnet* to open that weekend with substantially more numbers than we would have had if the video wasn't produced. I haven't seen it recently, but love the crunchy quality of the song."

In June 1987, the film came out and shot to the number-one spot at the US box office, beating out *Spaceballs*. Ultimately it made $67 million, more than *Spies Like Us* but nowhere near *Ghostbusters* money. Aykroyd was happy enough that it had connected with audiences; he made his own visit to a movie theater to see one of the movies that ended up overtaking *Dragnet*'s haul: Brian De Palma's *The Untouchables*. Coincidentally, Aykroyd had also spoofed the original *Untouchables* TV show on *SNL*, alongside John Belushi, playing G-men in a skit that aired the same year as his *Dragnet* send-up. "I really enjoyed it. I'd go back and see it again," he enthused of the De Palma film. There was only one thing that bugged him about the picture, and of course it had to do with law enforcement. "Being a Canadian, my grandfather was a Royal Mounted policeman . . . and in *The Untouchables* they didn't actually wear those tunics, they didn't ride cavalry-style," he said. "Apart from that, it was a great movie."

———

A WORRIER at the best of times, Steve Martin felt particularly tense when he considered the prospects of his next project. It didn't have the car chases of *Dragnet*, or the mind-blowing effects of his buddy Martin Short's new one, *Innerspace*. "This picture is so small compared to everything that's out there, and everything else has something humungous going for it," he fretted. "I don't know if we can compete against these pictures. I try to put myself in the audience's situation: 'We're looking for fun on Saturday night. Do we want to go see *Predator*, about an evil creature that kills everyone? Or do we want to go see what we've heard is a 'funny romantic comedy'?"

But he wasn't giving his new movie enough credit. It actually did have something humongous going for it: a nose the size and shape of a ski run.

Roxanne was a spin on Edmond Rostand's classic tale *Cyrano de Bergerac*, in which a soulful soldier with a facial blight helps a fellow cadet to woo the girl he himself is in love with. Martin had caught the 1950 movie adaptation starring José Ferrer on TV when he was twelve, and the sweetness of the set-up had stayed with him. The idea of updating it for '80s audiences had occurred to him in 1983, and he secretly beavered away on the screenplay between shoots, changing the huge-honkered hero from French aristocrat to American firefighter C. D. Bales. The project became an obsession, with Martin working from noon until midnight. It was not only the first script he'd ever written solo but an opportunity to transform his screen image. Rather than flinging gag after gag at the audience, *Roxanne* would be slower, gentler, with real soul and real heart. The only fake thing would be that nose.

"It had to be designed so that when you were shooting from the front it didn't look so bad," remembers director Fred Schepisi. "Not for vanity reasons or star reasons, but because that the beginning of the film we wanted you to see an ordinary person walking down the street. In fact, that's how Steve sold Dan Melnick on making the picture. He had somebody make a prosthetic nose for him, then he went around and knocked on Dan's door. Melnick said, 'Hey, Steve, this is a surprise.' And then Steve turned his head to reveal it."

By the time cameras rolled in the sleepy Canadian timber town of Nelson, British Columbia, Martin had written a staggering twenty-five drafts of the screenplay. Each character had been finely polished, from astronomer love interest Roxanne (Daryl Hannah) to doofus wannabe lothario Chris (Rick Rossovich) to the Greek chorus of firemen (played by an assortment of stand-up comedians). Accordingly, throughout the summer of 1986 the shoot ran like a well-oiled machine. To make Nelson feel like a glamorous ski resort, rather than the recession-hit burb it actually was, a deal was struck with Ray-Ban: actors throughout the movie would wear the company's sunglasses, in exchange for twenty attractive models who would parade up and down the main street. At times it felt more like a vacation than a tightly organized production. Even Martin was largely relaxed, cracking jokes with the crew.

One thing, though, was making him break into flop sweats: the movie's most crucial sequence, looming ever-closer, in which C.D. fires off a barrage of nose-based insults in a crowded bar, showing up a drunken idiot who has attempted to mock him.

From the beginning Martin had seen this as *Roxanne*'s key set piece, but it had to be note-perfect. "I think Steve wrote about seventy jokes, way more than he needed," says Schepisi. "He just kept trying them out on all his comedy friends. Anybody he came across, I think! We eventually whittled them down to about thirty-five or forty."

When the day arrived, more than a hundred people were packed into a Nelson bar, on two levels, with stand-up comics dotted around to warm up the crowd. Martin sat in the makeup chair for his daily ninety-minute prosthetic fitting, antsily rehearsing his jokes, which he had lived with for so long that he no longer found them funny. "He was very nervous, kind of like a thoroughbred horse, not wanting to get into the barrier," Schepisi recalls. "Because it meant so much to him, really. Finally time was running out. So I said to Steve, 'Look, let's just do five jokes and see how we go.' He headed in there, started, and *boom*: incredible laughter. He got through the first five jokes and it was going really well. I kept the camera rolling and he got through seven jokes. It was still going really well. He got through ten jokes.

Then he started looking at me through the corner of his eye: 'What the hell are you doing to me?!' So we stopped there. But he went for it and it was fantastic. I think he even chucked in a couple of new ones."

Like Eddie Murphy's bar scene in *48 Hrs.*, it's a chance to see a former stand-up back in peak form, dominating the spotlight and rolling with the reactions of the audience around him. And the nose jokes were gold, each themed around a different topic.

"OBVIOUS: Excuse me. Is that your nose, or did a bus park on your face?"

"POLITE: Ah, would you mind not bobbing your head? The orchestra keeps changing tempo."

"METEOROLOGICAL: Everybody take cover! She's going to blow!"

"PORNOGRAPHIC: Finally, a man who can satisfy two women at once."

"AROMATIC: It must be wonderful to wake up in the morning and smell the coffee—in Brazil."

The rest of *Roxanne*, though, was Steve Martin as people hadn't really seen him before: genuine, sweet, romantic, and not Jerky in the least. Reviews were ecstatic—Roger Ebert enthused that "what makes *Roxanne* so wonderful is . . . the way the movie creates a certain ineffable spirit. . . . Martin plays a man with a smile on his face and a broken heart inside—a man who laughs that he may not cry." Martin won a Writers Guild of America award, and there was even some Oscar buzz, though a nomination failed to come to pass. No matter: he was newly married, having got hitched to his long-term partner, Victoria Tennant, in Rome in late 1986, and on a roll professionally, recently boosted to the $5-million-a-movie bracket.

After *Planes, Trains and Automobiles*, which took up most of 1987, he took a job which would dispatch him to the South of France for several months of highly honed knavery. *Dirty Rotten Scoundrels* was a remake of the 1964 Marlon Brando–David Niven con-men two-hander *Bedtime Story*, originally commissioned as a vehicle for Mick Jagger and David Bowie. "They got lured out of the movie by Martin Scorsese saying he wanted to do something with them," says screenwriter Dale Launer, whose idea it was to update *Bedtime Story*. "So they dropped out of my project to go with the big dog. Scorsese's a bit of a groupie. But aren't we all?"

Finding stars to replace the two rock gods proved a difficult task. The project next went to Paramount and Eddie Murphy, the idea being that the tale would be transposed to the Ivory Coast. The studio, however, rejected it on the grounds that Michael Ritchie, director non gratis following the *Golden Child* fiasco, came as part of that package. Warren Beatty and Tom Cruise briefly showed interest. John Cleese loved the first half of the script but not the second. Richard Dreyfuss seemed interested, before drifting away. Finally, Steve Martin and Michael Caine were locked down—Martin in the role of gauche American grifter Freddy, Caine as highly refined British bullshit artist Lawrence, although Martin had originally read for the latter.

"It was really down to the wire," says Frank Oz, who came on board as director, eager to work with Martin again. "Steve and I flew by Concorde to London and went to Oxfordshire, where Michael was having a dinner party. He was wonderful and introduced us to everyone. Then we went to his study to read, and it was so obvious that he and Steve would be brilliant. Sometimes you try so hard for something and don't get it, and then something else happens which is better than you can ever believe."

Most of the first day's footage was thrown away at Martin's request, after he watched the dailies and decided he was playing it too broad. But otherwise the Riviera shoot, taking place under blazing sunshine, was a largely pleasant time for the stars. "It was one of the happiest films I've ever done," says Caine. "They rented me a villa on the Riviera between two of my closest friends, Roger Moore and Leslie Bricusse, the composer. And Steve is so wonderful. The problem with that picture was trying to stop laughing. I remember we did thirty takes on one scene because I couldn't stop laughing."

Martin's memories are equally fond. "*Dirty Rotten Scoundrels* was one of the fun experiences of my life," he says. "Michael Caine was hilarious, Glenne Headly, Frank Oz . . . we all just got along. We were shooting in the south of France and it would get dark at ten p.m. and we'd wrap at seven and have dinner outdoors. It was just paradise."

But paradise wasn't entirely trouble-free. Haunted by his experience with the ending of *Little Shop of Horrors*, which he'd had to reshoot at great expense, Oz agonized over the film's climax. As written, it saw Martin, Caine, and Headley as mark (and secret mastermind) Janet Colgate, pretending to be Japanese, complete with appliances on their eyes to make them look Asian. But Oz, nervous that it would be offensive, nixed it. "I couldn't fucking believe it," he says now. "Can you imagine? I didn't like it at all and there was no way to make it funny." He devised another ending with Launer and Martin, including a line in which Lawrence tells their new target that Freddy is a mute, a beat Martin loved.

One day, a quarrel broke out on-set between Launer and Martin. The subject of the disagreement was "Ruprecht the Monkey Boy," a persona that Freddy adopts in order to frighten off an heiress. Martin's idea was for Ruprecht to wear lederhosen, put Coke bottles on his fingers, and do a strange, simian dance.

Launer didn't think this went far enough. "I wanted to take the original and make it darker," he explains. "Lawrence brings this woman into a dungeon, completely dark except for a shaft of light. We hear a chain dragging. Then Ruprecht breaks through the light and he looks like Nick Nolte on a three-week bender. Hair everywhere, beard with food in it, urine stains around his crotch. I mean, he's just horrible. He gives her a huge hug and buries his filthy face in her cleavage. Lawrence makes a half-assed effort to pull him off, but Ruprecht wraps a leg around her and starts humping her like a dog."

Martin objected to the sequence, strongly.

"He thought it was gross," says Launer. "And to prove it wasn't funny, he bent his knees and went through a little humping motion. The crew was moving lights and cameras nearby, and when they saw Steve doing this they broke out laughing. He looked ashamed. I was embarrassed for him and felt I had to come in and rescue him in a way, even though I had won the argument. You know, if you win the argument with your star, you lose."

Ruprecht's intro was dialed down, but Martin was to come up with some new, edgy gags of his own for a later dinner set piece, including a moment in which Freddy/Ruprecht, wearing an eye patch and wielding a trident and a fork with a cork on the prongs, asks permission to go to the bathroom, then squeezes his eyes closed, strains and finally says, "Thank you." It's the funniest scene in the movie, Martin back at his wildest and craziest.

"I love Ruprecht from *Dirty Rotten Scoundrels*" is the star's take, decades on. "Ruprecht the Monkey Boy is one of my favorite things. The scene I always think of is the one at the dinner table, because we had nothing—we went in that morning with no material. I thought up the cork gag, which still tickles me . . . I don't know, I just love that sequence."

Martin's reservations about the leg-humping wasn't an isolated incident: as he entered his forties, he began thinking more and more about what he was putting up on-screen. Movie theaters were flooded with raunchy comedies throughout the 1980s—the *Police Academy* and *Porky's* films, *Hardbodies, Stewardess School, Hot Resort,* and so on and so on—and Martin was repulsed by the increasing reliance on cheap laughs.

"I think it's very easy to be avant-garde in films, but it's harder to get to the meat and do a nice clean movie with a beginning, middle, and end," he said in 1987. "I think when we look back at all the foul humor of the last few years, I don't think it's going to last; it's going to look dated and tacky."

Then he made a pledge: "I intend to work clean."

15

"WE'RE BACK!"

RICHARD DONNER, THE veteran director who had launched Christopher Reeve into the air for *Superman* and teamed Mel Gibson and Danny Glover as yin-yang cops in *Lethal Weapon*, was not a man prone to nerves. But late one afternoon in 1987, as he waited in his L.A. home for a guest to arrive, the fifty-seven-year-old realized he was feeling some serious jitters. This was due to the impending meeting, set up by his agent, with someone he admired greatly but had never actually met: Bill Murray.

"I was told he would stop by at six o'clock," Donner remembers. "But six o'clock passes. Seven o'clock. Eight o'clock. Nine o'clock. No Bill. And then the doorbell rang and it was Bill. He came in and I was awestruck. Because he is, I think, one of the greatest talents we've ever had."

There was nothing particularly unusual about Murray's tardiness that evening: he was not a man famous for his punctuality. But maybe, just maybe, the star was putting off the appointment due to nerves of his own. His meeting with Donner was, after all, to discuss the project that would mark his proper return to the big screen after four years away. Titled *Scrooged*, it was a darkly comic, modern-day spin on Charles Dickens's *A Christmas Carol* that would see the Ghostbuster get ghost-busted, visited by a series of macabre ghouls bent on turning his character into a nice guy.

The studio was Paramount. The writers were Michael O'Donoghue, the legendarily acerbic *Saturday Night Live* joke spinner, and Mitch Glazer, the former journalist who had been introduced to Murray by John Belushi in 1977 while working on a profile of the latter. Fortunately for all of them, on that evening in L.A. Donner and Murray clicked. "Everything we talked about, it was not only funny but very enlightening," says the director. "An extraordinarily bright man. By the time he said good night and left, I would have killed to do it."

As a comeback vehicle, *Scrooged* seemed tailor-made for Murray. His character, TV executive Frank Cross, was an even bigger asshole than Peter Venkman, but hilariously so: told by a terrified minion that they're having trouble gluing antlers onto a mouse for a cutesy Christmas film, he orders them to use a stapler. Yet as he falls apart, getting the dickens scared out of him by the trio of Dickens-inspired wraiths, that sarcastic veneer slides away, revealing a sweet core.

It was a solid arc to play: from what Murray called "a crumb, a pig" to a joy-filled do-gooder. Plus, they were shooting in New York, Murray's favorite place to be.

If Murray was feeling rusty, he didn't show it. He worked away at the script with O'Donoghue and Glazer, beefing up the romance between Frank and his true love, Claire (Karen Allen). On-set, surrounded by friends and family (*Scrooged* found roles for not only his former *SNL* compadre Paul Shaffer but all three of his brothers: Brian, John, and Joel), he ad-libbed up a storm, most notably dictating the way the movie ended, turning to face the camera during the climactic singsong and inviting the audience to join in.

"That was totally improvised by Bill," marvels Donner. "I don't remember how it was originally written, but this was an extremely well-written script. And whatever the end was, it was great. But Bill did that soliloquy of his and looked into the lens, and it was so moving that I just got carried away by it. As the camera pulled back, I kept pushing crew in. That's all the crew. That's me, holding a kid. I know it sounds bullshit to say it, but a lot of people on-set had tears in their eyes. And I think I was one of them."

The twinkle-eyed, fun-dispensing comedy Santa that was Bill Murray was back. But so, occasionally, was the truculent, difficult Grinch that was also Bill Murray.

Although Donner now says he remembers only the good times, *Scrooged* was an intensely tense set, with him clashing frequently with his star over the direction of the movie. Co-star Carol Kane, who as the Ghost of Christmas Present pummeled Murray mercilessly, burst into tears on more than one occasion. Murray himself made his increasing distaste at the whole endeavor clear, throwing the movie under the bus at every opportunity. "*Scrooged* was a miserable gig," he told *Starlog* in early 1989. "I had more fun on *The Razor's Edge*, which made no money. But I got to go around the world and meet all kinds of people. On *Scrooged*, I was trapped on a smelly and smokey set for three-and-a-half months, having a lousy time by myself, and just coughing up blood from the fake snow that was falling all the time. So, the work is everything."

Despite its star's disdain, it was a solid $60 million hit. Audiences went along and sang along to "Put a Little Love in Your Heart." And over the years it became a holiday classic, still the only Christmas movie to feature the line "The bitch hit me with a toaster!"

As for Donner and Murray, they never saw each other again, though the director hopes they'll run into each other one day: "I assume there would be a hug." Donner followed up *Scrooged* by making the first sequel to his buddy-cop hit *Lethal Weapon*. Murray, meanwhile, headed to Los Angeles for a crucial meeting. It looked like he might be making a sequel of his own.

JIMMY'S, A RESTAURANT located midway between Beverly Hills and Century City, had seen a lot of history since it opened in 1978. Rumor had it that the Kennedys once formed a conga line and danced past Ronald and Nancy Reagan as they ate dinner. Marlon Brando, who came in so often that he called Irish owner Jimmy Murphy "Il Patron," traipsed in late one night with Richard Burton and Clint Eastwood, the trio of titans parking themselves at the bar. Every St. Patrick's Day, the likes of Liam Neeson, Pierce Brosnan, and Gabriel Byrne swung by. It was a place where you could spot anyone, and where anything could happen.

An appropriate venue, then, for the gathering that occurred in late 1987, a lunch to discuss a project that had long looked impossible: *Ghostbusters II.*

One major hindrance had been Bill Murray, whom Dan Aykroyd had been badgering since 1985 but who remained reluctant to revisit a past glory. Another was David Puttnam, head of Columbia from 1986 to 1987, a forthright British filmmaker turned suit whose reaction to *E.T.: The Extraterrestrial* was to say the alien should have stayed dead. His thoughts on a *Ghostbusters* sequel were equally frank: he not only declared that the way to move forward was with a younger and cheaper cast, but insulted Murray during a speech at a welcome lunch for industry players, singling him out as an actor "who makes millions of movies but gives nothing back to his art. He's a taker." Given Puttnam had also tangled with Aykroyd over a movie called *Vibes*, which ended up being made with Jeff Goldblum, it looked like a lock had been slapped on the whole sorry affair. And there was no Keymaster in sight.

Then, suddenly, Puttnam was gone, replaced by savvy executive Dawn Steel. Her very first act was to salvage *Ghostbusters II*, which she described as "in the dollars-and-cents point of view, probably the most important, eagerly awaited sequel in the history of Columbia Pictures." The back room at Jimmy's was hastily booked and decorated with Ghostbusters toys, Slimers and Stay Puft Marshmallow Men that were scattered around in an attempt to pump up the nostalgia. Then in they filed: Ivan Reitman, Harold Ramis, Dan Aykroyd, CAA's Ray Kurtzman, superagent Michael Ovitz, and, incredibly, the Murricane himself. The six men sat around a table for four hours. By the time the check came, it was obvious that proton packs would be fired up once again.

"I think walking into the meeting no one really felt we'd make the movie," said Murray. "But in the course of lunch we had so many laughs and so much fun that it became clear we'd really enjoy working together again."

There would likely be big paydays; Reitman, Aykroyd, and Murray each agreed to work for a reduced fee, instead taking a percentage of the movie's profits. But there were other incentives too. For Murray, the thought of working in an ensemble again appealed: no more being the lone goofball, responsible for mustering up every laugh. As for Aykroyd, he would get to flex his writing muscles for the first time since *Dragnet*, reuniting with Ramis to figure out a new assignment for Venkman, Stantz, Spengler, and Zeddemore.

Their first ideas veered toward the bizarre. Aykroyd argued that New York had been done, and that the Ghostbusters should jump on a plane to Scotland instead, pursuing a kidnapped Dana. There, they would encounter a colony of fairies and travel through a two-thousand-mile pneumatic tube—a journey that would take three days. Ramis suggested that the story feature a creepy baby imbued with the agility of an adult, a notion he ultimately admitted was "just too horrible for a movie." Eventually they decided to keep the characters in New York, where, after battling evil way up at the top of a skyscraper at the end of their last adventure, the Ghostbusters would find it way down in the subterranean tunnels of the city's subway system. A river of pink slime, the physical manifestation of New Yorkers' negative energy, would provide the story with gloopy thrills; Vigo, a Carpathian warlord trapped in a painting, would be the new antagonist.

The first *Ghostbusters* had been a terror to make, with Reitman contractually obligated to deliver it within a year. The sequel was even worse. Filming was to begin on November 28, 1988, with a release date of July 1989, and Aykroyd and Ramis frantically hammered out the screenplay throughout the summer.

"The script is nowhere near ready, and we start shooting soon," Murray told a writer for *Starlog*, unhelpfully. "Jeez, more pressure. We'll figure it out . . . or we won't." If the movie's front man was trying to whip up hype for the long-awaited sequel, he was doing a truly terrible job at it. "It's not going to be called *Ghostbusters II*," he promised in the same interview. "We'll burn in hell if we call it *Ghostbusters II*. I've suggested *The Last of the Ghostbusters*, to make sure there won't be anything like a *Ghostbusters III*."

ORIGINALLY, *Ghostbusters II* was to open with its heroes still on top of their game, as idolized by New Yorkers as they had been at the end of the first movie. But Aykroyd, Ramis, and Reitman decided it would be more effective to have them split up and at a low ebb. Ray is running a dingy occult bookshop. Egon has sequestered himself away inside a lab. And Venkman is back to his low-rent ways, hosting a dodgy cable show called *World of the Psychic*.

Intentionally or not, it mirrored the stars' own career trajectories. While Murray had vanished from view, Aykroyd had been having a rocky time at the box office, suffering a series of embarrassing flops with the likes of *The Couch Trip* and *My Stepmother Is an Alien*. Ramis had had his own fallow patch, writing and directing tropical flop *Club Paradise*, while Ernie Hudson had been slumming in films such as *The Dirty Dozen: The Fatal Mission*. The *Ghostbusters* brand was a bigger draw than their own names to many people, as Ramis found out when they started to shoot on the streets of New York. "Shooting anywhere in New York in Ghostbusters gear is wild. . . . They bring their kids and hold them up to us like offerings," he said. "The strange thing is that the cartoon characters have been immortalized in plastic, so a lot of the kids only know us as the cartoon characters. They look at me and they go, 'Your hair isn't blond.'"

Still, the famous no-ghost logo brought more perks than ever. *Ghostbusters II*'s fortnight of location shooting in New York happened to coincide not only with the pre-Christmas shopping rush, but a historic three-day visit from Russian president Mikhail Gorbachev, but the city bent over backward to accommodate the production.

"When we had the uniforms on, we were above the law," said Murray. "We could do anything."

This applied particularly to him. On the first movie, the fifty-pound proton packs had proven so cumbersome that Murray complained his had bent his spine into curves resembling Mulholland Drive. For the sequel, their weight was reduced to twenty-eight pounds. He also declared early on that this time Peter Venkman would remain slime-free. Accordingly, he was absent from a scene shot at two a.m. on a freezing New York street, in which his fellow Ghostbusters emerge from beneath ground, covered in pink goo. "They poured buckets and buckets of sticky, watery slime over us—over our heads, over everywhere, because Ivan wanted it even in our eyes," Hudson complained. "He wanted us to look like we had really been swimming in slime." In fact, the story called for the creation of 100,000 gallons of the substance—a biodegradable jelly laced with red food coloring—so much that a "slime lab" was put in place to produce it.

A day spent shooting the quartet driving around the city in *Ecto-1* proved Murray's favorite: the star got a kick out of screaming at people who cheered when the car zipped past. Then cast and crew headed to L.A. for thirteen weeks at Burbank Studios, to shoot such locations as the fictional Manhattan Museum of Art, where Sigourney Weaver's Dana Barrett now works, and a ghost-infested courtroom, a recycled set from Reitman's 1986 comedy *Legal Eagles*.

One night, as they waited for Reitman to finish shooting a scene involving Egon jackhammering cement, Aykroyd and Murray sat in a corner sipping coffee and argued about a recent Eddie Murphy appearance on *The Arsenio Hall Show*. The host had asked Murphy if he'd ever work with John Landis again after their falling-out on *Coming to America*, to which the star had responded with a dark quip: "He has a better chance of working again with Vic Morrow than he does with me." This reference to the actor who had been decapitated on the set of Landis's portion of *Twilight Zone: The Movie* divided the

Ghostbusters stars: Aykroyd, who had not only worked with Landis five times but cameoed in *Twilight Zone*, thought it was in bad taste, while Murray freely chuckled.

"Come on," he said to his *Saturday Night Live* compadre. "You gotta admit it, that's funny."

IN 1984, *Ghostbusters* had mingled comedy and special effects in a way that had never been done before. Five years on, with the likes of *Back to the Future* and *Innerspace* upping the ante, the pressure was on to deliver an even more astonishing experience. And nobody felt that pressure more than Industrial Light & Magic's Dennis Muren, the effects supervisor on the sequel. "We had nearly 180 shots to complete," he said, "and considering they were still shooting with the actors two months before the film opened, it was definitely tight."

Aykroyd and Ramis had dreamed up numerous phantasmagorical delights for Muren's team to conjure up: the Statue of Liberty come to life, a phantom jogger, even the *Titanic,* docking at Pier 34 and unloading its ghostly passengers. But Murray felt that the original movie's fine balance between laughs and spectacle had tipped too far in the direction of the latter. "Those special-effects guys took over," he complained. "It was too much of the slime and not enough of us."

When it came out on June 16, pushed forward from its original date of July 4 to get out of the way of Warner Bros.'s *Batman*, many critics concurred. "This movie is a total disappointment. No thought went into it, no effort went into it, there's no comedy in it," stormed Roger Ebert. "I did go to see it in a real movie theater in Michigan with several hundred people. They sat through the entire movie, they were there to have a good time. And there was one laugh. One laugh, in two hours. . . . This is a demonstration of the bankruptcy of sequels."

These days Reitman is philosophical about it. "All the acting parts are really terrific—frankly better, I think, than in the first movie. But emulating the structure of the first movie as much as I did, that was a mistake. *Batman* was coming out and was the shiny new thing, cynical and dark and bloody. Ours was a family movie. And of course the tricks and wonderful surprises of the first movie, I didn't have at my disposal in the second one."

Aykroyd also offers up a fairly spirited defense, saying, "I think it holds up to the first movie about 75 percent. Maybe the ending broke down a little, but it's hard to follow up Mr. Stay Puft, you know?" But despite making a hefty $215 million, and becoming the eighth biggest film of 1989, it proved the final *Ghostbusters* film to feature the original lineup.

The *Saturday Night Live* and *SCTV* casts had prided themselves on coming up with fresh material week after week. But with Hollywood increasingly reliant on sequels—1989 also saw the release of *Back to the Future Part II*, *Indiana Jones and the Last Crusade*, and *The Karate Kid Part III*—they were feeling as much pressure as anyone to return to their past glories. It was a dangerous game, resulting sometimes in glory, sometimes in infamy.

Chevy Chase was about to experience both.

WHEN ASKED in interviews about his experience at the Betty Ford Center in 1986, Chase was rarely serious. "It was just awful," he told Barbara Walters when she visited his home to probe him with a concerned expression. "Betty staggering around . . . I just couldn't sober her up."

In reality, though, he *had* hated it: the endlessly recited self-help slogans ("Thank you for sharing with us"), the enforced discipline, and perhaps most of all the very public shame. His two-and-a-half-week stint in rehab was reported in every newspaper in the land, although the statement released by his publicist mentioned only his problem with painkillers, with nothing about cocaine. Reporters called the clinic for months afterward, trying to dig up more dirt.

Chase returned to his wife, three daughters, birds, and bunnies in late October 1986 with a clean system and new attitude. "We were told that if you take them you would know yourself better," he mused of drugs. "Fact of the matter is, all you know about yourself is what you're like when you're poisoned. It took a long time to learn that."

The next step was career rehab: a series of carefully calculated public appearances to establish that he was back on the top of his game. The first was a guest-host slot on *The Tonight Show* on October 31, taking over from Johnny Carson, who privately quipped to him, "You're the first Betty Ford graduate to host the show." Chase, who had previously shown off his tennis serve on the show, found it a terrifying experience—his monologue seemed to last forever. But he returned a few months later to sit on the couch next to film critics Roger Ebert and Gene Siskel. It had all the makings of a late-night car-crash: Ebert and Siskel had savaged many of Chase's films over the years, with Ebert most recently awarding *¡Three Amigos!* one star and saying, "Chase essentially seems absent most of the time."

But anyone expecting a brawl—or, more likely given Siskel and Ebert's trademark review system, a thumb wrestle—was disappointed. Asked by Carson to pick their favorite Chevy Chase picture, Siskel chose *Fletch*: "I have thought that on occasion he has played a character that seems a little bit too smug. And he seems like a nice guy. In *Fletch* he was a nice guy pursuing a goal. And I felt warm for him and I had a rooting interest in him."

Then, as Ebert expounded his own thoughts, Chase slipped into one of his old *SNL* gimmicks, looking into the camera and aping the critic as he earnestly spoke. Raucous laughter from the studio audience.

"I hope you were kind to me," said the owlish Ebert, turning to Chase, "because after all, we haven't brought up *Oh! Heavenly Dog.*"

Next was something less expected. Paul Simon had released his album *Graceland* in September 1986, with the single "You Can Call Me Al" dropping out of the charts after fourteen weeks. Simon had been unhappy with the original music video, a performance of the song he had done on *SNL* filmed on a video monitor, and griped about it to his friend Lorne Michaels. One day, when Chase was visiting Michaels at his home on the easternmost point of Long Island, the *SNL* boss suggested that he do a new video with Simon. "So within a couple of days, I just learned the song and we went in there to shoot it for next to nothing, while other people were shooting videos that cost hundreds of thousands of dollars," said Chase.

The concept was simple: the tall comedian and the short musician strode into a pink room, sat down in white chairs, shook hands, and then Chase started to lip-sync with the song, with Simon left to twiddle his thumbs, only joining in for the choruses. The combination of the brilliant simplicity, Chase's mugging (at one point he pretends to mistake a drum stand for a table, dropping a glass of water on the floor) and the infectiousness of Simon's ditty made the video a phenomenon. So much so that Simon and Chase were to reunite in 1990 for another music video, "Proof," drafting in Steve Martin to dance in baggy, MC Hammer–inspired outfits.

Chase's biggest and most intimidating public appearances, however, were as host of the Academy Awards two years running. On March 30, 1987, he divvied up the duties with *Crocodile Dundee* star Paul Hogan and his old pal Goldie Hawn, kicking off his monologue by looking at the star-strewn audience and saying, "Welcome to *Monday Night Live*." Then he ran through some of the night's major contenders, giving a Chevy Chase spin on each. *Platoon*: "A recruiting film for conscientious objectors." *The Mission*: "The story of the liberation of the Guaraní Indian tribe in the jungles of South America, mapped out on a corner table at the Polo Lounge at the Beverly Hills Hotel." *Hannah and Her Sisters*: "In which Woody Allen plays a hypochondriac and Michael Caine plays with the sisters."

He was a hit. Less successful was his reprise a year later, in which he headed to the Shrine Auditorium, Oscars venue for the first time in forty years, to host the 60th Academy Awards alone. It was Chase's bad luck that a Writers Guild of America strike had struck shortly before the event, meaning that no member of the guild (including himself) was allowed to work on the script for the event. Many comedians were drafted in to improvise their way through presenting duties, leading to Eddie Murphy's anti-racism tirade, but Chase was left largely adrift. After starting the evening roving the red carpet, microphone in hand, cornering the likes of Charlton Heston for awkward small-talk, he strode onstage with the words "Good evening, Hollywood phonies," explaining the situation and claiming, "My entire monologue was generously donated by five Teamsters."

Unlike the previous year, Chase looked flustered as he faced the starry audience, which included Tom Cruise, Dustin Hoffman, Jack Nicholson, Sean Connery, Michael Douglas, and Mel Gibson. "The women are beautiful and many of the men have showered," he quipped, before struggling through scads of thin material, including an unfunny assault on film critics and a desperate moment where he drops his trousers after engaging in banter with Paul Newman, prompting Newman to say, pointedly, "Well, there's something to be said for comedy."

The show ran an excruciating three and a half hours, despite Chase's claim at the top of the show that the writers strike would ensure it would be nice and tight. He would not be called back by the Academy for the next year, or ever again. In his mind, it was the trouser-dropping that had sealed his fate.

HIS DOUBLE OSCARS stint and talk-show bons mots boosted the Chevy Chase brand. But he knew that where it really counted was at the box office. Post-rehab, Chase decided it was time to stop with the double-act pictures and return to a solo vehicle. Hence *Funny Farm*, the tale of a wannabe novelist, Andy Farmer, who moves to a small Vermont town for the peace and quiet and is, inevitably, driven mad by the locals. "Citizens of Redbud," he announces to the townsfolk, "we came to Redbud filled with hopes and dreams for a better life and a better place. Basically, we've seen those hopes and dreams crushed and shattered before our very eyes."

This is of course just a prelude for a happy ending, in which Farmer and his wife cancel their looming divorce and end up in an idyllic house covered in snow. The project itself had a less happy climax, making just $25.5 million domestic, Chase's weakest haul since *Deal of the Century*. Siskel and Ebert were unlikely champions, perhaps still feeling the afterglow of their chummy talk-show-sofa joust with the movie's star when the former described it as "the best film Chase has made" and the latter as "a small miracle." Most other critics were less kind, one newspaper writer slamming it as "about as funny as picking cotton on a 103-degree August day" in an article titled *"Funny Farm Not Funny at All; Chevy Chase Needs Better Stuff."*

Feeling the strain again, Chase beat a retreat. His next three movies were all sequels to hits he'd had earlier in the decade. But if he thought this meant they were guaranteed earners, he had a tough lesson coming. *Caddyshack II*'s ignominious roots lie not in a pitch from the creatives to the studio, but the other way around. "The Shack is back!" the Warner Bros. suits whooped at Harold Ramis. "No, I don't think so," Ramis replied. But he realized that the original's cultural cachet had swelled during the '80s to the point where a follow-up was inevitable, with or without him, and he decided he may as well try to make the damn thing work. He stuck around for a couple of drafts before running for the hills.

The endeavor was doomed from the start. Warner wanted to build the project around Rodney Dangerfield, the wild man of the original, but after reading the script Dangerfield shook his head. Making matters worse, there was a writers' strike in process, meaning a polish was out of the question. Desperate to still get the picture out in July 1988 to capitalize on summer audiences, Warner execs flew director Allan Arkush out on the studio jet to New York to see another stand-up, Jackie Mason, in action. "He was funny," remembers Arkush, "but he wasn't connecting with the audience, wasn't making eye contact. I went backstage and talked to him and there was just something in his personality that made me worry a little bit." But when the director returned to L.A. and voiced his concerns to producer Jon Peters, he was told, "Don't turn a go movie into a development deal." There was no going back.

Bill Murray refused to have anything to do with *Caddyshack II*, wary of sullying the good name of Carl Spackler. The groundskeeper was written out, replaced by a deranged Marine explosives expert, played by Dan Aykroyd, who decided to play the role with a high-pitched voice, channeling military historian Oliver North. As for Chevy Chase, he made it very clear he was only returning for an extended cameo as Ty Webb (this time with a diamond stud in his left ear) as a favor, and because he was being paid a sackload of cash.

On-set, Jackie Mason drove everyone crazy, unable to remember his lines; ultimately Arkush had to shoot him in close-up so he could feed him readings from off-camera. And the director clashed with Chase from the start. "Chevy was best friends with the head of the studio, so Chevy got whatever Chevy wanted," Arkush recalls. "The first day I was working with him was on the golf course. I'd come from episodic TV, *Moonlighting* and a lot of other big shows, and was used to leaving actors who had played their character before alone. But he started in on me: 'Well, don't you have a point of view? Don't you know what you want from me? I can't work like this.' So the next scene I did with him, I'd done a lot of homework and gave him specific notes. And he said, 'You're not giving me any room to have fun here. You're telling me what to do every second.' It went on and on like that."

Watching dailies, Chase griped about the cinematography, which was being overseen by Oscar-nominated veteran Harry Stradling Jr., complaining that the lighting in a scene where he played pool made his tan look bad. "That was Chevy's big preparation for the film," says Arkush. "He'd worked on that tan very hard." And in the edit suite, after scanning the footage, an unhappy Chase reportedly commented, "Call me when you've dubbed the laugh track."

Genuine laughter was not forthcoming. This time the Shack was an unstable structure, and the sequel bombed, making less than $12 million and earning Aykroyd a Golden Raspberry Award (Worst Supporting Actor). "I wish the movie was funnier. I wish I could have done a better job," says Arkush. "But I've found over my career that I do my best work when I'm part of a team. And there was no team on *Caddyshack II*. After doing that movie I ended up in therapy for a year. Then I went back into TV and never tried a movie again."

Chase's next project, *Fletch Lives*, was better, but only because it couldn't be worse. The shoot took the star down to the swampy environs of Louisiana, mixing him up in another convoluted mystery, this time involving a televangelist and the Ku Klux Klan. With more disguises, silly fake names, and a *Gone with the Wind*–spoofing poster, featuring Chase embracing a buxom belle with a gun held to his head, it did little more than repeat the formula with a Deep South twist. There were some amusing set pieces, like a dream sequence sending up the "Zippity-Doo-Dah" song from Disney's *Song of the South*, but many more lazy clichés. And at the middle of it all was another dead-pan, detached, weightless performance from Chase, floating through the movie without leaving a footprint or generating an emotion.

Even hardcore *Fletch* fans felt let down, not least Gene Siskel, who had rhapsodized to Chase's face about the original film. "This thing is just Joke City. He just walks through it tossing off one-liners, and they're not really very funny," he lamented on his TV show. "Too often he just wants to be in a movie as if he's guesting on a talk show," chimed in Roger Ebert. "He's got to be willing to be in the movie if we're going to be willing to be interested in it."

It was, if Chase was adding it to his tally, another four thumbs down.

WITH THE END of the 1980s approaching fast, Chase had to conclude that it had been a rough decade. Some of the movies he had been in-volved with had bloomed into roses—*Caddyshack, National Lampoon's Vacation, Fletch*—but around them was a whole lot of mulch. Privately, he was as hard on himself as any critic—he felt as if he'd fallen into a slump as soon as he'd left *Saturday Night Live* and never bounced back. But he tried to stay positive. "I feel I'm going to come out of it," he said. "No, I can't act, but I can make a lot of people laugh and I can perform."

Perhaps it was desperation that led him to renege on an oath he'd made in 1985. Back then, he'd sworn that he would never return as hapless family man Clark Griswold. Warner, however, despite the *Caddyshack II* debacle, was eager to add another installment to the franchise. Especially when John Hughes agreed to adapt his own short story, *Christmas '59*, into a screenplay, and in no time at all turned in a dazzling draft.

"John was the fastest typist I've ever seen in my life," says director

Jeremiah Chechik, who worked with Hughes on cracking the story. "You could hardly read the script while he was at the computer. I mean, it was rolling off the screen. I'm not going to take any credit for that screenplay, because John Hughes was a force of nature in terms of his perceptive genius and ability to twist family realities just a little, so that a situation was both recognizable and extreme at the same time."

For this *Vacation*, the Griswolds wouldn't even have to leave the house. Instead, their crackpot relatives would come to them, for a Christmas break destined to be plagued by calamity. Returning to the series would be Uncle Eddie (Randy Quaid); his wife, Catherine (Miriam Flynn); their trailer-trash offspring; and their Rottweiler dog, Snots. New to the fray, and not helping things run any more smoothly, were cigar-wielding Uncle Lewis (William Hickey) and Aunt Bethany (Mae Questel). Nicholas Guest and Julia Louis-Dreyfus, on the cusp of becoming a massive star with *Seinfeld*, were cast as the Griswolds' yuppie neighbors, a duo for Clark to battle in his obsessive quest to win Christmas. New Griswold kids were cast: future stars Johnny Galecki and Juliette Lewis. The central location, the Griswold abode, was built on the Warner Bros. back lot in L.A., next to a house used in *Lethal Weapon*.

Chechik was as stunned as anyone when the studio offered him the director's chair. For one thing, he'd seen neither of the previous *Vacation* movies. For another, he'd never made a film, only a series of commercials so moody and sultry that he started jokingly referring to himself as "the Prince of Darkness." He had at least visited a few sets, including *Scrooged*, which was ample demonstration to him that just because a film was about the joy of the holidays, it didn't necessarily follow that there'd be joy behind the scenes. "I definitely felt the tension there," he says. "Though I didn't really attribute that to Bill Murray."

His own headline star, it turned out, would not be a problem. Chase was on good behavior throughout, trucking on even after he broke a finger punching a plastic reindeer, taking Galecki to visit the nearby sets of *Harlem Nights* and *Ghostbusters II*, and executing some of his most inspired physical comedy yet. One morning he was handed an empty cardboard box, with the challenge of creating the illusion that it contained a rowdy cat. Chase retired to a quiet corner, considered the box, and returned a half hour later with some perfectly timed shtick, egged on by his director making meowing sounds off-camera. Schrödinger's Cat has nothing on Chevy Chase's Cat.

Not that it was a wholly tension-free set. Beverly D'Angelo, returning as Ellen Griswold, was unsure about the material and suspicious of Chechik's credentials. "She was very unhappy about doing what was, in her mind, a stupid comedy," the director says. "I was shooting a sub-master early on and gave Beverly a note, and she just went off on me. Like, 'Who the fuck are you to give me a note? You've not directed anything. I've worked with Schlesinger and Scorsese' and all the rest of it. I just had to bite my tongue and shrug my shoulders."

Another difficult moment followed, where his on-screen husband and wife unleashed a blizzard of invective at each other. "It was a pretty fucked-up day," Chechik recalls. "We were rehearsing the scene where Chevy and Beverly look out the window at Randy pumping out shit in the RV. And at that point in the movie they were not getting on. They were fighting like cats and dogs and there was a lot of hostility, a lot of shit between them. We were getting ready to go, and they were having final touches, but they were still at each other's throats. So I said, 'OK, roll . . . and action!' And *bam!*—they snapped into character and hit those comedy moments out of the park. I had this appreciation that they could feel all that Sturm und Drang about each other, but yet hit their beats perfectly."

At "Cut!" the sniping began afresh.

HUMAN NATURE may have threatened to derail things on-set, but actual nature came a lot closer to doing so. Midway through the *Christmas Vacation* shoot, an earthquake rocked the Griswold home, making the lighting rigs shake and forcing cast and crew to run for cover. But incredibly, far more stress was caused by a garden-variety squirrel.

In the story, the rodent invades the house and is chased around by Uncle Eddie's dog. So, once the sequence had been extensively storyboarded, a squirrel was procured and brought onto the set during every lunch break for training. For weeks the bushy-tailed beast was coached through its movements, persuaded to dart around the rooms from point to point. Finally, the morning designated for shooting the scene arrived. And with it an unanticipated problem.

"I remember this so clearly, it could have happened yesterday," says Chechik, wincing. "I drive into the lot and park. Then I look up to see the line producer and my AD and the animal trainer, huddled together, looking grim." The squirrel, it turned out, had expired only hours before its big moment. "It was a disaster. I go, 'We fucking need a squirrel!' And I kid you not, we shot that scene with a random squirrel. We fucking winged it. I didn't ask where they got it. I didn't want to know."

On the studio lot, fake snow transformed an L.A. summer into a festive wonderland. But real snow was needed for a sledding scene, so after some serious scouting the filmmakers decided to head to the small town of Breckenridge, Colorado. Except, by the time all the production trucks had parked up, it was obvious that the Curse of the Squirrel had traveled with them. All the snow that had recently coated the town had melted: there was not an icicle to be seen.

"It was very, very stressful," says Chechik. "In the end we ordered enormous truckloads of snow and ice to be hauled in from some mountaintop somewhere. Then, while all that was on its way, it started to snow. And snowed and snowed and never stopped snowing. It snowed so much the roads closed and you couldn't move. There was like ten feet of it. Then *our* snow arrived, which was really a joke."

But with the arrival of the blizzard, the entire mood of the production changed. Cast and crew reverted to a kid-like state, none more so than Chevy Chase, who performed his sledding shots with a big goofy grin on his face. And when the movie opened, the euphoria spread to movie theatres: after debuting at number two (behind *Back to the Future Part II*), in its third week it took the top spot. Chase received the news while at a party at the home of Martin Short. As for Chechik, he and his comedy mentor James L. Brooks bought tickets for a public showing in West Hollywood. There, he listened to the paying audience laugh during the opening sequence, even before the first joke had arrived. As the first act rolled on, chuckles turned into howls. Then, as Clark tried to activate his turbo-powered Christmas lights to no avail, the crowd let out a collective sigh of disappointment.

"That's when I knew we had them," Chechik says. "They weren't just there for the laughs; they were carried forward by the emotional commitment of the main character, despite the fact he's a clown. That's what I had focused on: this man destroying his family because of his obsession with creating the greatest Christmas ever. And in no small part thanks to Chevy, it paid off. No matter how stupid he was, they wanted him to succeed."

16

EXIT THE NICE GUYS

THE YEAR 1990 was rushing up fast, and with it a fresh decade. It had been a breathless ten years for the *SNL* and *SCTV* stars who had made it big, and a lot more craziness lay ahead. But they were all different people from the ones they had been at the start of the ride. Middle age had arrived. Bill Murray was thirty-nine, Steve Martin forty-four, Chevy Chase forty-six. There were wives now, houses, kids, sagging bellies, and graying hair, though Martin was way ahead with that last one.

As young men, their white-hot fame and near-constant jet-setting had been a kick. But was that really what they wanted for the rest of their lives? Rick Moranis, for one, wasn't entirely sure.

He had cut his teeth up in sleepy Edmonton, goofing about with friends in a ramshackle studio. Now he was thirty-six years old and his face was on a McDonald's cup, part of the hysterical promotional campaign for *Ghostbusters II*. He'd been a toy before, for the first movie, but this was different: kids all over America were slurping Coca-Cola out of his face. It both amused him and weirded him out.

"There were two phases of it," Moranis says of his movie career.

"The phase where I was being hired to be a comedian, to make things as funny as I could with the other comedians on the set. You felt nothing other than the fun of making a comedy. When I crossed that line and became a commodity, when the executives swarmed in, it became a different kind of animal that wasn't enjoyable to me."

His role in *Ghostbusters II* had been severely cut, including a string of scenes where his returning character, Louis Tully, straps on a proton pack and hunts Slimer. But Moranis's ascent into the Hollywood firmament, as meteoric as it was unlikely, continued nevertheless. It probably didn't hurt that he was garnering a reputation as one of the most decent people in Hollywood, a rare comedian not riddled with neuroses and insecurities.

In fact, he clung to normality with both hands, continuing to clip grocery coupons, picking up Pampers for his two young kids, and driving a sensible Chevrolet Lumina rather than a sports car. Whomever he encountered, he was unfailingly polite.

"He's a lovely human being," says producer Trevor Albert, who worked with Moranis on *Club Paradise*. "Kind and grounded and down to earth. Combine that with a searing wit and ability to improvise brilliantly. I have a memory of watching him and Eugene Levy doing a scene on a beach where they put suntan lotion on. Just jaw-droppingly funny improv."

Perhaps because of his *Ghostbusters–Little Shop of Horrors* double-whammy, multiple roles in science-fiction blockbusters came his way. In Mel Brooks's 1987 *Star Wars* send-up *Spaceballs*, Moranis stole the show as Dark Helmet, the nebbish wannabe ruler of the galaxy, who sports an absolutely enormous piece of evil headwear. (In an early draft of the script, the character spent most of his screen time *inside* an even bigger helmet.) "I was only on *Spaceballs* for six weeks, but that was wild," recalls Moranis. "Working with Mel Brooks is like the best ride at the amusement park."

His next movie, though, would prove so huge that it ended up *becoming* a ride at an amusement park, specifically EPCOT Center at Florida's Walt Disney World. The project had gone through several changes of title, from *Teenie Weenies* to *Grounded* to *The Big Backyard*. But Moranis was tickled by the on-the-nose-ness of its final moniker: *Honey, I Shrunk the Kids*. "The title says it all," he said at the time. "That's the era we live in. *Three Men and a Baby*? You knew what the movie was about. . . . *Ninotchka*—what was that? An eggplant dish or something? *Gone with the Wind*: the story of a kite?"

Even more so than *Little Shop of Horrors*, Moranis was the front man, playing the lead character—Wayne Szalinski, an inventor who accidentally miniaturizes his children—in a big summer Disney picture. Despite the fact that the story took place in and around a house in the California suburbs, the shoot took place on the back lot of Churubusco Studios in Mexico City, where a sleepy US neighborhood had been painstakingly created. So Moranis packed his suitcase, said goodbye to his costume-designer wife, Ann, and two kids, and flew south. "You drive on the lot, it's exactly like shooting anywhere else, except there are a couple of guys eating a dog," he deadpanned to David Letterman on his chat show. "Or a couple of dogs eating a guy."

Ever cautious and aware of how much was riding on him this time, he was careful with his diet, drinking bottled water and boiling fruit before eating it. This was not how John Belushi would have handled the situation. A film buff, Moranis got a buzz from the fact he was filming next door to the new James Bond movie, *Licence to Kill*, and in the same place where *The Treasure of Sierra Madre* had shot back in the '40s. And though he wasn't involved in the "shrunk" sequences, he savored the fact that he was making a movie in which someone falls into a bowl of Cheerios.

When Disney finalized the poster, Moranis's face dominated, with the four young cast members leaping off his nose and onto that of the family dog. He was dispatched around the world on his very first global press tour, discovering that in Japan the movie was called *Micro-Kids*. From interview to interview, he refused to take any of it seriously, vigorously endorsing the novelization ("You can put it right between Hemingway and the Iacocca autobiography . . . *Honey, I Shrunk the Plymouth*"), cueing up clips from the Gregory Peck movie *Old Gringo* instead of *Honey*, and pointing out, with a big grin, that one of the reviews sent to him by Disney had misspelled the film's title as *Honey, I Struck the Kids*.

Asked what the best perk of the movie had been, he replied that it was getting to keep his character's shoes: a pair of brown loafers with tassels.

MORANIS LIKED to go to matinee screenings of his movies, to see them with a paying audience. He was rarely recognized. When he stumped up the cash for a ticket to *Honey, I Shrunk the Kids*, he was delighted to see people's reaction: they cheered the special effects, expertly coordinated by first-time director Joe Johnston, and howled when Wayne timidly informs his wife that he's thrown their children out with the trash. Not as hip or as inventive as *Ghostbusters*, it still combined laughs and high-concept spectacle in a similarly effective way, and was rewarded with a $222.7 million gross. Disney immediately started plotting sequels.

In the meantime, Moranis decided to have some fun. He made three movies back-to-back with Steve Martin, whom he had long admired and even been compared to back when he was a guitar-strumming stand-up. In *Parenthood* he played another scientist. For *My Blue Heaven*, a not entirely successful oddity in which Martin plays an Italian gangster in a sharkskin suit and Moranis a fastidious FBI agent, he carried a gun for the first and last time. And in *L.A. Story*, he cameoed as a gravedigger, turning up on-set for his single scene with a Cockney accent nobody was expecting.

Next up was his very first western, a project called *City Slickers*, about three urban schmoes who deal with their joint midlife crisis by venturing into the wild for a two-week cattle drive. Moranis started practicing horseback riding with co-stars Billy Crystal and Bruno Kirby, ready to start galloping through canyons in New Mexico and Colorado.

But then he received devastating news: Ann, his wife since 1986, was diagnosed with cancer. He pulled out of *City Slickers* to take care of her, but she died in February 1991, just thirty-four years old.

Moranis got back to work, completing the second *Honey* movie, *Honey, I Blew Up the Kid*, which featured a giant baby, and making a daft comedy called *Splitting Heirs*, which was conceived when he bumped into Eric Idle in an Italian restaurant near his New York home. But the tragedy was to change everything. Now a single parent, he wanted to spend as much time as he could with his kids, and became pickier and pickier with his projects. One script he turned down was a weird thing called *Ace Ventura: Pet Detective*, which would end up starring an old acquaintance from the Toronto comedy-club scene: Jim Carrey.

"It was a perfect vehicle for Carrey, this rubber-bodied crazy guy I used to watch flinging himself all over the place, but it wasn't what I was looking for," says Moranis. "I wanted to know, 'Who else is in this thing? Who can I battle with?' I didn't really take to the idea of being the lead, with nobody else in it to play with."

But he did say yes to one more mega-budget fantasy blockbuster: *The Flintstones*, which Universal was positioning as their big summer hope for 1994. Back at *SCTV*, there had been a card on the ideas board that read FLINTSTONES HUMANOID SHOW, not because the cast were particularly fans of the iconic Hanna-Barbera cartoon, but because they wanted to force the producers to build seventeen identical living rooms so Moranis and his cast mates could run past the same scenery (alas, it never happened). Now he was offered the chance to play Barney Rubble, in a genuine live-action adaptation, produced by no less than Steven Spielberg, whose credit at the front of the movie read "Steven Spielrock." He took it.

Everything about *The Flintstones* was enormous, not least the pressure. As vast prehistoric sets were erected and Jim Henson's Creature Shop built animatronic dinosaurs, a small army of writers tapped away feverishly at the script, pumping out draft after draft, including one based on John Steinbeck's *The Grapes of Wrath*. Director Brian Levant, a *Flintstones* enthusiast with a sizable collection of merchandise from the original show, hired writers from shows such as *Family Ties* and *Happy Days*, calling it "a sitcom on steroids." *City Slickers* writers Lowell Ganz and Babaloo Mandel did two days' work on the script, pocketing $100,000. Even Moranis was invited by to throw in his two cents.

Somehow, all that time and manpower (one estimate has the total at as many as thirty-five writers) resulted in lines such as "Look at him, drunk as a skunk-o-saurus!" relentless Stone Age punning (the Flintstones go to see a movie called *Tar Wars*, directed by "Gorge Lucas"), subplots about embezzlement and extramarital affairs, and a character called Sharon Stone, who was written for the actual Sharon Stone but ultimately played by Halle Berry. On-set, Moranis and John Goodman, as Fred, tried to re-create their 2D equivalents' manic movements, but ended up feeling like madmen, trying to figure out how to channel cartoon cavemen. The production values were phenomenal, but it felt like the natural order had switched around: the sets had become the stars, and the humans on them mere ornamentation.

Audiences lapped up the spectacle and bought into the feverish marketing blitz, for which the atrocious punning continued, turning McDonald's into "RocDonald's." *The Flintstones* made over $340 million worldwide, becoming the fifth biggest film of 1994. For Moranis, though, who had suffered a peroxide dye job for the shoot, it was yet another flimsy showcase of his talents. On paper he had succeeded beyond his wildest dreams, but he still wasn't happy.

"I don't know that it's productive to name them, but toward the end there were experiences that were not good," he says. "I was being well paid, but the fun was gone. It started to feel more like 'business' than 'show.' And there was a period where the fame and power was affecting me negatively."

He made a couple more small appearances in movies, and one last *Honey* sequel called *Honey, We Shrunk Ourselves*. Then, incredibly, Rick Moranis pulled the chute, vanishing completely. After 1997, he would appear only as a voice in the odd animated movie. Retiring to his New York home, a lavish apartment in a prewar co-op building with a view of Central Park, he focused entirely on his family, leaving

Hollywood behind and falling out of touch with his fellow comedy stars and former directors, with the sole exception of Frank Oz. Even Steve Martin, his most frequent co-star, didn't cross paths with him again: "Loved him. I don't know where Rick is. He sort of quit show business."

From Poindexter to prince, Moranis's singular Hollywood career spanned just eleven years.

DAN AYKROYD, CHEVY CHASE, and Bill Murray had all been briefly considered for the role of Fred in *The Flintstones*. They were each deemed too skinny to play the caveman wastrel, however, and their names were crossed out. One person who was more seriously talked about was John Candy. It wasn't to be—Spielberg was determined to cast John Goodman, with whom he'd worked on *Always*—but it would have been an inspired move. Embued with the energy and warm simplicity of a cartoon character, Candy had even sung the *Flintstones* theme tune in *Planes, Trains and Automobiles*.

As the '80s turned into the '90s, Candy's filmography remained patchy. *The Great Outdoors*, in which he co-starred with Aykroyd and a 1,400-pound Kodiak bear named Bart, was a bust, with the two human stars failing to establish an effective comedic dynamic. *Who's Harry Crumb?* was a lousy mystery, with Candy cast as a bumbling PI (tagline: "Nerves of steel. Body of iron. Brain of stone"). The less said about *Cannonball Fever*, a clunky clone of *Cannonball Run*, the better.

Fortunately, there was one filmmaker who did understand how to effectively deploy Candy's man-child charm and butterball physique. For John Hughes, Candy wasn't just a fat guy who looked funny falling over, but a complex clown with deep emotions swirling beneath the surface. The two men were a lot alike: not only had they each married their high-school sweethearts, but they both chain-smoked, stayed up late, and had endless energy. "I remember on *Uncle Buck* they shot something like a million feet of film," says Bob Crane, who ran Candy's production company, Frostbacks. "It was twelve-hour days, easy. I was dying, but they would just keep going and going and going."

Planes, Trains and Automobiles had showcased Candy at his most heartbreaking, but his definitive role was as the title character in 1989's *Uncle Buck*, also written and directed by Hughes. A shambolic, ill-disciplined calamity of a man, the forty-year-old Buck munches cheese, washes socks in a microwave, gambles, and drives around in a smoke-belching Mercury Marquis Brougham. He also has a unique approach to quitting smoking: "I'm onto a five-year plan. I eliminate the cigarettes, then I go to cigars, then I go to pipes, then I go to chewing tobacco, then I'm onto that nicotine gum."

Due to a family tragedy, Buck is summoned, as a last resort, to look after his two nieces and nephew (one of whom has a poster for *¡Three Amigos!* on their bedroom wall). There are many laughs squeezed from his uselessness, but Candy's performance is thoroughly moving too: it's clear that Buck cares, deeply, about both the children and his long-suffering fiancée, but has major fears he is grappling with. From the outside his life looks like a wreck, but the character, like Candy himself, is a bright-eyed optimist, ever ready to deploy an earthy chuckle. The star tweaked the script himself to find the right balance: "There was a harder edge to him initially. We shaved a lot of that off and gave him more of a vulnerability."

Reviews were strong. "Candy once again seems as ferociously creative as he was on the old *SCTV* television series," wrote Dave Kehr in his *Chicago Tribune* review. "*Uncle Buck* is a great, happy mass of urban, ethnic funk." And it hit the number-one spot at the box office, the first solo Candy vehicle to make it that big.

Screenplays poured into Frostbacks, though many failed to transfer from paper to celluloid. *Bartholomew vs. Neff* was a comedy that would have starred Candy and Sylvester Stallone as feuding neighbors, battling over their garden fence. *Our Father*, based on an idea by Candy himself, would have seen him put on robes to play a priest transferred from his cushy West Hollywood parish to inner-city Detroit, a coincidental reversal of *Beverly Hills Cop*. *Haulin' Ashes* was about a pencil-pusher for a big advertising agency who is assigned to spread the ashes of his dead boss, traveling to locations specified in his will.

Out of the films that did get made, there were two that meant a special amount to Candy. One was *JFK*, a formidable challenge: as New Orleans district attorney Dean Andrews, he had eight solid pages of dialogue, facing off against Kevin Costner in a French Quarter restaurant. Candy was so excited about being asked to do a meaty dramatic role in Oliver Stone's film that he said yes without even seeing a script; before filming, he was horrified to see a giant cold sore emerging beneath his mouth. "John was really anxious, because he took that performance so seriously," says Crane, who ran off to buy a variety of medicinal creams for the star. "But he did a fantastic job. I do wonder if he would have gone the Bill Murray route and done some interesting drama pieces. I think he could have done anything."

The second was *Only the Lonely*. It got mixed reviews and only grossed $25 million, but the Chris Columbus drama was special to Candy in that it treated him like a regular person. With no jokes about his weight (his character, a cop, only mentions in passing that he's switching from Danishes to yogurt for breakfast) plus a sweet romantic throughline between him and co-star Ally Sheedy, it's a film that could have been written for Tom Hanks.

"That was a wonderful experience for John," says Dave Thomas. "He felt he was evolving more into the character that he saw himself as and that he wanted to play. Also he was a movie buff and couldn't stop raving about working with Maureen O'Hara."

As for Sheedy, she was thoroughly charmed by her unconventional leading man. Asked if it was harder to do love scenes with the bulky Candy than men like Sean Penn and Matthew Broderick, she shook her head and replied, "John has a way of making you feel like the most beautiful actress he's ever worked with."

VISITORS TO CANDY'S L.A. HOME, which spread over three acres in Brentwood's tranquil Mandeville Canyon, tended to quickly notice an object by the swimming pool. It was hard to miss: a seven-foot-high stone replica of the Statue of Liberty, holding her miniature torch aloft in the direction of the water.

For the star, the sculpture was a tribute to the country that had welcomed him and given him so many opportunities. When he sat poolside, sipping on a rum and Coke, he would reflect on the unlikely rocket ride that had taken him to this sunbaked paradise.

When he was up on his farm with his four horses (named Peaches, Cream, Uncle Buck, and Harry Crumb), he enjoyed the tranquility. But when he was in California he liked to party. Frostbacks HQ, on San Vicente Boulevard, was both a vast office and Candy's personal clubhouse. Drinks were served from behind a seventy-year-old curved mahogany bar he had found in a St. Louis watering hole; visitors could cut loose on a jukebox, pinball machines, or air-hockey table. A veritable Candy Land, it was a souped-up version of the 1063 Avenue Road hangout where the *SCTV* crew had gathered back in the day. "We nicknamed it the Frostbacks Bar & Grill," says Bob Crane. "You'd see everyone there from Oliver Stone to the L.A. Kings hockey team to random agents dropping by on their way home. John liked playing the godfather role—Don Candy."

When he was on the road, filming or promoting a movie, the don brought the party with him. Candy enjoyed devising names for his publicity tours—"Guns N Snakes," "Just the Facts"—and would get hats and T-shirts made up for everyone who traveled with him. "He was a one-person rock 'n' roll band; he had the energy of the entire Guns N' Roses band," Crane says. "We'd constantly be doing fun, crazy things on the road; there was never any boredom." While in Calgary for bobsledding comedy *Cool Runnings*, Candy booked the entire crew on the real Olympics bobsled run. In Jamaica another time, he found the house at Round Hill where Paul McCartney had stayed and threw a massive shindig there.

He looked like the jolliest, most laid-back guy in Tinseltown. When he wasn't kicking back, he used his celebrity for good, promoting charities and on one occasion ensuring that a skeletal-looking scleroderma sufferer was positioned so close to him during a paired TV interview that she couldn't be edited out. But as with Rick Moranis, not everything was as idyllic as it seemed from afar.

For one thing, Candy was still not addressing his health issues, continuing to smoke copiously and feast on pizza and hot dogs. Anyone who brought up the subject of dieting was quietly banished from his inner circle, until nobody dared mention it.

Then there were his series of poor investments and unwise loans. His beloved Toronto Argonauts, the football team he co-owned, was sold without him knowing, causing him to go on a two-day tequila binge. Other people borrowed money and never paid him back. "John was so gregarious and generous that people took advantage of him all the time," says Dave Thomas. "It was only late in the evening, around midnight, when he switched from rum and Coke to Courvoisier or Remy, that his personality would change and he'd get a lot darker. Under the magical key of Remy or Courvoisier the door would open, and you'd get a glimpse of how John really felt about the people taking advantage of him."

Only once did Bob Crane witness Candy lose his cool in public: it was at a Chicago nightclub where Dan Aykroyd and John Belushi had frequently hung out while shooting *The Blues Brothers*. After taking photos with fans, signing autographs, and dispensing hugs on the street outside, he started heading into the club. Then a drunk guy yelled, *"John Candy sucks!"*

Candy froze. He'd been heckled before, onstage and on the street, but for some reason this one got to him. He marched over to the man, grabbed him by the throat, and lifted him up off the ground, pinning him against a brick wall.

"That was the most furious I ever saw John during the thirteen years I knew him," Crane says. "It was literally like a cartoon, with the guy's feet dangling above the pavement. That's how strong John was. You know, John's thing was to make everybody feel good and have a laugh. So when he heard that, I guess it went against his whole being, his whole philosophy, and he couldn't believe it."

Despite the setbacks, the betrayals, and the anxiety attacks that started when he hit forty, the future looked bright for Candy. He made lists in his head of filmmakers he wanted to work with, serious dramatic sorts such as Martin Scorsese and Francis Ford Coppola. On a private jet heading back to Los Angeles from the set of *JFK*, he and Gary Oldman had cooked up a plan to put on live Shakespeare in the park: Oldman would play Macbeth, Candy would be Falstaff. His career had been sagging in the early '90s, but 1993's *Cool Runnings* was a comeback hit, getting him back into the $4-million-a-picture bracket. He was even considering directing.

Then, on March 4, 1994, the unthinkable happened. In a hotel just outside Durango, Mexico, where Candy had just finished filming the comedy *Wagons East*, the star went to sleep and never woke up. He'd had a massive heart attack, the one he'd feared all of his life. Weighing in at 330 pounds, he was aged just forty-three.

The reaction, from Hollywood and the world, was tumultuous. Unlike Belushi, whose demise was easy to see coming, the beloved Candy had been full of life to the last. "I thought, despite being overweight and the drinking and the smoking, this guy is probably going to outlast everyone, just because he's a bull," says Crane. "So when I got the phone call from his driver, Frankie Hernandez, down in Mexico, I could not believe it. I mean, I had no reason to not believe he would live to be seventy-five or eighty, and still doing voices for cartoons. This guy was just going to go forever."

The funeral was held at St. Martin's of Tours, on Sunset Boulevard. Among the mourners were Bill Murray, Chevy Chase, Tom Hanks, Rita Wilson, Jeff Bridges, Ed Harris, and Martin Short. Dan Aykroyd, the comedian who had considered becoming a priest, stood up in the pulpit and delivered a brilliantly written, energetically delivered ten-minute eulogy, incorporating the lyrics of the Canadian national anthem, making attendees laugh and cry. Then, as paparazzi snapped photos, the funeral procession headed on its nine-mile journey to the cemetery in Culver City.

Amazingly, their route on the 405 freeway was entirely clear. "It was entirely shut down. At noon. On a Wednesday," Crane marvels. "That is unheard-of. People said to me, 'This only happens when the president is going through.' We all started looking around us, and then we spotted Highway Patrol on the on-ramps, holding back traffic. It had nothing to do with Rose, John's wife, or the cemetery or anything. It was just a thank-you from them to John for being a regular guy and helping them out a few times."

Candy's friends were left bereft, swapping their favorite stories of the star who lived large in every sense. Aykroyd and Thomas had one warm memory in particular, of the time Candy had flown them and Jim Belushi to Toronto to see the Argonauts play at Dome Stadium. Before the game, in front of a crowd of fifty thousand people, Candy had walked onto the field, eliciting a deafening roar of approval. Back in his private box, Aykroyd had turned to the others with a huge grin.

"He did it," he said. "He's Johnny Toronto."

17

GETTING SERIOUS

SITTING IN HIS West Hollywood home in the early 1990s, Steve Martin saw two things on his TV that elicited a strong reaction. The first was news footage of American troops on the front lines in Saudi Arabia. Martin was suddenly struck by a sense of guilt: here he was on his plush furniture, rich and at ease, while fellow countrymen were risking their lives. So he and his wife, Victoria Tennant, decided to make a personal visit, in the style of World War II entertainer Bob Hope.

Arriving at Camp Midway in the Gulf aboard a UH-60 Black Hawk helicopter, clad in camo fatigues, Martin greeted five hundred troops sitting on a sand dune, then climbed aboard a tank and wise-cracked, "We're going to put a condo here." The soldiers cheered. One of them asked him to sign a "Steve Martin for President" poster. Only a single moment darkened the tour, when Tennant removed her fatigue jacket in a car and got screamed at by a Saudi guard, furious she was revealing her arms.

The second thing he saw on his TV was a film: Tony Scott's action thriller *The Last Boy Scout*. Martin had got hold of it on LaserDisc, but when he put it on was appalled by its coarse laughs and violent shocks. "It's very ugly," he told *Playboy*. "It's about a family falling apart. The wife is having an affair and the husband is a detective who's always at work. The daughter is just plain repellent. Her language is horrible."

It certainly wasn't the type of movie Martin wanted anything to do with. Instead, in his mid-forties, he was now looking for projects with depth and meaning, whether it was encouraging servicemen in the Middle East or making a film that resounded with him personally. He wasn't trying to shake his image as a funnyman: an autograph card he handed out to fans during this period, as a way to avoid awkward protracted encounters, read, "This certifies that you have had a personal encounter with me and that you found me warm, polite, intelligent and funny." But after *Roxanne* his mission was to play *real* characters, not exaggerated, silly ones. The big nose and Amigo hat had been put into cold storage.

The first of these characters, Gil Buckman, was the hero of *Parenthood*, a 1989 ensemble piece whose sprawling cast included Rick Moranis, Keanu Reeves, and Mary Steenburgen. Off-screen, Martin still had no children, a subject that was off-limits in interviews but which he would occasionally discuss with his closest friends. "Victoria wanted children. He was afraid to have children," Carl Reiner says. "I once said, 'Why?' He said, 'Well, I know how I am about art. And I know if I have a kid I'll become so focused on them I'll give it up.' He was frightened of losing that intense interest in art."

On-screen, however, Martin slipped effortlessly into the role of a doting dad. *Parenthood* delved deep into the issues that arise between parents and kids, with Martin playing a highly strung businessman who is terrified he'll mess up his children. "Well, great!" he tells his wife when she reveals she's pregnant for the fourth time. "Let's see how I can screw the fourth one up! Hey, let's have fun—let's have six. Let's have a dozen and pretend they're doughnuts!"

It was not only one of the most emotionally complex roles Martin had taken on—in scenes like the above, the neurotic Gil is downright unlikeable—but one with real resonance for him. Just as Gil struggles with his relationship with his own father, a remote figure played by Jason Robards, Martin had never managed to strike up a rapport with his dad, Glenn. After emerging from a screening of *The Jerk* back in the late '70s, somebody had asked Glenn Martin what he thought of his son's performance. "Well, he's no Charlie Chaplin," he had replied.

"The number of funny or caring words that had passed between my father and me was few," Martin wrote in his 2007 memoir. "He had evidently saved his vibrant personality for use outside the family." A thick undercurrent of sadness runs through his scenes with Robards.

But there's hilarity in *Parenthood* too. The movie's most famous scene—other than the moment in which Gil's sister (Dianne Wiest) accidentally brandishes a vibrator in a black-out, thinking it's a flashlight—sees Gil transform himself into "Cowboy Gil" to save his son's birthday party, since the real entertainer, Cowboy Dan, has failed to show up. Employing many of the old tricks he learned as a child working in Frontierland, Martin does thumb tricks, yodels, even rides a horse. "After I blow a hole in somebody and slip around on their guts," he tells the awestruck children, "I always like to make balloon animals." The misshapen balloon monstrosity he presents one kid with is, he quickly ad-libs, "Your lower intestines."

Parenthood was a hit, a massive one. In fact, it was Martin's biggest commercial success since *The Jerk*. "What I liked about the movie was that it presented the incredible virtues of the average man," he said. "It takes a tremendous effort to raise children and figure out what's right. It's so common to everyone, but no one realizes how magnificent it truly is." He would go on to play another fretful dad in a *Father of the Bride* remake, alongside a supremely hammy Martin Short. But it also launched an era of grand experimentation, as Martin, emboldened, played a succession of men with complex psychologies.

In *My Blue Heaven*, he played a dark-haired mob boss named Vincent. In *Grand Canyon*, he played a movie producer who specialized in violent action flicks, just like *The Last Boy Scout*. *Leap of Faith* saw him tackle a purely dramatic lead role for the first time since *Pennies from Heaven*, as a huckster evangelist named Jonas Nightengale. Prancing around a stage in a glittering suit, backed by a gospel choir as he bawls, "The more you give, the more you live!" to an audience of dupes, it was the closest he'd come to reliving his heady stand-up days. The film bombed, but it showed what Martin could do: bringing to life a sad, seedy man as compelling as his clowns.

WITHOUT DOUBT, though, of all the Steve Martin movies of the 1990s, the *most* Steve Martin movie was *L.A. Story*. It was his second solo screenplay, following *Roxanne*; like that one it fused highbrow with lowbrow, and as with that one Martin churned through draft after draft, spending seven years trying to get it just right. But this was a weirder, more abstract proposition, without the easy laughs afforded by a protagonist with a giant nose.

It was also an acutely personal project for the star. Harris K. Telemacher, the hero, is a weatherman famous for his wacky shtick, who off-screen is a quiet, serious, often morose fellow. His love interest, a British newspaper reporter named Sara on assignment in Los Angeles, was to be played by Martin's wife, Victoria. And all of the star's passions—for paintings, art-house cinema, philosophy, stupid jokes—are layered in. There's even a sequence set in the L.A. County Museum of Art, as Harris roller-skates past priceless murals that Martin no doubt coveted for his collection.

Others, setting a comedy in L.A., would have gone for cheap laughs, lampooning the city's lack of culture. But while Martin came up with inspired moments of satire—a waiter offers "diet or regular" dental floss; a gun battle kicks off on a freeway; a beverage order is for "a half-double decaffeinated half-caf, with a twist of lemon"—*L.A. Story* is actually a paean to the place's peculiar appeal. "Whenever I'd visited before I thought it was vulgar, shallow, showy," says Mick Jackson, the Englishman Martin picked to direct the film. "But when I met Steve to discuss the film we ended up driving around L.A. at night in his car. He put on these CDs of French songs from the 1930s and '40s, and showed me areas that he had fallen in love with."

They drove to a place near Century City called Boystown, a gay community where everyone had turned their house into the place of their dreams, whether it be a Gothic castle or a thatched medieval cottage. They checked out a big marble building on Melrose and La Cienega, striped with white, black, and red marble in a style that Martin described as "Iranian urinal." And they took in unusual views of the city, spots where the star liked to sit and think. "I saw the mood of the movie immediately," Jackson says. "Which is a kind of sun-filled easefulness and insouciance. L.A. as a magical entity. The whole thing is like *A Midsummer Night's Dream*, with two crazy, mixed-up couples and magic happening in the forest that is L.A. I guess that makes the talking freeway sign Puck."

Shakespeare gets a nod in the movie, in the form of a headstone for the Bard inexplicably located in a Hollywood cemetery. But that's just the start of its references. The opening, with the camera tilting up from a swimming pool to find a helicopter, is a riff on the opening of Federico Fellini's *La Dolce Vita*, although in that the chopper is carrying a statue of Christ rather than a large inflatable hot dog. The pair of stone lions that nod at Harris and Sara at one point are a surreal homage to Jean Cocteau's *La belle et la bête*. Then there are tips of the hat to Eisenstein, Tarkovsky, Botticelli, Hockney, and countless others. Rather than focusing on the laughs, the game plan was to make the film look like a French Impressionist painting. Cinematographer Andrew Dunn even had silk Dior stockings flown in from Paris and draped over the camera lenses, to give the images a soft, sun-dappled quality.

It was Martin the aesthetician, unfettered. One day, Dan Melnick, Martin's regular producer, lost his nerve watching a scene being shot in which the star walked through a poorly lit area in the TV studio set. "I should tell you this—we don't do dark scenes like that in comedies," he told Jackson. "It should all be brightly lit." Martin overheard, came up to the director, and said, "Shoot it the way you want to shoot it. Be brave."

Jackson, who had never made a comedy before and in the nuclear-annihilation drama *Threads* had made one of the least funny movies ever, was blown away by what his star was capable of. "I think only he could have carried this off," he says. "I don't know of any other actor who could have done the pathos, the really awful one-liners and puns, the slapstick pratfalls that even Chaplin would admire, the range of references to art and cinema and music. It's a tour de force, I think, for one guy."

For the art-gallery scene, Martin taught himself how to roller-skate from scratch, donning protective knee pads outside his Beverly Hills house and falling over again and again until he could do it perfectly. At LACMA, where he had secured permission to shoot largely by dint of the fact that he was a trustee, the gallery administration stood watching, practically wetting themselves, as a movie star zipped by priceless marble busts and paintings, as surreal a sight as any of their Salvador Dalís. If Martin was nervous, he didn't show any signs of it.

But when the time came to actually show people their unusual concoction, which Martin sometimes described as "*Manhattan* West," referencing Woody Allen's love letter to New York, Martin finally started sweating bullets. "There's an extra chill that sets in every time the movie starts to screen," he said. "Maybe because I don't want to go down in flaming disgrace. Writing is so blind, and there's no precedent for something like this." He turned up to test screenings in a bizarre disguise—thick pebble glasses, a long red pageboy wig, and a French beret—so as not to distract the audience. "I can't think of anything more guaranteed to attract attention at the back of the theater," says Jackson. "But he didn't want them to know he was there."

If the beret was unnecessary, so were his jitters. At a preview for his comedian friends, guests including Mike Nichols, Neil Simon, Buck Henry, and Martin Short were ecstatic in their responses. Carl Reiner couldn't stop saying, "It's a piece of art. It's a piece of art. It's a goddamn piece of art!" The movie also won over Roger Ebert, Martin's longtime critical nemesis, who had written in 1984 that seeing Martin on-screen made him feel like someone was raking their fingernails down a chalkboard. In recent years Ebert had a damascene conversion. "The lack of subtlety in early films like *The Jerk* has now been replaced by a smoothness and unforced intelligence," he wrote. Although Martin had canceled his subscriptions to *Variety* and the *Hollywood Reporter*, sick of seeing movies reduced to box-office numbers, he would have been pleased to find *L.A. Story* grossing $28 million, not bad at all for a movie with a homage to the Peter Brooks art-house film *Marat/Sade*.

The movie would, however, prove difficult for him to revisit over the coming years. In 1994, Victoria Tennant asked for a divorce, a shock that came out of the blue for Martin—a year earlier, he had told a *Playboy* reporter, "We're a couple forever." Tennant would go on to marry entertainment lawyer Kirk Stambler two years later. As for Martin, the separation plunged the forty-seven-year-old into a bout of fearful soul-searching. "I was very screwed up at the time," he said later. "It was a bad time for me." Having written a wry, funny, critically acclaimed play called *Picasso at the Lapin Agile*, he considered giving up movies and becoming a playwright full-time. Haunted by images of being old and alone, he started to see a therapist and read self-help books with titles such as *How to Survive the Loss of a Love*, *Care of the Soul*, and *The Drama of the Gifted Child*.

He also bought a dog, a yellow Labrador retriever called Roger. With his new constant companion by his side, he would go for long walks, slowly getting back to his old self, thinking about life, love, the next great joke.

For Roger, Steve always had a treat. For everyone else, he had an autograph card.

EDDIE MURPHY also saw a movie in the early '90s. But unlike Steve Martin and *The Last Boy Scout*, he loved it. The movie was *Boyz n the Hood*, and Murphy sat through its packed premiere at the Cannes Film Festival in May 1991, wearing an electric-blue suit and leading the cheers as John Singleton's edgy urban masterpiece received a twenty-minute standing ovation. Movie stars tend to attend film festivals only if they have something in competition. But Murphy had decided to visit the South of France purely to lend support to black American filmmakers. As well as *Boyz n the Hood*, a searing coming-of-age story set in a neighborhood troubled by drugs and guns, he hung out with Spike Lee, who was there with the interracial romance *Jungle Fever*, and checked out Bill Duke's *Rage in Harlem*, starring Forrest Whitaker and Robin Givens.

Murphy's sojourn to Europe was no isolated event. It was emblematic of his new career strategy: he not only wanted to watch edgy, groundbreaking films but to make them too. It's telling that when he had his handprints put in cement on Hollywood Boulevard in 1987, he scrawled the words "Be Free" into the cement. Like Martin, he wanted to stretch his screen image in interesting new ways, to mix things up, to stop running around with a gun and a smirk for a while.

Unlike Martin, however, he had a major film studio heavily invested in him, and Paramount was not so keen for their prize star to change the formula. "Eddie Murphy is our Kellogg's Corn Flakes," declared Frank Mancuso, the studio's chairman in June 1989. Now Murphy had decided he wanted to try being a different brand of cereal altogether. Paramount executives prayed he wasn't about to turn himself into All-Bran.

The first experiment did not bode well. 1990's *Harlem Nights* was a gangland drama set in the late 1930s, with Murphy headlining opposite his idol, Richard Pryor. The pair-up got comedy fans salivating, but it turned out to be a disappointingly muted affair, with Murphy's nightclub owner Quick delivering few memorable lines, and Pryor turning in a performance so low-energy it barely registered. Part of the problem was that Murphy had decided to not only star but write and direct the project too. His script relied heavily on not particularly creative cursing, while the production felt light on texture, perhaps because production designer Lawrence G. Paull, who had had nine months to prep *Blade Runner*, was charged with whipping up sets for *Harlem Nights* in seven weeks. Paramount suits, who hadn't wanted Murphy to do the picture in the first place, grumbled behind the scenes about some of the story's edgier moments, as when Quick shot off an old woman's pinkie toe, or killed another woman before she could dispatch him.

It made money, but also provoked a critical backlash more punish-

ing than any Murphy had experienced before. He was nominated for a
Razzie Award for Worst Director, and won one for Worst Screenplay.
He'd bitten off far more than he could chew, and having invested
himself so personally in the project, he was particularly wounded by
the drubbing. "*Harlem Nights* was the first time I did a movie that
flopped," he said. "It didn't flop on a monetary level, but it was like,
'Ugh, did you see that piece of shit?' And I had never gone through
that."

He would never direct again. And his reaction to the *Harlem Nights*
fiasco was to retreat—despite having bought the film rights to the
award-winning Broadway play *Fences*, he instead signed up for the
48 Hrs. sequel that Paramount had been pressuring him, Nick Nolte,
and director Walter Hill to do for years. The result, *Another 48 Hrs.*,
pleased few. "It was a nice payday, but a mistake," said Nolte afterward.
"The whole thing was out of fear," admitted Murphy. And Hill, who
had privately joked that there had already been a sequel to *48 Hrs.*—
Beverly Hills Cop—says now that they knew going in it wasn't going to
match the original. "I don't think we got the script right," Hill says. "I
thought we did it just a little bit too much the same. But suddenly we
had [release] dates and we couldn't seem to wiggle through." While
Another 48 Hrs. hewed close to the beats of its predecessor, even finding Murphy's character in prison again, and once again singing the
Police's "Roxanne," the zesty interplay between his con and Nolte's cop
had gone flat.

A decade after his debut in the original *48 Hrs.*, things were looking pretty grim. The man once dubbed "Mr. Box Office" by *Newsweek*
had taken to wearing a charm bracelet on his wrist, complementing
his gold cross necklace and St. Christopher medal, but it wasn't doing
an effective job of warding off bad luck. "I was fucked up. I was really
trippin'," he told *Premiere* in 1992 of a glum period he'd recently gone
through. "I was depressed about my work . . . I wasn't getting along
with my family, and I wasn't getting along with my daughter's mother
[model Nicole Mitchell, the mother of his child Bria and his wife from
1993], and I couldn't find a movie."

On a trip to Half Moon Bay in Jamaica to celebrate his thirtieth birthday, Murphy meditated. The friends and relatives around him were surprised to find him staying still for a change, sitting on the beach rather than running around clubs and chasing girls. Even more surprising was the moment where he broke his teetotal rule again and downed a fruit punch. Unlike the occasion years earlier when he'd downed vodka because of his *Coming to America* woes, there was a new sparkle in his eye, and when he returned to America he arranged a meeting with producer Brian Grazer.

"I want to go back to being funny again," Murphy told him.

The decision he'd made was to go in a softer, more female-friendly direction. Off-screen, he had acquired a reputation as somebody who struggled to deal with women as equals, something that had begun because of his comments onstage and in interviews, and intensified when a $75 million lawsuit was filed against him by a twenty-two-year-old actress on *Harlem Nights*, Michael Michele Williams, who alleged that he had tried to make moves on her on-set, then fired her when she declined. (The suit ended up being dropped.) Now Murphy decided to tone down the profanity, stop surrounding himself in movies with tough men, and make a movie about love.

That movie was *Boomerang*, a story about a slick lothario who falls for his boss and gets a taste of his own medicine. Given his womanizing in his private life, it was fairly remarkable that Murphy's romantic liaisons on-screen had been so chaste. The star had fought for his character in *The Golden Child* to have a sex scene with his love interest, having heard that Paramount was opposed to it and suspecting the reasons for that were racial. Based on an idea by Murphy and written by two old *SNL* collaborators, Barry Blaustein and David Sheffield, *Boomerang* was an opportunity to finally play a man with seduction techniques as deft as his own—while giving the primary female character, played by Murphy's old girlfriend Robin Givens, considerable power. Moreover, it was a chance to do a screwball comedy with a predominantly black cast.

"It's a movie about how a dog becomes a man," said director Reginald Hudlin. "It's personal for Eddie in the same way that *Annie Hall* was for Woody Allen."

Some bad press was generated by Murphy's habit of arriving massively late to the *Boomerang* set, due largely to overrunning recording sessions for his new album, *Love's All Right* (guest vocalists for which included Michael Jackson, Elton John, Paul McCartney, MC Hammer, and Jon Bon Jovi). But the higher-ups claimed that when he did arrive, he was livelier than he'd been on a soundstage for several years. "Eddie might show up two hours late, but he contributes to rewriting the script and does brilliant things," insisted Brian Grazer.

Surrounded by comic talents (Martin Lawrence, Chris Rock, Geoffrey Holder) and pop-culture icons (Grace Jones, Eartha Kitt), Murphy was back in form, slimmed down to 170 pounds, and engaged with the material. He even got a kick out of the audience reaction to a scene where Halle Berry slaps his horn-dog marketing executive, Marcus Graham, saying, "The audience cheers like, '*Somebody* finally slapped him for all those years. . . .'" But in the end *Boomerang* only made $70 million domestically, getting trounced by comedic competition such as *Home Alone 2: Lost in New York*, *Sister Act*, and *Wayne's World*. Murphy's first non-Paramount film, *The Distinguished Gentleman*, a political satire that he took to Disney, didn't light up the box office either.

Other stars might have shrugged off the declining receipts, but for a man with the nickname "Money" it was truly a crisis point. It was time to break glass in case of emergency. So Eddie Murphy collected himself, then summoned the last person in the world anyone could have expected.

JOHN LANDIS HADN'T SEEN, or spoken to, Eddie Murphy since the *Coming to America* premiere. He had, however, seen Murphy's snipes about him in the press, such as his claim to *Rolling Stone* that "I was going out of my way to help this guy, and he fucked me over." So when he received a call from Paramount chief Sherry Lansing one day in 1993, explaining that a second sequel to *Beverly Hills Cop* had been green-lit and asking if he wanted to direct, he wondered for a moment if he was being pranked.

"Do you want to do it?" asked Lansing.

"Who's playing Eddie Murphy?" Landis replied, incredulous.

It turned out that the only thing that could eradicate memories of a testicle-grabbing, throat-choking fight between a Hollywood star and a Hollywood director was the prospect of a golden payday. For a long time, *Beverly Hills Cop III* had looked impossible, with Murphy saying in 1989, "There's no reason to do it. I don't need the money and it's not gonna break any new ground. How often can you have Axel Foley talk fast and get into a place he doesn't belong?" He had followed that up with a statement that was candid, even for him. "In fact, if I do a *Cop III*, you can safely say, 'Ooh, he must have got a *lot* of money.' Because we're *whores*." That turned out to be an accurate prediction: Murphy's wages for the threequel would amount to $15 million, more than double his usual $6 million Paramount fee. The studio was confident it was a safe investment for bringing back Axel for one more spin.

Beyond the title and the star, however, they didn't have much. Writer after writer had had a crack at creating an exciting premise. One early draft saw Foley head to London to rescue his superior, Captain Bogomil, when the latter gets captured by terrorists. Robert Towne, of *Chinatown* acclaim, proposed a team-up between Murphy and Sean Connery, who would play a Scotland Yard detective. Both were scrapped. Finally, Murphy decided to bring in some bigger guns, people who had been part of his earlier successes.

His first suggestion, that they should lure back *Beverly Hills Cop* director Martin Brest, didn't pan out. But he did manage to entice aboard the writer and producer of *48 Hrs.*, Steven E. de Souza and Joel Silver. Though only one of them would end up staying the course.

"Joel and I visited Eddie's house, where he was cutting an album," explains de Souza. "We were waiting five minutes . . . ten minutes . . . twenty minutes. . . . At twenty-five minutes Joel jumps up and goes, 'I'm tired of this shit! I made this kid a movie star. I'm not going to sit here and be treated like an asshole!' As he's ranting, I realize that Eddie's wife has come out to give the baby to a nanny, and she's hearing the whole thing. After another twenty minutes, we're told, 'He's very busy with his album. He'll see you tomorrow on the studio lot.' So anyway, within a week Joel was gone. He said he was gone because they slashed the budget, which they did. But this may have had something to do with it."

By this point a story had been settled on: Foley would take his young niece to Disneyland, where he would stumble on a criminal conspiracy and shoot a lot of people. But despite this ambitious premise and the huge amount of cash going to Murphy, the project was allotted around $55 million for production costs, no small amount for a comedy but not nearly as much as its summer action-movie competitors (*True Lies* came in at over $100 million, *Clear and Present Danger* at $62 million).

De Souza maintains that at one point it was set to be a lot higher: "Eddie had several movies fail in a row, so the studio kept cutting the budget." And that wasn't the only way in which Murphy's flops affected *Beverly Hills Cop III*. "*The Distinguished Gentleman* was about a little girl who got leukemia from a cell-phone tower, which was one of those urban myths," recalls de Souza. "The movie tanks, probably because there are bald children in it. So [Paramount] say to me, 'You've got to take the kid out of the movie.' So now he was dating a girl who works at Disneyland. Then he had a second movie fail, called *Boomerang*, a romantic comedy. And they said, 'Take out the romance.' So the script kept getting altered to avoid any resemblance to the previous movies that had failed."

By the time Landis came on, the hotly anticipated return of Axel Foley was looking like a hot mess. "The picture was in trouble," the director says. "It was a bad script and they wanted to go right away." One of his concerns was that the screenplay was toothless: after two edgy, expletive-packed outings, Axel was going PG-13, a decision agreed on by the studio (who saw bigger profit margins) and Murphy (who saw it as being in line with his new, gentler image). So the savage satire cooked up by de Souza—"We wanted to tear Disneyland a new asshole"—was toned down considerably. The setting became a generic theme park called Wonder World, and the climax of the movie, which originally saw Foley being chased by villains into an animatronic Old South, full of racial stereotypes for him to inflict damage on, was turned into a lame shootout in an Ice Age–themed ride.

Landis's second, and even more significant, concern was that Murphy no longer seemed to want to be funny. A fact that, as cameras rolled on an expensive summer comedy, boded ill.

"Literally the first week, I went, 'Oh fuck,'" says Landis. "Because I gave him a gag to do and he said, 'I don't want to do that. I'd be a wiseass.' I said, 'Excuse me, Axel Foley is a wiseass.' He went, 'Yeah, yeah, he was, but he's a man now.' My theory is that at that moment in time, there were a lot of big action films with Wesley Snipes and Denzel Washington and Samuel L. Jackson. And he wanted to be an action hero too. He was totally professional—he just didn't want to be funny. If you look at that movie, there are setups and he literally steps around them. It was disheartening."

De Souza recalls a memo sent by one of Murphy's brothers to Paramount, explicitly asking them to start removing jokes from the screenplay. "Eddie decided he wanted to be a serious actor on that movie, in the middle of it," the writer confirms. For Paramount, it was a waking nightmare: *Beverly Hills Cop III*, the movie that should have been a golden goose, was being torpedoed from within. The budget ended up spiraling north of $70 million; it made just $119 million, far less than *Another 48 Hrs.* had mustered. And critics were quick to identify the lack of laughs as the problem. "Eddie Murphy needs to shoot off his mouth," wrote Richard Schickel in *Time*. "It's his best weapon, and the one that's unique to his arsenal. When a movie mostly requires him to shoot off a gun he becomes just another action star, and another talent wasted in lazily miscalculated material."

It was an ignominious swansong for Murphy's signature character, who, a decade earlier, had even run rings around the Ghostbusters. But it wasn't enough to force a course correction for the star, as the writers for his next project (his final one for Paramount under the terms of his contract) found out. During the first meeting for *Vampire in Brooklyn*,

Chris Parker and Michael Lucker were told, "We want this movie to be funny. Eddie Murphy does not want this movie to be funny. It's your job to trick him into being funny."

The two twentysomethings took in the information, looked at each other, and gulped.

TIME OUT

AS THE 1990S began, Dan Aykroyd found himself a haunted man. Quite literally. The 4,828-square-foot Hollywood Hills home he and Donna Dixon had bought at the start of their married life was protected by formidable security gates, but it turned out that there was no way to stop ghosts getting in. According to Aykroyd, two spirits plagued the couple: a man who had died in the house decades before and Mama Cass, the legendary singer from the folk-rock group the Mamas and the Papas, who had passed away in London in 1974 but apparently found her way home.

The poltergeists were as mischievous as Slimer: they particularly liked to turn on the Stairmaster in Aykroyd's gym and slide Dixon's jewelry across her dresser. And when the *Ghostbusters* star was in bed alone, both of them enjoyed getting in there with him. As he recalled of one of these nocturnal visits, "I felt the mattress behind me depress, like something was sitting on it. I thought, 'Well, this is not the cat, it's not the dog, the kids aren't home, my wife's not here. This has to be the guy who died in the house in the '60s.' Not meaning to discriminate,

I just wiggled right up next to him and it was a rump-to-rump sleep for the night." Dixon sighed every time he told the story, aware of how much harder it was going to make it for them to sell the mansion down the line.

Weird things had always happened to Aykroyd, not that he minded one bit. Long ago, back in the small hours of an evening in 1977 when he was still on *Saturday Night Live*, he had been driving through upstate New York when he got pulled over by a state trooper for speeding. Instead of issuing him a ticket, the officer ordered the star to join him on a journey, driving through eight miles of thick forest and ending up at a huge, run-down old house. "I was taken to see a judge at three in the morning," Aykroyd says. "And she had a big old spooky fucking room with a desk, and she liked me."

She liked him so much, in fact, that after fining him $50, the unhinged justice of the peace forced him to stay for tea and a chat. "She kept me there for a couple of hours talking, and I thought, 'Fuck, man, I could be dropped through the floor and I'd never be seen again,'" says Aykroyd, shivering. "I had nightmares about it."

Lying in his bed more than a decade on, Mama Cass floating around somewhere nearby, he remembered the incident, and began to believe that it could be the beginnings of a film. After all, his biggest success had been inspired by the peculiar things he had heard and seen as a kid—"I wrote *Ghostbusters*," he liked to say, "because I grew up with it." This was right in his whacked-out wheelhouse, and after telling the tale of the creepy judge to his brother Peter, the two Aykroyds started turning it into a screenplay.

His own personal nightmare, it turned out, would become a nightmare experience for many others.

The *Valkenvania* script commences with a businessman meeting an attractive female lawyer at a party in his Manhattan penthouse. The two hit it off and embark on a road trip to Atlantic City, but after taking a detour off the New Jersey Turnpike, they end up in a bizarre place called Valkenvania. There, a 106-year-old judge puts them on trial and, yes, drops them through the floor, into a prison cell that's also a terrifying theme park, run by goblinlike creatures and featuring a deadly roller coaster called Mr. Bonestripper.

Replete with deranged characters, ghoulish jokes, and an outlandish role for Aykroyd as the decrepit judge, it made him chuckle as he and his sibling fleshed out the scenario. In fact, so excited was he that he rang up Chevy Chase, asking if he'd play the businessman, a slick customer who becomes increasingly bedraggled as he's subjected to Valkenvanian torments. Chase agreed, without seeing the script. John Candy, willing to do any favor for his old buddy, also confirmed he would play the two roles Aykroyd had in mind—the town's chief of police and the judge's grotesque granddaughter—if the money came together.

It was an odd project, to say the least. But after hawking the script around town to no avail, Aykroyd found a curious party in Warner Bros., who had worked with him before on *Spies Like Us* and *Caddyshack II*. There on the Burbank lot, during a meeting to discuss potential casting, a fatal die was cast. "OK, who's going to direct?" a Warner executive asked.

Aykroyd, brimming over with enthusiasm and desperate to get the project rolling before it could be killed, blurted out, "I'll do it!"

He had never been behind a camera before, had never particularly wanted to be behind one. He also knew that *Valkenvania* would require a mastery of tone and flair for effects. But his instincts told him that the offer was the quickest way to get the thing green-lit. The Warner Bros. suits huddled, held a brief conference, then agreed. After all, this *was* the guy behind *Ghostbusters*. He'd even recently been nominated for an Oscar for his performance in *Driving Miss Daisy*. What was the worst that could happen?

Aykroyd's palms started to sweat. In fact, he was perspiring all over. "I was as complete a wreck as a person could be," he revealed a year on. "I was disturbed and worried right up until the first day of shooting. But it was on that day I realized, 'How lucky can a first-time director get?'" He had huge stars in Chase, Candy, and Demi Moore, who had been lured on to play the sexy lawyer. He had veteran

Hollywood craftsmen, including special-effects technician Michael Lantieri and cinematographer Dean Cundey, guys who usually worked on Steven Spielberg's and Robert Zemeckis's crews. And he had the kind of budget that only the guy behind *Ghostbusters* would be given for his directorial debut.

"I have never, ever felt any tension over what the studios have to pay to make the artistic vision come to reality," he says. "I thank them, I'm grateful for it, but I feel no tension. And in fact I joyously spent $80 million of Warner Bros. money on the movie I directed."

But if he was joyous, others were feeling less positive after reading the finished script. According to Chevy Chase's authorized biography, "Chevy knew it was going to be the worst film he would ever make. He got himself into a jam by agreeing to star in it before Dan Aykroyd had written enough of it to confirm Chevy's worst fears." Moore, who had just starred in the more conventional tale of the unexpected, *Ghost*, turned up bemused by what she'd gotten herself into, a state of mind that didn't change. Because as soon as the cameras started to roll, *Valkenvania* made like Mr. Bonestripper and flew off the rails.

"Let me preface this by saying I am a Dan Aykroyd fan," says Bob Crane, who arrived with John Candy and witnessed much of the shoot. "I loved him since the original *Saturday Night Live* run. I thought he was brilliant. But this movie in a word: disaster. It was pure excess. A huge production for Dan to bite off as his first directorial effort. The premise just got too far-out, the egos were rampant, and they were given too much money. They were in way over their heads."

Aykroyd's goliath, maniac scripts had in the past been tamed by the likes of John Landis and Ivan Reitman. But there was nobody here with the clout to suggest the judge's prosthetic nose look just a little less like a human penis, or to ask if it was really necessary to have two disgusting-looking, troll-like creatures torment Moore, or to inquire about the incongruous cameo from rapper Tupac. No matter how distressing or inexplicable, it all made the cut. And exacerbating things was the situation on-set.

Instead of Aykroyd alone calling the shots, each actor had been given their own video monitor, so they could play back takes and give comments. Sometimes Chase had a note, other times Candy or Moore. With everyone focused on their own performance, or hair, it resulted in a Kubrickian number of takes and the production rapidly falling behind schedule. When two veteran directors, John Hughes and Tom Mankiewicz, visited the set, they were shocked at the sight. "You've got to get rid of these monitors," each of them whispered to Aykroyd. "You can't have a committee voting on each take."

Adding to the delays was the fact that Aykroyd mostly gave orders from beneath grotesque and time-consuming David Miller makeup, either as the judge or one of those troll-like creatures, the "Infant Bodies," who resemble giant babies dipped in radioactive waste. Moore and her beau, Bruce Willis, who visited the set more than once, surely made a few concerned calls to their agents.

As for Chase, he had his own way of giving feedback on the process. "I was standing onstage one day with a bunch of other people, waiting for the cast to walk in for rehearsal," says Crane. "And Chevy walked in and just blasted a fart, which echoed off the walls of the soundstage. I guess it was just his looseness, no pun intended, and probably his dissatisfaction with what was going on at the time. He just didn't give a damn. So I thought, 'OK, that's his comment, I guess, on what's happening.'"

AS *VALKENVANIA* FELL a week behind schedule, the movie's title changed to *Nothing But Trouble*. The obvious jokes were made. *The Blues Brothers* and *Ghostbusters* had been gigantic but controlled; this was Aykroyd's undiluted vision, direct from his prefrontal cortex.

In early 1991, the Warner Bros. marketing department was faced with a tough challenge in selling the project, not helped by the fact their director-star was talking up the unhinged spectacle as if it were neorealism. "What transpires in this film really comes from American life," he told *Starlog*. "There are crazy old country judges sitting out there in the woods capable of any kind of behavior and there's a family I know where the two brothers are literally Infant Bodies who are so fat they're not allowed in the house. So people may look at

Nothing But Trouble and think it's totally made up. But I know that there are people like this out among us."

It came out on February 15, a cold Friday night, and tanked, making just $8.4 million. The critics were as baffled by its gonzo funhouse stylings as the film's yuppie heroes. "Most of the jokes are so lame that Chevy Chase can't even be bothered to look nonchalant," said Owen Gleiberman of *Entertainment Weekly*, summing up the general mood.

Aykroyd was, and is, philosophical. "We lament, but we lament with no lachrymosity," he says. "If there was any flaw, it would have been maybe the darkness of the tone. But for me, a big part of it was, 'Don't throw us up against *Sleeping with the Enemy* and *Silence of the Lambs*.' Demi Moore would have brought a huge female contingent in, if those two stars hadn't been in the marketplace that week."

Be that as it may, *Nothing But Trouble* was seen as a rejection of *Saturday Night Live*–style comedy—the wild characters, the sketch-style set pieces, the exaggerated makeup. The underperformance of Aykroyd's next movie, a big-screen spin-off of actual *SNL* skit *Coneheads*, only reinforced that.

Chase and Aykroyd had ruled the 1980s. Now it was clear that their box-office clout was fading. Aykroyd would never direct again—as star, writer, and director, the failure of *Nothing But Trouble* was laid squarely at his feet. Acting-wise, he began to focus on supporting roles in dramas, buoyed by his *Driving Miss Daisy* success: over the '90s he popped up in *My Girl*, *Sneakers*, *Chaplin*, and *North*. Assisting others and stealing the odd scene, the onetime utility player was back in his comfort zone.

AS FOR CHASE, *Nothing But Trouble* was embarrassing, but true humiliation came via the small screen. In 1993, in the talk-show vacuum left by the retirement of Johnny Carson, Fox offered a late-night show to Dolly Parton. Her manager declined, but suggested Chase instead. Way back in 1975, a cover story for *New York Magazine* had quoted a network executive as calling him "the first real potential successor to Johnny Carson when he gives up the *Tonight Show*." Almost two decades later, Chase got the chance to prove that potential. It did not go well.

Hype levels for *The Chevy Chase Show* were through the roof. At an expense of $1 million, Fox renovated the selected Hollywood venue, the Aquarius Theatre. They also changed its name to the Chevy Chase Theatre, in a high-profile ceremony during which Chase christened the building by firing a water balloon full of Champagne at it using a slingshot. As for the show itself, no expense was spared. Chase's deal was a rich one: $3 million. Big stars were booked for the first six weeks, including Robert De Niro, Pamela Anderson, Burt Reynolds, Whoopi Goldberg, and Chase's two-time co-star Goldie Hawn. A vast set was constructed, complete with fish tank, fake palm trees, a basketball court, and an electric keyboard for Chase to mess around on between interviews.

On Tuesday night, September 6, 1993, the first show began with the lanky, middle-aged funnyman loping out onto the stage and throwing a basketball at the hoop. It missed. He jogged toward the audience, was passed the ball again and missed for a second time. The tone had been well and truly set.

Chase looked stiff and flustered throughout his monologue, and failed to work up much chemistry even with Hawn, who in the episode's oddest moment sang a serenade to his face, before boogying with him in front of the cringing crowd.

"One of the great things about the movie . . . are the actors in it," he floundered during an interview with De Niro, there to shill his first directorial effort, *A Bronx Tale*, a couple of weeks later.

When Whoopi Goldberg swung by, her own late-night series having just been canceled after one season, he started with the question, "What are you doing with yourself, now that your show's going the way mine is about to go?"

The self-assured guy who had clowned from behind the "Weekend Update" desk on *Saturday Night Live* was AWOL. This Chase was awkward and downbeat, so much so that even the show's network couldn't stand it. On October 17, Fox Broadcasting's chairwoman, Lucie Salhany, did an extraordinary interview with the Associated

Press, admitting, "The shows weren't good. He was very nervous. It was uncomfortable and embarrassing to watch it." Chase himself blamed Fox, saying he'd wanted a darker, more improv-centric setup. But whoever was at fault, *The Chevy Chase Show* was sunk, lambasted by critics and deserted by the curious few who had tuned in in the first place. After five weeks on the air, the plug was pulled. And within forty-eight hours of the final show, the new name of the theater had been painted over.

On the big screen, too, Chase was struggling, though he did his best not to show it. In the early 1990s, Steven E. de Souza wrote a script for Joel Silver to produce that he thought would be perfect for Chase; titled *Thin Ice*, it was about a dirty Chicago cop forced to pair up with a squeaky-clean Mountie, a role for which Silver was considering John Candy. But a meeting with Chase's manager did not go well. "He came in and pissed all over this script," says de Souza. "I've never seen anyone do such an evisceration. And so he left and Joel said, 'This guy clearly doesn't think Chevy needs the movie.'" Instead, Chase released such little-loved films as *Memoirs of an Invisible Man*, *Cops and Robbersons*, and *Man of the House*. He'd once been one of the most buzzed-about stars in America. Now, increasingly, he was becoming an invisible man himself.

THE GOLDEN AGE, it seemed, was over. The immense surge of comedic energy that had come out of New York and Toronto had slowed to a weak pulse. Belushi, Moranis, and Candy were gone. Chase, Murphy, and Aykroyd were still active but hardly the unstoppable powerhouses of invention they once were. The snow-haired Martin was as sharp as ever but tame now, playing dads and middle-aged men vexed by newfangled things. Meanwhile, a generation of younger, hipper comedians, forged in the blockbuster era these '80s superstars had created, was starting to overtake them. These rising stars included Mike Myers and Dana Carvey (two *Saturday Night Live* veterans themselves, who blew up when they turned their McKenzie Brothers–esque "Wayne's

World" sketches into a 1992 film), Adam Sandler (another *SNL* alumnus, who had been gifted the small role of Carmine Weiner in Aykroyd's *Coneheads* movie), and Jim Carrey (who, after taking the Ace Ventura role Moranis had turned down, became an unstoppable comic force, mesmerizing audiences with the Elvis-on-amphetamines antics he'd displayed, early in his career, on Johnny Carson's *Tonight Show*).

Out of the original *SNL* and *SCTV* crews, only one man still had his edge. Time had battered him, but it had not bridled him. At the age of forty-two, he remained capricious, inconstant, a puckish, wild, and mercurial being.

And Bill Murray was about to make a masterpiece.

Not that *Groundhog Day* was written for him. Screenwriter Danny Rubin actually had somebody very different in his head while writing his tale of an asshole weatherman stuck in a temporal loop, unable to escape from February 2. "The only person I had in mind was a young Jimmy Stewart," he says. "When I told Harold Ramis, he said, 'I don't think he's available.'" Ramis, who had come on board as director, suggested a still-living alternative: Chevy Chase. It was a prospect that filled Rubin with dread. "Chevy had never shown any aptitude for depth. He could comment on a character, but he could never *be* a character. So the fact they were considering him was making my stomach churn."

Chase, it turned out, wasn't interested. And neither was Tom Hanks, who was also offered the part. Hanks would run into Ramis on a street in New York shortly after *Groundhog Day* opened, telling him, "I was right to say no. Because everybody knows me as a nice guy. So if you see me coming in and being a jerky fellow, you know I'm going to be a nice guy at the end of it. With Bill Murray, you have no idea what's going to happen."

On *Groundhog Day*, that last sentence proved accurate right from the get-go. Ramis sent Murray a copy of the script in late 1991, almost certain that they'd never hear from him, at least anytime soon. But within forty-eight hours he had called his fellow Ghostbuster back, saying, "Yeah, pretty good. I'll be in L.A. Let's meet."

Murray got together with Ramis and Trevor Albert on the Sony lot in Culver City. The three bullshitted for a while, with Albert feeling he was being eyed with a little suspicion, the kid gofer from the *Caddyshack* set now all grown up and a powerful producer. One topic wasn't being raised: the actual movie. Then, at about five p.m., with the sun going down, Murray said, "Hey, will you guys walk with me?"

He led them into the parking lot toward his vehicle, finally asking a few questions about the project. Still talking, he got into the car. Revved the engine. Then, as Albert and Ramis exchanged concerned looks, he said, almost as an aside, "I want to do it." And sped off.

"We were left there going, 'Did that just happen?'" remembers Albert.

They had their star. But the script still needed plenty of work. Even the first draft had wowed both producer and director, Albert saying, "By the time I got to page twelve and realized the day was repeating, it blew my mind." It began inside the time loop, with it not apparent what's going on until the hero, Phil Connors, falls off a cliff and wakes up back in his bed. The executives at Columbia, though, fretted that this comedy about a man's existential crisis, which includes several suicide attempts, would be too challenging for general audiences. "I think there was a lot to my script that meandered in a way that was pleasing and enjoyable," says Rubin, "but it didn't have those sharp dramatic edges that Hollywood seems to require."

So the writer had been taken off the project, much against his will. By the time Murray signed on, Ramis himself had done an extensive rewrite, with some assistance from associate producer Whitney White, who suggested that the story start the day before Phil gets trapped in time. It was fussy work, even leaving aside such suggestions from the studio as the addition of a gypsy curse to explain the time loop. "A major headbanger" is how Albert puts it. "It was the most delicate script imaginable—if you change one thing, it could potentially bring the whole thing down."

Finally, everyone was happy. *Groundhog Day* was green-lit, casting commenced, and sets began to be built in Woodstock, Illinois, subbing for Punxsutawney, Pennsylvania. But they had forgotten one thing: Bill Murray. On his earlier movies he'd flung screenplays aside, or barely read them before showing up. This time, the opposite was true. While Ramis was scouting locations with cinematographer John Bailey, Murray had been secretly doing his own work on the script, molding it into the tale he wanted it to be.

In early February 1992, Rubin, who had thought he was completely off the movie, was suddenly summoned by the star to Northern California, where Murray was competing for the first time in the AT&T Pebble Beach National Pro-Am. (The star made headlines by devouring a Polish sausage and downing a beer at the first tee.) "It was surreal," Rubin recalls. "I met him right after he's finished doing the golf tournament he does every year. This is only the second time I've met him in person. And all of a sudden we drive to an airfield and get on a private plane. And it's just him and me, flying through the night to the middle of nowhere, some refueling station, and then off again. On the ride we're talking about story structure. Like, he had spoken to Elaine May or one of his highfalutin writer friends and she had told him what the script needed and he was sort of explaining it to me."

This was the beginning of an intense collaboration between the two men, undoing much of what Ramis had done to the script. For two weeks in New York, they would show up every morning to an office in the Directors Guild Building on West Fifty-Seventh Street, Rubin arriving first, Murray rocking up at about ten o'clock.

"He wouldn't really talk to me. He would just grunt and pace and smoke cigars and read the newspaper," Rubin says. "And after about an hour of puttering around he would sit down next to me and say something like, 'OK, if I agree to do this movie . . . what do you suppose Phil would say here?' I mean, they were already building sets!"

The countdown to the start of the shoot was ticking. But if Murray was feeling any pressure, he didn't show it. After a page or two had been done, he would invariably invite Rubin on an errand. They went to the bank together, bought Murray's wife a dress. One day Murray peeled hundred-dollar bills off a roll, handing them out to homeless people on a Manhattan street. And there were adventures too.

"The most surreal thing was at one point we got side-by-side shiatsu massages," says the writer, "and he and I broke out into song. The Korean masseuses were nonplussed. Another time we ended up playing basketball with Dan Aykroyd and [*Saturday Night Live* writer] Tom Davis. We were all in our socks, even though it was winter, sliding all over the place. And the only thing I remember from that game is Bill passing the ball to Dan, full-force, but through the space where my head had just been. I really quickly moved my head to get out of the way. And after that Bill started treating me with more respect. It was like, 'Hey, good reflexes.'"

Ramis, who by this point had found out about the unauthorized rewrite, was livid. He called Rubin frequently from Woodstock, where he was supervising the set builds, asking, "How far along are you? Where are those pages?" Once he asked the writer to put Murray on the phone. Murray refused.

For the people trying to get the movie filmed on schedule and on budget, these developments were alarming. "It's every producer's nightmare," says Albert. "It was devastating. Terrifying. Harold and I were apoplectic. Danny and Bill's draft got sent to us two and a half weeks away from shooting, and the delicate balance that we had achieved had been disrupted significantly. I can't remember what had changed exactly, but the script came and we were freaked out by it. Some new lines were good, but mostly it was like a grenade had been thrown into the middle of everything."

It's an apt analogy, for the set of *Groundhog Day* was to become a war zone.

A WEEK AND A HALF before the cameras rolled on March 15, Murray arrived in Woodstock. Ramis arranged a meeting, which quickly became heated. It appeared that they each had a different vision for *Groundhog Day*: Ramis wanted the film to be warm and romantic, while Murray was pushing for it to be a little chillier and more existential. The push and pull would continue throughout the shoot.

Something else was apparent right away: Murray was having a hard time in his personal life. His marriage to Mickey Kelly was disintegrating (they would divorce in 1994) and it was leading to some dark moods. Perhaps this midlife ennui was why he was pushing for the movie to have more complex shadings than his previous rambunctious blockbusters. It was certainly making life trickier for those working with him.

Stephen Tobolowsky, a gangly Texan actor, had been cast as Ned Ryerson, an old acquaintance of Phil's who gets by turns snubbed, punched, and caressed. Flying in from Paris, California, where he had been shooting another movie called *Calendar Girls*, Tobolowsky was excited to unleash his take on the nebbish character; as he'd told Ramis, "The way I'm playing this part is big enough to work in the Roman Coliseum." But he was nervous too about how it would go down, not least because all his scenes were opposite Bill Murray.

Having gotten just three hours of sleep, he left his hotel room and headed to the town square, where five hundred Woodstock locals were gathered to watch the encounter between Phil and Ned. There he sighted the movie's star.

"Bill's a big guy," Tobolowsky says. "He's taller than me, like six-five. And he can be quite grumpy. His demeanor can be quite rough. So I came over to Harold, who gave me a big hug and said, 'Let me introduce you to Bill.' And Bill kind of pushed Harold away and said to me directly, 'Show me what you're going to do. Right now.' So I started going through the first speech with him, doing the Ned noises and everything. My heart was beating a little bit. Nervous, nervous. Bill didn't laugh but he said, 'Stop. OK. You can do that.'"

Just a few minutes later, the other, more charming side of Murray emerged. Surveying the crowd on the other side of the rope, he looked at Tobolowsky, still no flicker of a smile on his face, and said, "You know what these people need?"

"No, sir," Tobolowsky replied.

"Doughnuts." A beat, then: "Follow me."

The two actors ran in costume over to the nearest bakery, on the corner of the town square. There, Murray pulled out a wad of cash and said, "I want every doughnut, every bear claw, every Danish you got." Returning to the set with towering boxes of pastries in their hands, he and his new acquaintance proceeded to distribute them to the people of Woodstock.

"Bill, in his flamboyant Bill way, started throwing handfuls of doughnuts into the air, like it was chum into water full of sharks," says Tobolowsky. "People started screaming and grabbing for them. And I thought, 'Is this the most brilliant man in the world?' I mean, in one instant Bill did more than any big movie production working in a small town could do to get goodwill on our side. Those people loved us after the doughnut fling."

One person who probably didn't get a delicacy from Murray was Ramis. The affable director, a convert to Buddhism who wore meditation beads, was having his Zen mind-set severely tested by his onetime friend. In fact, communication between the two quickly broke down completely. "He's raging, angry, and full of grief and unresolved emotions," Ramis reflected later of Murray. "He's volcanic." Finally the director was forced to make an official request for an assistant for Murray, so that messages could be conveyed between the two. A young lady subsequently arrived on-set, selected by Murray. There was one small hitch: she was deaf.

"To many people it seems like a hilarious thing," says Albert. "You insist to an anarchist that they find someone to help bridge the gap of communication, and the next thing you know they've found someone who can't communicate to be the go-between. It's like an existential joke. But the victim of that joke was the young woman, more than anyone else. She was in the middle of that thing and had no fricking idea what was going on. And it exacerbated the situation on-set. You know, it was the Everyman thing; fuck the Man. But Harold and I weren't really the Man."

Danny Rubin was only in Woodstock—"cold as fuck"—for the first week of filming, but picked up on the discordant mood. "I never really understood what was going on," he says. "And it wasn't really between Harold and Bill—it was Bill. There was something going on with him. Because Harold seemed as bewildered by the whole thing as I was. Bill had decided I was on his team and he liked me, so it was all right, but it was also always a little edgy too."

Even with all the tension boiling over behind the scenes, every-one was taking *Groundhog Day* seriously. What could have been a silly romp—a high-concept *Animal House* in which Bill Murray cuts loose without consequences—was instead emerging as a mature, even pro-found comedy. The stages that Phil goes through as he revisits the same day over and over again are akin to the Kübler-Ross stages of grief: denial, anger, bargaining, depression, and finally acceptance.

Ramis, meanwhile, was fully aware of the story's spiritual qualities. "Bill destroys all meaning for himself," he said years later. "Buddhism says our self doesn't even exist." A sequence of sheer debauchery, in which Phil chainsaws a bed in half and shaves his hair into a Mohawk, had been written to establish that the time loop undoes even the crazi-est antics. While it was filmed, it was ultimately replaced by a simple shot of Murray snapping a pencil. Elegance, replacing excess. The bad boys of the '80s were truly growing up.

Enthuses Tobolowsky, "That decision took away what you expect of a Bill Murray film, the comedy chaos, and replaced it with poetry. It changed the tone of the movie and of Bill's character. He wasn't this crazy, wild, eccentric guy. He's this poor fellow trapped in time. That's what made Bill's performance so mighty: he's suddenly a real guy with a very unreal problem."

In the story, Phil slowly learns to become calm, kind, even altruis-tic. That arc was not reflected by the mood on-set, which continued to be spiky as arguments raged between Murray and Ramis and icy tem-peratures wore down the crew. By day forty-five, pretty much everyone was looking forward to escaping *Groundhog Day*. But there was one more major standoff to come. Murray and co-star Andie MacDowell were due in the hotel-room set for the movie's big climactic scene, in which Phil wakes up alongside love interest Rita, slowly realizing that Punxsutawney is blanketed in snow and February 3 has arrived at last. It seemed like a straightforward day, until Murray walked in and an-nounced, "Not shooting it."

He was, it turned out, vexed by one particular issue: his costume. Or rather, whether he should be wearing one at all. It hadn't been established whether Phil had slept with Rita, as well as alongside her, or not. So should he be clad in just his underwear, or all of his clothes from the night before?

Sensing another long and painful debate simmering, Ramis looked around the room and said, "Why don't we put it to a vote?"

And they did. It came down to a tiebreaker, with one vote outstanding: a lowly assistant set decorator, on her very first movie. Nervously, but with conviction, she piped up: "They're both wearing exactly the clothes they were in the night before. If you do anything different, it'll ruin the movie."

Ramis chuckled. Murray cracked a smile. MacDowell breathed a sigh of relief.

They shot the scene as instructed.

THERE'S LITTLE DOUBT that Murray took the movie seriously. On February 2, 1992, a month before shooting began, he flew to the actual Punxsutawney and watched from the crowd as the actual Groundhog Day ceremony unfolded at Gobbler's Knob, with legendary rodent Punxsutawney Phil roused from sleep at 7:20 a.m. As the master of ceremonies announced that Phil predicted six more weeks of winter, everyone—including Murray—booed. He also brought specificity to his weatherman role. "He was more well informed than I was," admits Rubin. "I'd done as little research as I could get away with, but Bill was actually a big watcher of the Weather Channel. That was just something he did as a pastime."

Yet a month after the release of *Groundhog Day*, Murray still hadn't got around to watching it. A no-show at the Hollywood premiere at Mann's Village Theater on February 4, 1993, he showed little interest in catching a public screening either, telling an incredulous reporter, "Just haven't had the time." His dim enthusiasm, fortunately for the film, was not matched by that of the paying public. *Groundhog Day* was the second biggest comedy of 1993, defeated only by the unstoppable, duster-wielding force that was *Mrs. Doubtfire*, and ruled the box office for two straight weeks, wending its way to $70.9 million domestic.

But Murray had had hits before. Where this differed was in the

kind of reaction it was getting. A couple of days after the movie
opened, Trevor Albert got a phone call telling him that a group of
Hasidic Jews had gathered outside a movie theater that was showing
it, brandishing signs. His first thought was that they were protesting.
But when he arrived on the scene, he realized it was quite the opposite.

"They were celebrating *Groundhog Day*," he marvels. "Because
there's a thing in Judaism called mitzvah, which is a word describing a
good deed, woven into the fabric of Judaism. And that movie personi-
fied mitzvah."

Then letters began arriving from Christian organizations, enthusing about the comedy's message of redemption and spiritual values.
And Buddhists too, from all over the world, wrote about its cranky
hero's journey to enlightenment. "All these religious groups thought it
was a specific expression of their teaching or philosophy," says Albert.
It took the film's makers aback—few stories featuring a girl-chasing
schmuck are revered as holy text—but they were happy to accept the
praise.

Words from more worldly critics were just as kind. "Such a fiendishly clever premise that it would work even if it didn't star Bill Murray," thrilled Robert W. Butler in the *Kansas City Star.* "The story's
premise, conceived as a sitcom-style visit to *The Twilight Zone*, starts
out lightweight but becomes strangely affecting," Janet Maslin concluded in the *New York Times.* Todd Camp of the *Fort Worth Star-
Telegram*, like many, thought Murray's character arc was very similar
to the one he'd had in *Scrooged*, but was still blown away by the star's
chops: "Murray returns to familiar stomping grounds and delivers another powerhouse performance."

His characters had always had edge, but in the first half of *Groundhog Day* Ramis had trusted Murray's natural charm enough to let him
go full asshole. In pre-production, Danny Rubin had questioned one
line of dialogue that the director had added, where Phil Connors slams
a chubby guy against a wall and says, "Don't mess with me, pork chop!"
He worried that the moment was too mean and would turn viewers
off. But Ramis held firm, saying gently, "Don't worry: Bill can get
away with it." And he did. Murray's performance is wholly believable

as it swings from glibness to anguish to that rarest of Murray emotional states: earnestness. "Let's live here," Phil tells Rita, surveying the street that earlier had seemed like purgatory and now looked like paradise.

If his on-screen avatar was staying still, Murray was doing just the opposite. In *Groundhog Day* are the seeds of a transformation, from big-screen clown to something more complex, with far more range. Two years on, he would appear in Tim Burton's *Ed Wood* as sad-eyed drag queen Bunny Breckinridge. Three years after that, he would make his first film with indie auteur Wes Anderson, *Rushmore*, playing a steel tycoon so depressed that he plunges into a swimming pool fully dressed. And in 2003 came *Lost in Translation*, with another midlife crisis–struck businessman, marooned not in a time loop but in a high-end Tokyo hotel. The subtle, weighty roles he had craved back in his *Where the Buffalo Roam* days had arrived at last. And it all began with that damn groundhog, who looked like a distant nephew of the furry fiend he had hunted in *Caddyshack*.

Murray did, in the end, sit down and watch *Groundhog Day*. And it melted his heart too. "I think it's an extraordinary movie," he said in 2017. "The kid whose idea it was, Danny Rubin . . . I mean, he was touched by God when he wrote that. He really was." In the summer of that same year, he went along to the August Wilson Theatre in New York with his brother Brian, to take in a performance of the Broadway musical based on the film, which Rubin had co-written with Tim Minchin. Murray tipped the lady at the bar $50 for a glass of water, exchanged quips with other theatergoers, and pumped his fist in the air as the show began and Stage Phil met Stage Ned. By the time the curtain fell on the first act, Murray was weeping like a baby.

Twenty-four hours later, as if a time loop had been conjured up on West Fifty-Second Street, he was back in line to see it again.

EPILOGUE

LATE ONE WINTRY night in Midtown Manhattan, Chevy Chase and Bill Murray faced off against each other again. It was February 20, 1999, almost exactly twenty-one years to the day after they had taken swings at each other backstage at *Saturday Night Live*, and they were back in the same building for another episode of the show. But this time, they were in front of the camera—and the live studio audience—and the only jabs they were aiming were verbal ones of the gentlest kind.

"Toga! Toga! Toga! Toga!" chanted Chase enthusiastically, dressed up as Ty Webb from *Caddyshack* and clutching a golf club.

"No, no, no," sighed Murray. "That's *Animal House*, buddy. We weren't in that one."

The skit was titled "The Quotable *Caddyshack*" and riffed daffily on the slapstick comedy's pop-cultural omnipresence. "You're a white male between the ages of fifteen to forty-one," intoned an announcer to tee it off, "chances are you love quoting lines from *Caddyshack*." But for the two middle-aged stars, returning to their old haunt, the building in whose corridors they'd once rattled around with infinite energy, it was a bittersweet moment of reflection. Their funniest, breeziest movies were behind them: this was a victory lap, plus a public piece of truce-making. Still, they were going to make it funny, even if it meant savagely making fun of their own foibles.

"We got a pool in the back. We got a pond and a pool. Pool would be good for you," said Chase, deliberately (or maybe not?) misquoting his own iconic line.

As for Murray, who had recently made a few questionable career decisions in the form of *Larger Than Life*, *Space Jam*, and *The Man Who Knew Too Little*, he wasn't above presenting himself as a man of monumental avarice. "Order the Quotable Caddyshack now," he told viewers. "Thirty percent of the profits go to the Ted Knight Slow Burn Foundation. The other seventy percent goes to me."

Then, swinging into his Carl Spackler drawl, the kicker: "I got that goin' for me . . . which is nice."

Bill Murray had, of course, much more goin' for him than that. And so did his comedy cohorts. The legacy they were leaving behind was nothing short of stunning: a blueprint for fresher-faced, up-and-coming Hollywood jokers—from Will Ferrell and Ben Stiller to Chris Tucker and Adam Sandler—to study and follow. Murray, Chase, Murphy, Aykroyd, and the rest had stepped out of television and set fire to the silver screen, making cinematic comedy vital, dangerous, unpredictable, *huge*. Somehow, they had managed to both keep alive the subversive spirit of their own heroes—funny forefathers like Jerry Lewis, Abbott and Costello, Richard Pryor, Jack Benny—and channel it into unbelievable commercial success.

Hollywood would never be the same again. Because what was possible, this scruffy and slightly shambolic band had proven, was absolutely anything. They had battled ghouls, made a giant action movie based around blues music, set the template for the buddy-cop film, and inspired millions around the world to memorize and repeat their quips. They had even, on occasion, made people cry.

Not all of their material has aged well, and some of it wasn't even funny at the time. But there is no denying that their vast ambition, raw talent, and total disregard for the rules combined to create a movement that was beloved, influential, and truly special. Their movies have been remade, spun off, and homaged to death, and fans still dress up as Ghostbusters, Blutos, and Blues Brothers (the mutant troll-babies from *Nothing But Trouble*, not so much). Hollywood scouts now keep a close eye on TV sketch shows, particularly *SNL*, as well as web series on the cutting edge of comedy, in the hopes of finding the next big star. And studio comedies have become raunchier, weirder, bigger, and looser, always chasing that elusive alchemy that happened in the 1980s, when a bunch of very silly men were given very large sums of money and allowed to go play.

BILL MURRAY made such a successful transition to serious actor that he even got an Oscar nomination for *Lost in Translation* (and grimaced when Sean Penn won instead for *Mystic River*). He's worked with indie darlings Jim Jarmusch and Cameron Crowe, as well as his frequent collaborations with Wes Anderson (for one of which he portrayed a badger). Still, he never turned his back on his 1980s heyday. In 2009's *Zombieland*, playing himself as the celebrity survivor of an undead apocalypse, he donned a proton pack and re-created scenes from *Ghostbusters* before being accidentally shot dead. After many torturous efforts to secure him, he also agreed to cameo in the female-led 2016 *Ghostbusters* reboot, as a paranormal debunker who again gets violently killed mid-film.

Most glorious of all, though, are the *Caddyshack*-themed restaurants (one in Florida, the other near his hometown of Chicago), which he's opened with his brothers. The eateries' catchphrase: "Eat, Drink and Be Murray."

CHEVY CHASE fronted another theatrical hit with 1997's *Vegas Vacation*, the final adventure for Clark Griswold and his brood, but otherwise largely faded into supporting roles in movies such as *Snow Day*, *Goose on the Loose*, and *Hot Tub Time Machine*. (He claims that he turned down the lead in 1994's *Forrest Gump*.) In 2015, he reprised the role of Clark for a cameo in a soft reboot of *Vacation*, alongside Beverly D'Angelo, quipping, "Beverly's hilarious and I would not do it without her, of course. Unless there was somebody better."

A mini-comeback occurred on TV, in the form of *Community*, the acclaimed sitcom in which he played moist-towelette tycoon Pierce Hawthorne for eighty-three episodes. That experience ended prematurely when, following a long feud with show runner Dan Harmon, his angry voicemails were played by Harmon on his podcast. *Community* co-star Joel McHale ended up playing Chase, with Chase's blessing, in 2018's *A Futile and Stupid Gesture*, a dramatization of the early days of *National Lampoon*.

He calls *Funny Farm* his favorite of his own movies. He still hasn't seen *Oh! Heavenly Dog*.

DAN AYKROYD achieved much after the calamity of *Nothing But Trouble*, including predicting both the rise of the forty-fifth president of the United States and the actor who would lampoon him on *Saturday Night Live*. "The villain was based on Donald Trump," Aykroyd said in 2016 of his screenplay for *Ghostbusters 3: Hellbent*. "I wanted Alec Baldwin to play the devil in the thousand-foot black onyx tower overlooking the hell-pit mine of Central Park." He still holds out hope that *Hellbent* might get made in some form, but in the meantime has popped up in Paul Feig's *Ghostbusters* reboot as a taxi driver, as well as lending technical advice. He has also written an as-yet-unproduced comedy for himself and Chase called *Run for the Roses*, with Chase as a broke Kentucky horse breeder and Aykroyd as his valet.

In 1992 he founded the House of Blues, a chain of live-music venues that currently has eleven locations in North America. He has also successfully launched a high-end spirits brand, Crystal Head Vodka, which comes in a skull-shaped bottle and is based on ancient artifacts said to be of extraterrestrial origin. The vodka, Aykroyd maintains, will leave you hangover-free.

RICK MORANIS resides mostly these days at his apartment on New York's Upper West Side, with a view overlooking Central Park. Poking fun at his own homebody tendencies, two lines from his 2006 comedy country album, *The Agoraphobic Cowboy,* go, "I like conditioned air, man/I never go nowhere."

Still, while he has only done voice acting for a few animated films since 1997, he claims he's not officially retired. "Why would I retire? How could I be retired?" he says. "If there's another movie, I wouldn't not do it, but it's got to be good. It's got to be interesting to me. It's got to be a deal I would want to make."

STEVE MARTIN has gone on to host *Saturday Night Live* fifteen times to date, outdone only by Alec Baldwin. In a 2013 skit called "The Five-Timers Club," he peacocked around a secret hosts' lounge in a smoking jacket, ordering a drink from the celebrity bartender (Dan Aykroyd), tutting at the clumsy celebrity waiter (Martin Short), and studiously ignoring the fellow club member befuddled by a landline phone (Chevy Chase).

On-screen, alternating between broad comedies and serious works, he has earned consistently warm reviews (and an honorary Oscar in 2013). Off it, he's won a Grammy for his first solo music album, 2009's *The Crow: New Songs for the 5-String Banjo,* and written novels, a novella, two children's books, more plays, and a musical. And, a true Renaissance man, he took to Twitter so deftly that his posts have been turned into a book, *The Ten, Make That Nine, Habits of Very Organized People. Make That Ten: The Tweets of Steve Martin.* Sample: "Tired of sitting on my butt. Trying my shoulder."

In 2007 he remarried, to *New Yorker* writer Anne Stringfield, and finally became a father five years later, at the age of sixty-seven.

EDDIE MURPHY teamed up with Steve Martin for 1998's *Bowfinger,* the Frank Oz comedy that introduced the world to the phrase "chubby rain." It garnered Murphy some of his best reviews since the '80s for his dual role as neurotic movie star Kit Ramsey and simpleminded look-alike Jiff. Less beloved by critics, but still huge at the box office, were his multi-performances in *Norbit* (three Murphys) and the *Nutty Professor* franchise (seven Murphys). And his clout was boosted considerably by dint of voicing a dragon and a donkey in *Mulan* and the *Shrek* films, respectively.

Dreamgirls bagged him a Best Supporting Actor nomination at the 2006 Academy Awards for his portrayal of soul singer James "Thunder" Early. But his return to the Oscars stage as host in 2012 was not to be: three months before the event he dropped out, during the furor created after his friend Brett Ratner, who was producing the show, made a homophobic remark to reporters.

Fans were disappointed, but not as disappointed as they have been by the multiple aborted efforts to get Axel Foley back on the beat. A fourth *Beverly Hills Cop* was announced in 2013, with Murphy claiming it would be both set and shot in Detroit. And a pilot episode of a TV series about Foley's son was filmed the next year for CBS. Neither, however, has made it to the screen. Which begs the question: has someone checked for a banana in the tailpipe?

ACKNOWLEDGMENTS

I was a child of the 1980s who grew up surreptitiously watching cuss-packed Eddie Murphy movies and perfecting my Slimer impression, and getting to chronicle this period of comedy history has been an incredible voyage. The characters within these pages only get more fascinating—and funnier—the more you learn about them.

There are many people who made this book possible, and I am hugely grateful to all of them. My first thank-you goes to Sanam Jehanfard, who went above and beyond, fixing me up with an unscheduled sit-down with Bill Murray, the white whale of funnymen, at the Cannes Film Festival back in 2012. Without that conversation, accompanied by a plate of cookies, this book might well not exist.

Enormous thanks, of course, to all of the talented actors, directors, writers, and producers who have spoken to me, offering their memories and occasionally documents from the time. A full list can be found in the Notes section, but I am particularly grateful to three of them: Steven E. de Souza, for opening up his archives for *48 Hrs.* and *Beverly Hills Cop III;* John Landis, for a series of epic phone conversations and even more epic anecdotes; and the frankly delightful Rick Moranis, for inviting me into his home in 2013. I'm not sure a nicer human being exists.

For arranging and facilitating interviews, my appreciation goes to Victoria Male, Zach Book, John Singh, Joe Dante, Bess Scher, Cece Neber, Jeff Field, Andy Jones, Amy Roy, Jeff Sanderson, Kirk Honeycutt, and Paul Alan Smith.

I have been fortunate enough to work at *Empire* magazine for the past fifteen years, surrounded by endlessly wise and witty colleagues. For all the encouragement and spirit-reviving counsel, I thank Simon Crook, David Hughes, Ian Freer, Ian Nathan, James Dyer, Terri White, Chris Hewitt, Olly Gibbs, James White, Helen O'Hara, and Dan Jolin.

It's been a joy to work with such a brilliant team on my first book: Felicity Blunt and Lucy Morris at Curtis Brown; my razor-sharp editor Matt Inman, as well as Angeline Rodriguez and Amelia Zalcman at Crown Archetype; and Paul Baggaley, Paul Martinovic, Kishani Widyaratna, and Jon Mitchell at Picador. Thanks to all of you for guiding me through the process so expertly. And very special Three Amigos salutes to Steve Schofield, Natasha Bardon, and Emlyn Rees.

Finally, a whole lot of gratitude to my friends and family for putting up with four years of Chevy Chase chatter—not least the ever-hilarious Steve Levin, the ever-mellow Nat Backhouse, and my wonderful brothers, Phil and Chris. And to Daniela Phillips: thank you for accompanying me down the Holiday Road.

NOTES

PROLOGUE

xi   **Nobody saw the punch coming:** This account of the events of February 18, 1978, is based on interviews the author has done with people present, including Bill Murray, John Landis, and Dave Thomas. Details are also drawn from Murray's interview on *The Late Show with David Letterman* on June 7, 2012; Chevy Chase's interview on *The Howard Stern Show* on September 18, 2008; and eyewitness accounts in various books.

xii   **"Money. Lots of money":** Doug Hill and Jeff Weingrad, *A Backstage History of Saturday Night Live* (Untreed Reads, 2011), chapter 19.

xii   **"There was no love lost":** Author interview with Dave Thomas, September 13, 2017.

xiii   **"It was a huge altercation":** Author interview with John Landis, April 18, 2016.

xiii   **"It was really a Hollywood fight":** Author interview with Bill Murray, "Pint of Milk: Bill Murray," *Empire*, August 2012.

xv   **"It came on and I thought":** Tom Shales and James Andrew Miller,

Live from New York: An Uncensored History of Saturday Night Live (Little, Brown, 2002), 63.

xvi **"I think the '80s"**: From Quentin Tarantino interview on *The Nerdist Podcast*, Episode 774, December 18, 2015.

xvi **"When I started playing stadiums"**: Author interview with Steve Martin, "In Conversation with Steve Martin," *Empire*, March 2009.

xvii **"I'm not too proud"**: Chevy Chase interview on *West 57th*, CBS, 1989.

1: MR. CAREFUL AND MR. FUCK IT

1   **"He's a cartoon"**: Josh Karp, "Animal House: The Movie That Changed Comedy," *StumpedMagazine*, 2003, http://www.stumpedmagazine .com/articles/animal-house/.

1   **"The other guys were backups" and following quotes in present tense**: Author interview with John Landis, April 18, 2016.

2   **"goddamn suicide missions"**: Mitch Glazer, "Saturday Night's All Right for Fighting," *Crawdaddy*, June 1977.

2   **"You cannot put an actor"**: Tom Burke, "Live, from New York . . . It's NBC's Saturday Night!," *Rolling Stone*, July 15, 1976.

2   **"I chose him because"**: Charles M. Young, "John Belushi: Son of Samurai," *Rolling Stone*, August 10, 1978.

4   **"*War and Peace* on speed"**: Matty Simmons, *Fat, Drunk, and Stupid: The Inside Story Behind the Making of Animal House* (St. Martin's Press, 2012), 41.

4   **"Everybody is drunk"**: Ibid., 46.

5   **"I was trying to create an ambience"**: Laura Sobel, *Animal House: The Inside Story*, documentary, Pangolin Pictures, Biography Channel, 2008.

5   **"Bullshit money, no points"**: Timothy White, "Messin' with the Kid," *Rolling Stone*, February 22, 1978.

5   **"He made everyone"**: Giulia D'Agnolo Vallan, *John Landis* (M Press, 2008), 70.

6   **he'd sometimes turn up high:** Ellin Stein, *That's Not Funny, That's Sick: The National Lampoon and the Comedy Insurgents Who Captured the Mainstream* (W. W. Norton, 2013), 117.

6   **"The audience went berserk"**: Author interview with Matty Simmons, December 22, 2017.

7   **"It was the marking point"**: Author interview with Ivan Reitman, August 14, 2017.

7   **"I like Bluto a lot"**: John Belushi on *The Carolyn Jackson Show*, KTBC, 1978.

7   **"John was sure"**: Stein, *That's Not Funny*, 254.

7   **"I make more money"**: Bob Woodward, *Wired: The Short Life and Fast Times of John Belushi* (Simon & Schuster, 1984), 198.

8   **"I really thought"**: Laurent Bouzereau, *The Making of 1941*, documentary, Universal Home Video, 1996.

9   **"It reminded me"**: Young, "John Belushi: Son of Samurai."

9   **"He reached in his pocket" and details:** Judith Belushi Pisano and Tanner Colby, *Belushi: A Biography* (Rugged Land, 2005), chapter 1.

11   **"He's Mr. Careful"**: White, "Messin' with the Kid."

11   **"A remarkable, wonderful"**: Tasha Robinson, *AVClub*, July 21, 2014, https://www.avclub.com/john-landis-1798208456.

11   **"If it weren't against the law"**: Gene Siskel, "Doctor Detroit Will See You Now . . . & Vice Versa," *Movie Magazine*, Spring 1983.

11   **"You look at the floor"**: Doug Hill and Jeff Weingrad, *A Backstage History of Saturday Night Live* (Untreed Reads, 2011), chapter 20.

12   **"She objected to liquefying"**: John Blumenthal and Lindsay Mara-
     cotta, "The Cast of *Saturday Night Live*," *Playboy*, May 1977.

13   **"Man, we're in it"**: Mitch Glazer, "The Legend of Jake and Elwood,"
     Crawdaddy, 1978.

13   **"There was a lot"**: Bouzereau, *The Making of 1941*.

13   **"John's got a real Judy Garland personality"**: Glazer, "Saturday
     Night's All Right for Fighting."

14   **"I get incredibly straight"**: Ibid.

14   **"Working with John Belushi"**: Bouzereau, *The Making of 1941*.

14   **"*Animal House* Goes to War"**: *Time*, April 16, 1979.

14   **"Fuck the critics"**: Woodward, *Wired*, 174.

14   **"On about the 145th day"**: Todd McCarthy, "Sand Castles," *Film
     Comment* 18, No. 3, May–June 1982.

2: THE JERKS

17   **"Now, a lot of dogs watch TV"**: Steve Martin on *The Carol Burnett
     Show* (CBS), Season 11, Episode 21, March 5, 1978.

18   **"Our acts are similar in that we have no segues"**: Jerry Buck, "The
     Innocent from Ork," *Sarasota Herald-Tribune*, September 2, 1979.

18   **"Another comedian will do anything to get a laugh"**: William P.
     Moore, "Have You Got a Pair of Cat Handcuffs?," *Port Arthur News*,
     November 5, 1977.

18   **Martin collected his paltry fee:** This story is told in the article "Steve
     Martin: King of Hearts" by Dave Felton, *Rolling Stone*, December 1,
     1977.

19   **"I call them the war years" and following quotes in present tense:**
     Author interview with Steve Martin, "In Conversation with Steve
     Martin," *Empire*, March 2009.

19   **"I walked onstage":** Steve Martin, *Born Standing Up* (Scribner, 2007), 171.

20   **"This isn't comedy":** Felton, "Steve Martin: King of Hearts."

20   **"I bought some pretty good stuff":** Steve Martin, *Let's Get Small* (Warner Bros., 1977).

20   **"The act is funny on stage":** Steven X. Rea, "Move Over, Bogart! Take That, Cagney! Drop the Roscoe, Ladd!," *Prevue*, June 1982.

21   **"What I realized":** Jeff Silverman, "Steve Martin Is Serious About Comedy," *Chicago Tribune*, November 1, 1984.

21   **"There was no whiter man" and following quotes in present tense:** Author interview with Carl Reiner, June 15, 2016.

22   **"My memory is" and following quotes in present tense:** Author interview with Carl Gottlieb, March 3, 2018.

22   **"It wasn't a parody":** Adam Gopnik, "Steve Martin: The Late Period," *New Yorker*, November 29, 1993.

25   **"*The Jerk* is all gags":** Roger Ebert, *Chicago Sun-Times*, June 1, 1979.

25   **"Steve Martin is a friend":** Bill Murray on "Weekend Update," *Saturday Night Live* (NBC), Season 5, Episode 7, December 15, 1979.

26   **"I'm still bitter about this" and following quotes in present tense:** Author interview with Bill Murray, "Pint of Milk: Bill Murray," *Empire*, August 2012.

26   **"No drunken audience":** Lewis Grossberger, "Bill Murray: Making It Up as He Goes," *Rolling Stone*, August 20, 1981.

26   **"One of my strongest childhood impressions":** Bill Murray, *Cinderella Story: My Life in Golf* (Doubleday, 1999), 18.

26   **the Murray Christmas tree:** Details drawn from "The Rumpled Anarchy of Bill Murray" by Timothy White, *New York Times Magazine*, November 20, 1988; and "Bill Murray Is Ready to Laugh Again" by Mitch Glazer, *Vanity Fair*, November 3, 2015.

27   **He routinely defied:** Details drawn from Murray's interview with
      Jim Ferguson for KMSB Fox 11, 1981, available at https://www.you
      tube.com/watch?v=kB9u2jSpV6Q.

27   **"I was an underachiever":** Timothy Crouse, "Bill Murray: The *Roll-
      ing Stone* Interview," *Rolling Stone*, August 16, 1984.

27   **on his twentieth birthday:** Details of Murray's arrest are taken from
      a report in the *Chicago Tribune*, September 22, 1970.

28   **"We drank Champa Tampas":** Crouse, "Bill Murray: The *Rolling
      Stone* Interview."

28   **"He's fearless and physically strong":** Author interview with Dave
      Thomas, September 13, 2017.

28   **"Because he can come at you with hurricane force" and follow-
      ing quotes in present tense:** Author interview with Ivan Reitman,
      August 14, 2017.

29   **"I became the second cop":** Tom Shales and James Andrew Miller,
      Live from New York: An Uncensored History of Saturday Night Live (Lit-
      tle, Brown, 2002), 110.

29   **"I'm a little bit concerned":** Bill Murray on "Weekend Update," *Sat-
      urday Night Live* (NBC), Season 5, Episode 7, March 19, 1977.

31   **"One advantage was":** T. J. English, "Bill Murray: The King of
      Comedy," *Irish America Magazine*, November 1988.

3: HIT IT

36   **"When I saw *Trainspotting*":** Tom Shales and James Andrew Miller,
      Live from New York: An Uncensored History of Saturday Night Live
      (Little, Brown, 2002), 124.

36   **"I couldn't stop playing the stuff!":** Mitch Glazer, "The Legend of
      Jake and Elwood," *Crawdaddy*, December 1978.

37   **"The glasses are crucial, man":** Ibid.

37   **"Boy, that was a dog performance"**: Timothy White, "The Blues Brothers: Jake and Elwood's Secret Life," *Rolling Stone*, February 22, 1979.

37   **"We haven't eaten one meal"**: Glazer, "The Legend of Jake and Elwood."

38   **"When they finished"**: Author interview with Dave Thomas, September 13, 2017.

38   **"It was incredible" and following quotes in present tense:** Author interview with John Landis, April 18, 2016.

38   **"At SNL, Lorne was always warning"**: Author interview with Dan Aykroyd for *Empire*, June 2016.

38   **"It's too good to be a parody"**: Abe Peck, "The Blues Brothers Ask the $32 Million Question," *Rolling Stone*, August 7, 1980.

38   **"Those guys were like bloody meat"**: Ibid.

40   **"It might be a little big"**: Ibid.

40   **"I wrote a heavy, urban experience"**: David Standish, "On the Set with the Blues Brothers," *Oui*, August 1980.

41   **"He phoned around three"**: Judith Belushi Pisano and Tanner Colby, *Belushi: A Biography* (Rugged Land, 2005), chapter 9.

41   **"Seven dollars and 98 cents' worth" and following:** Standish, "On the Set with the Blues Brothers."

44   **"The critics will gun us down"**: Peck, "The Blues Brothers Ask the $32 Million Question."

44   **"They were wearing white shoes"**: Ibid.

45   **"A $30 million wreck, minus laughs"**: Charles Champlin, "'Blues': A $30-Million Wreck, Minus Laughs," *Los Angeles Times*, June 20, 1980.

45   **"A ponderous comic monstrosity"**: Gary Arnold, "Oh, Brothers!," *Washington Post*, June 21, 1980.

4: DR. GONZO AND THE GOPHER

47   **"My father was the funniest guy"**: Cal Fussman, "Chevy Chase: What I've Learned," *Esquire*, October 2010.

48   **"I lived in fear all the time"**: Rena Fruchter, *I'm Chevy Chase . . . and You're Not* (Virgin Books, 2007), chapter 1.

48   **"I can't discuss that"**: Chase interview on the *Today* show (NBC), October 7, 2009.

49   **"There's this intense"**: Mitch Glazer, "I'll Pay You $40 Cash Money If You Call My Piece . . . Mr. Funny!," *Crawdaddy*, September 1978.

49   **"He goes into a pothole"**: Tom Shales and James Andrew Miller, *Live from New York: An Uncensored History of Saturday Night Live* (Little, Brown, 2002), 33.

50   **"Chevy's falls were incredible"**: Author interview with Carl Reiner, June 15, 2016.

50   **"The prop guy"**: Chase interview on *Gilbert Gottfried's Amazing Colossal Podcast*, November 16, 2015.

51   **"I know that I had sex appeal"**: Shales and Miller, *Live from New York*, 89.

51   **"Acting's the most tenuous"**: Tom Burke, "Live, from New York . . . It's NBC's Saturday Night!," *Rolling Stone*, July 15, 1976.

51   **"It's bullshit to think"**: Glazer, "I'll Pay You $40."

51   **"I met with John Landis"**: Philip Wuntch, "Movie Flops Help Chevy Chase Chill Out," *Dallas Morning News*, August 7, 1983.

52   **"It's not an easy thing to overcome"**: Vernon Scott, "Chevy Chase Getting Hang of Movies," *Hutchinson News*, August 13, 1983.

52   **"Made me realize I don't want"**: Lawrence Grobel, "Steve Martin," *Playboy*, January 1980.

53   **"The last thing I wanted to do"**: "Whatever Happened to Chevy Chase?," *Chicago Tribune*, November 2, 1980.

54 **"In the first half of the '70s":** Doug Hill and Jeff Weingrad, *A Backstage History of Saturday Night Live* (Untreed Reads, 2011), chapter 20.

55 **"It finally got to where":** T. J. English, "Bill Murray: The King of Comedy," *Irish America Magazine,* November 1988.

55 **"They were worried":** Author interview with Dave Thomas, September 13, 2017.

56 **One night in December 1979:** Account of the conversation between Hunter S. Thompson and Ralph Steadman taken from "Gonzo Goes to Hollywood: The Strange and Terrible Saga of *Where the Buffalo Roam*" by Ralph Steadman, *Rolling Stone,* May 29, 1980.

56 **"An embarrassing piece of hogwash":** David Felton, "When the Weird Turn Pro," *Rolling Stone,* May 29, 1980.

56 **"Horrible pile of crap":** Sara Nelson and Sean Dooley, FarGoneBooks, 1997, http://www.fargonebooks.com/hunter.html.

56 **"I wanted to know how long":** Chris Heath "Johnny Depp's Savage Journey into 'Fear and Loathing in Las Vegas,'" *Rolling Stone,* June 11, 1998.

57 **Chevy Chase hadn't seen Bill Murray:** Details drawn from Chase's interview on *The Howard Stern Show* on September 18, 2008.

58 **"I thought there should be":** Bill Murray, *Cinderella Story: My Life in Golf* (Doubleday, 1999), 191.

59 **"Robin Williams has said":** Matty Simmons, *Fat, Drunk, and Stupid: The Inside Story Behind the Making of Animal House* (St. Martin's Press, 2012), 185.

59 **"It was a recipe for calamity" and following quotes in present tense:** Author interview with Trevor Albert, June 16, 2017.

59 **"Heavy enough to carry a baby's head":** Chase interview on *Gilbert Gottfried's Amazing Colossal Podcast,* November 16, 2015. Further details taken from Chase interview for *Drunk Stoned Brilliant Dead: The Story of the* National Lampoon, Douglas Tirola, documentary, 4th Row Films, Diamond Docs, 2015.

60 **A quick scene:** Described by Chase in Murray's book *Cinderella Story*.

60 **"He just scares you":** "Whatever Happened to Chevy Chase?"

61 **"I didn't know that Bill":** Chase on *The Howard Stern Show*, September 18, 2008.

5: A RISE AND A FALL

63 **"John Candy is perfectly named":** Pauline Kael, *New Yorker*, March 19, 1984.

63 **"Once, backstage at Second City" and following quotes in present tense:** Author interview with Dave Thomas, September 13, 2017.

63 **"My grandmother was Polish":** Bob Crane, "20 Questions: John Candy," *Playboy*, August 1989.

64 **"There's relief in acting":** Dotson Rader, "The Day the Acting Bug Bit Me," *Parade*, May 1992.

64 **"John liked to have a drink":** Mike Thomas, *The Second City Unscripted: Revolution and Revelation at the World-Famous Comedy Theater* (Northwestern University Press, 2009), chapter 4.

65 **"A lot of *Saturday Night Live*":** Phil Dellio, "Some Candy Talking!," *Graffiti* 3, No. 1, 1985.

65 **"I was in a bad hotel room":** Judith Dagely Flaherty and John LaRose, *To John with Love: A Tribute to John Candy*, documentary, Second City Entertainment, A&E Television Networks, 1995.

66 **"All of us partied there":** Thomas, *The Second City Unscripted*, chapter 4.

66 **"You'd eat at 2 a.m.":** Karen S. Schneider, "Exit Laughing," *People Weekly*, March 21, 1994.

66 **"I'm the one who has to look":** Cutler Durkee, "John Candy Surfaces in the Big Pond," *People Weekly*, July 13, 1984.

66 **"For some reason I started"**: Bob Crane, "Sweetmeat," *Oui*, August 1982.

67 **"There are any number of leeches"**: Martin Knelman, *Laughing on the Outside: The Life of John Candy* (Viking, 1996), 74.

67 **"All of a sudden the idea" and following quotes in present tense:** Author interview with Ivan Reitman, August 14, 2017.

68 **"They gave up on 50 points"**: Bob Thomas, "Ivan Reitman Had Sudden Inspiration for 'Stripes,'" *Playground Daily News*, June 28, 1981.

68 **"The biggest moose head"**: Chris Chase, "Bill Murray: A Black Sheep Now in *Stripes*," *New York Times*, July 3, 1981.

68 **"I don't want to be doing movies when I'm 50"**: Ibid.

69 **"I had to do it for the team"**: Candy interview on *Later* (NBC), August 1989.

70 **"It was 1980"**: Author interview with Sean Young for *Empire Online*, May 12, 2016.

70 **"A magnificently irreverent comedy"**: Ken McMillan, *Star-Herald*, July 23, 1981.

70 **"Old-fashioned and arrogant"**: James Andrew Miller, *Powerhouse: The Untold Story of Hollywood's Creative Artists Agency* (Custom House, 2006), chapter 2.

71 **"Jerks like that"**: Durkee, "John Candy Surfaces in the Big Pond."

71 **"I went from macaroni and cheese"**: Ibid.

72 **"a piece of shit"**: Gene Siskel, "John Belushi: New Film Turns Bluto into Nice Guy," *Chicago Tribune*, September 13, 1981.

72 **"That's just Animal House"**: Dick Kleiner, "Man of Laughs Tries a Different Role," *Havre Daily News*, October 30, 1981.

73 **"My mother had always told me"**: Ibid.

73 **"I had to hold myself back"**: Ibid.

73 **"We were in rehearsal"**: Joan E. Vadeboncoeur, "Comedians Duck Prime Time TV," *Syracuse Herald-Journal*, December 17, 1981.

74 **"I was shocked"**: Author interview with Carl Gottlieb, March 3, 2018.

74 **"a little Hitler"**: Bob Woodward, *Wired: The Short Life and Fast Times of John Belushi* (Simon & Schuster, 1984), 213.

75 **"brilliant" and following**: Roger Ebert, *Chicago Sun-Times*, December 28, 1981.

75 **"Without question Bill Conti"**: David Ansen, *Newsweek*, January 5, 1982.

75 **"This guy's a dip"**: From Chase interview on *Tomorrow* (NBC), December 17, 1981.

76 **"It was terrible"**: Bernie Brillstein, *You're No One in Hollywood Unless Someone Wants You Dead: Where Did I Go Right?* (Little, Brown, 1999), 204.

77 **"I was actually writing a line"**: Author interview with Dan Aykroyd, "Gremlins or Ghostbusters?," *Empire*, January 2007.

77 **"I genuinely loved him"**: Author interview with John Landis, April 18, 2016.

77 **"John represented messy bedrooms"**: Todd McCarthy, "Sand Castles," *Film Comment* 18, No. 3, May–June 1982.

6: CONFIDENCE MAN

79 **"Thirty-three years old and dead"**: David Rensin, "Playboy Interview: Eddie Murphy," *Playboy*, February 1, 1990.

80 **"Don't be a tightass"**: From Eddie Murphy interview on *The Hollywood Reporter's Awards Chatter Podcast*, August 20, 2016.

80 **"He looks in that mirror"**: Joseph Dalton and David Hirshey, "Eddie Murphy: The Prince of Comedy," *Rolling Stone*, July 7, 1983.

80 **"Girls started screaming"**: Gene Lyons and Peter McAlevey, "Crazy Eddie," *Newsweek*, January 7, 1985.

81 **"When I was at high school"**: Rensin, "Playboy Interview: Eddie Murphy."

81 **"I'm there Monday night"**: Chet Flippo, "Eddie Murphy Live," *New York Magazine*, October 11, 1982.

81 **"He would call every day"**: Tom Shales and James Andrew Miller, *Live from New York: An Uncensored History of Saturday Night Live* (Little, Brown, 2002), 213.

82 **"Talent was just shooting"**: Ibid.

82 **"It was just tokenism"**: Rensin, "Playboy Interview: Eddie Murphy."

82 **"Eddie . . . you're black"**: Bill Murray on *Saturday Night Live* (NBC), Season 6, Episode 12, March 7, 1981.

82 **"Hey, I'm funny"**: Shales and Miller, *Live from New York*, 246.

83 **"His face lit up"**: Ibid., 215.

83 **"How many people"**: Eddie Murphy on *Saturday Night Live*, Season 6, Episode 6 (NBC), January 10, 1981.

83 **"If I throw up a ball"**: Dalton and Hirshey, "Prince of Comedy."

83 **"A happy goose"**: Richard Corliss, "The Good Little Bad Little Boy," *Time*, July 11, 1983.

83 **"Eddie has no fear"**: Flippo, "Eddie Murphy Live."

83 **"Eddie Murphy has stolen"**: Tony Schwartz, "How an Amiable Youth Became a Star," *New York Times*, October 26, 1981.

84 **"When Eddie wasn't at a read-through"**: Shales and Miller, *Live from New York*, 256.

84   **"I went through a stage":** Rensin, "Playboy Interview: Eddie Murphy."

84   **"This is the last time we fly coach":** Quote taken from Richard Zoglin, *Comedy at the Edge* (Bloomsbury, 2008), 216.

84   **"Am I going to be a burn-out":** Eddie Murphy on *Saturday Night Live*, Season 6, Episode 8 (NBC), January 24, 1981.

85   **"But he didn't want to be a cop" and following quotes in present tense:** Author interview with Walter Hill, October 25, 2016.

85   **"He came in to meet me" and following quotes in present tense:** Author interview with Steven E. de Souza, June 25, 2016.

86   **"The studio wanted to fire him" and following quotes in present tense:** Author interview with Larry Gross, September 22, 2016.

87   **"Worst comes to worst":** Larry Gross, "The 48 Hrs. Journals," published on MovieCityNews.com, May 22, 2008, http://moviecitynews .com/2008/05/the-48-hr-diaries-week-one/.

88   **"Mr. Murphy runs away":** Janet Maslin, *New York Times*, December 8, 1982.

88   **"Call it Bitch Constantly":** Will Swagel, *Daily Sitka Sentinel*, February 25, 1983.

88   **"I left the theater":** Christopher Connelly, "Eddie Murphy Leaves Home," *Rolling Stone*, April 12, 1984.

88   **"When Nick got here":** Eddie Murphy on *Saturday Night Live*, Season 8, Episode 9 (NBC), December 11, 1982.

89   **"If you think of the '60s":** Dalton and Hirshey, "Prince of Comedy."

7: NEW-MODEL CHEVY

91   **"It was the closest":** Myron Meisel, "Mr. Middle Class: Chevy Chase Sinks His Teeth into Life," *Rolling Stone*, October 13, 1983.

92 **"Cary Grant is brilliant"**: Chevy Chase interview on *Tomorrow* (NBC), September 1980.

92 **"I don't think the whole mess"**: John Blumenthal, "Playboy Interview: Chevy Chase," *Playboy*, June 1988.

92 **"That movie split the audience"**: Roger Ebert on *Saturday Night Live* (NBC), Season 10, Episode 15, March 2, 1985.

92 **"I just don't understand"**: Blumenthal, "Playboy Interview: Chevy Chase."

93 **"Goldie Yawn"**: Arthur Thirkell, *Daily Mirror*, December 19, 1980.

94 **"I read the script"**: Blumenthal, "Playboy Interview: Chevy Chase."

94 **"The frame teems"**: Joe Morgenstern, "The Long Road from Munchkin Land," *Rolling Stone*, April 16, 1981.

94 **"That was probably the height"**: Sam Adams, *AVClub*, September 13, 2011, https://www.avclub.com/carrie-fisher-1798227374.

95 **"I remember going on the set"**: Author interview with Mike Medavoy, September 7, 2016.

95 **"They're half the size"**: Blumenthal, "Playboy Interview: Chevy Chase."

95 **"Chevy Chase, once"**: Pat H. Broeske, *Register*, Friday, July 31, 1981.

95 **"His performance as a romantic lead"**: Dann Gire, "No Pot of Gold at End of Rainbow," *Daily Herald*, Friday, August 14, 1981.

96 **"Look, I'm clammy" and other details**: Rena Fruchter, *I'm Chevy Chase . . . and You're Not* (Virgin Books, 2007), chapter 10.

96 **"What's your name?" and other details**: Meisel, "Mr. Middle Class."

97 **"At times he looks"**: Carlos Clarens, *Soho News*, December 1, 1982.

97   **"Five years and six movies"**: Bob Thomas, "Chase Handles Delay in Achieving Stardom," *Ottumwa Courier*, January 13, 1983.

97   **"I knew my career"**: Fruchter, *I'm Chevy Chase*, chapter 11.

98   **"Chevy was the first one" and following quotes in present tense**: Author interview with Matty Simmons, December 22, 2017.

98   **"There's one scene"**: Dale Pollock, "Lampoon Tries to Repeat *Animal House* Success," *Kenosha News*, August 11, 1983.

100   **"I just absolutely adored him"**: Author interview with Daryl Hannah for *Empire Online*, May 15, 2016.

8: BRAIN POWER

101   **"And now *you're* funny"**: Steve Martin on *Parkinson* (BBC), March 27, 1980.

101   **"He called me up" and following quotes in present tense**: Author interview with Steve Martin, "In Conversation with Steve Martin," *Empire*, March 2009.

102   **"When I look at it now"**: David Sheff, "Playboy Interview: Steve Martin," *Playboy*, January 1993.

103   **"What I saw in Steve"**: Ben Fong-Torres, "Why Is This Man Smirking?," *American Film*, June 1982.

103   **"I just don't think"**: Ben Fong-Torres, "Steve Martin Sings," *Rolling Stone*, February 18, 1982.

103   **"The script is now"**: Barry Koltnow, "Steve Martin Easing into Serious Role," *Orange County Register*, December 22, 1992.

104   **"I would not allow myself"**: Fong-Torres, "Steve Martin Sings."

104   **"the most emotional movie"**: Pauline Kael, *New Yorker*, December 21, 1981.

104 *"Pennies from Heaven* **is all flash"**: Roger Ebert, *Chicago Sun-Times*, January 1, 1982.

104 *"I have never spent":* Nathan Rabin, "Pennies from Heaven," AVClub .com, August 16, 2007, https://film.avclub.com/my-year-of-flops -case-file-59-pennies-from-heaven-1798212264.

104 **"I must say that the people"**: Fong-Torres, "Steve Martin Sings."

105 **"Like all good things" and following quotes in present tense**: Author interview with Carl Reiner, June 15, 2016.

105 **"We wanted personalities"**: Steven X. Rea, "Move Over, Bogart! Take That, Cagney! Drop the Roscoe, Ladd!," *Prevue*, June 1982.

106 **"I didn't want to act like Bogart"**: Ibid.

106 **"I felt like nudging Carl"**: Fong-Torres, "Why Is This Man Smirking?"

109 **"I really don't understand"**: James Wolcott, "The Man with Two Brains," *Texas Monthly*, August 1983.

109 **"I got stunned again"**: Dale Pollock, "Steve Martin: A Wild and Serious Guy," *Los Angeles Times*, September 16, 1984.

109 **"I'm like a loaded gun"**: Ibid.

110 **"I mean, it was craziness" and following quotes in present tense**: Author interview with Rick Moranis, May 24, 2013.

110 **"We were kinda awed by that" and following quotes in present tense**: Author interview with Dave Thomas, September 13, 2017.

113 **It was Silver who approached Moranis**: Details of conversation taken from author's interview with Moranis.

113 **"I've never even met him" and following quotes in present tense**: Author interview with Walter Hill, October 25, 2016.

114 **"Rick Moranis drove me out of my mind"**: Jeremy Smith, Michael Paré interview on Ain't It Cool News, March 21, 2011, http://www .aintitcool.com/node/48946.

9: CROSSING THE STREAMS

117 **"What's blue and sings alone"**: Gene Siskel, "Doctor Detroit Will See You Now . . . & Vice Versa," *Movie Magazine*, Spring 1983.

118 **"When I saw him come"**: David Michaels, "Aykroyd and Belushi: The Best of Friends," *Esquire*, December 1982.

118 **"While in Chicago"**: Dan Aykroyd, "Memories of Carrie," *Empire*, March 2017.

118 **"It was pretty grim"**: Author interview with Dan Aykroyd, "Gremlins or Ghostbusters?," *Empire*, January 2007.

119 **"As an eight-year-old"**: Author interview with Dan Aykroyd, "The Ghost Writer," *Empire*, June 2016.

119 **"It was set in the future" and following quotes in present tense:** Author interview with Ivan Reitman, August 14, 2017.

120 **"I really wanted to do it"**: Justin Bozung, "Interview with Writer/ Director Robert Boris," TV Store Online (blog), 2015, http://blog .tvstoreonline.com/2015/04/interview-writerdirector-robert -boris_30.html.

121 **"Danny made a lot"**: Author interview with Carl Gottlieb, March 3, 2018.

121 **"I did just what Franny said"**: Donna Dixon and Dan Aykroyd interview on *The Fran Drescher Tawk Show* (Fox), Episode 2, November 29, 2010.

121 **"I showed her the single-wide trailer"**: Ibid.

122 **"You come on this planet"**: Siskel, "Doctor Detroit Will See You Now."

122 **"Richard unfortunately set himself on fire" and following quotes in present tense:** Author interview with John Landis, April 18, 2016.

123 **On one particularly arctic morning:** Details of conversation be-

tween Eddie Murphy, Don Ameche, and Ralph Bellamy taken from author interview with John Landis.

124 **"The question has to be asked"**: Vern Perry, "Dan Aykroyd Tries, but 'Doctor Detroit' Is Just a Movie Pretending to Be a Comedy," *Register*, May 6, 1983.

124 **"It makes Eddie Murphy a force"**: Richard Schickel, *Time*, June 13, 1983.

125 **"I expected another"**: Rex Reed, *New York Post*, June 8, 1983.

125 **"For that first draft"**: Author interview with Dan Aykroyd, "The Ghost Writer."

125 **"The house is up on a hill"**: Ibid.

126 **"I don't know why John didn't wind up in it"**: Author interview with Rick Moranis, May 24, 2013.

127 **"I'm going to do *The Razor's Edge*"**: Gene Siskel, "Goofy, Successful Comedies Give Bill Murray the 'Edge'": *Chicago Tribune*, June 24, 1984.

128 **"It's a beautiful place"**: Timothy Crouse, "Bill Murray: The Rolling Stone Interview," *Rolling Stone*, August 16, 1984.

128 **"The nervous anticipation"**: Author interview with Dan Aykroyd, "The Ghost Writer."

129 **"We owned New York"**: Author interview with Dan Aykroyd, "Gremlins or Ghostbusters?"

129 **"They'd send three sets"**: Crouse, "Bill Murray: The Rolling Stone Interview."

130 **"Any of his scenes"**: Author interview with Dan Aykroyd, "Gremlins or Ghostbusters?"

130 **"This is the only movie"**: Roger Ebert, "Uniforms Making 'Ghostbusters' Out of Successful Actor-Writers," *Gazette Telegraph*, January 29, 1984.

130 **"One day I borrowed a bike"**: Author interview with Dan Aykroyd, "Gremlins or Ghostbusters?"

130 **"He looked at me and just said"**: Ibid.

131 **"It was like hitting a gusher"**: Author interview with Dan Aykroyd, "The Ghost Writer."

132 **"That summer was great"**: Ibid.

10: MURPHY'S LAW

133 **"If you had asked me"**: Aljean Harmetz, "Hollywood: The Marriage of Studios and Stars Is Back," *New York Times*, January 8, 1984.

134 **"I love it that"**: Richard Corliss, "The Good Little Bad Little Boy," *Time*, July 11, 1983.

136 **"I think it's unfair"**: Sylvia Rubin, "After 15 Years, Actor Apologizes for Gay Slurs," *San Francisco Chronicle*, May 11, 1996.

136 **"They're wasting their money"**: Christopher Connelly, "Eddie Murphy Leaves Home," *Rolling Stone*, April 12, 1984.

136 **"There are no icons"**: Aldore Collier, "Ebony Interview with Eddie Murphy," *Ebony*, July 1985.

137 **"I can't wait to leave"**: Connelly, "Eddie Murphy Leaves Home."

139 **"You see more of Murphy"**: Roger Ebert, "Total Defeat for 'Best Defense,'" *Chicago Sun-Times*, July 23, 1984.

139 ***Best Defense* turned out"**: Eddie Murphy on *Saturday Night Live* (NBC), Season 10, Episode 9, December 15, 1984.

140 **"Nobody knows how"**: Evelyn Renold, "Season's Top Film Originated from a Routine Traffic Ticket," *New York Daily News*, December 22, 1984.

140 **"He had an overall deal" and following quotes in present tense:** Author interview with Dan Petrie Jr., July 10, 2017.

140 **"I thought they'd sent it"**: Harry Knowles, Sylvester Stallone interview on Ain't It Cool News, December 3, 2006, http://www.aintitcool.com/node/30865.

142 **"We wanted Eddie to look"**: Lindsey Gruson, "Exit Stallone, Enter Eddie Murphy," *New York Times*, December 16, 1984.

142 **"Everything he had"**: From the Martin Brest DVD commentary for *Beverly Hills Cop*.

142 **"Every time, he came up"**: Gruson, "Exit Stallone."

143 **"Of all the characters I've played"**: David Castell, "Confidence Is High for Mr. Murphy," *Photoplay*, May 1985.

143 **"He is the perfect Brechtian"**: Steven Berkoff, *Tough Acts* (Robson Books, 2003), 51.

144 **"This is the year"**: Aljean Harmetz, "'Beverly Hills Cop' Wins at Christmas Box Office," *New York Times*, December 29, 1984.

144 **"Studebaker-grille smile"**: Paul Attansio, "Comedian Eddie Murphy Lets Loose in New Movie 'Beverly Hills Cop,'" *Washington Post*, December 10, 1984.

145 **"Everybody seems to love it"**: D. L. Stewart, "'Beverly Hills Cop' in a Category with Garfield, MTV, Jogging," *Colorado Gazette Telegraph*, March 31, 1985.

145 **"Me and my friend"**: Author interview with Chris Rock for *Empire*, April 29, 2015.

145 **"Both days were really cold for me"**: Cindy Pearlman, "No Sweat," *Daily Herald*, July 15, 1988.

146 **"Eddie can hear the rustle"**: Richard Corliss, "The Good Little Bad Little Boy," *Time*, July 11, 1983.

146 **"We're gonna have"**: Connelly, "Eddie Murphy Leaves Home."

11: EUROPEAN VACATIONS

148 **"They scream your name"**: Dale Pollock, "This Ghostbuster Finally Harnessed a Serious Role," *Los Angeles Times*, October 25, 1984.

148 **"I went to dinner with my agent"**: Author interview with Bill Murray, "Pint of Milk: Bill Murray," *Empire*, August 2012.

148 **"We'd go out to some bar"**: Rick Lyman, "He Ain't 'Fraid of No Ghosts, but Fame Is Sort of Spooky," *Elyria Chronicle Telegram*, October 22, 1984.

149 **"I get the same number"**: Joan E. Vadeboncoeur, "Murray Going Dramatic in 'The Razor's Edge,'" *Syracuse Herald American Stars Magazine*, September 30, 1984.

149 **"There are no dancing gophers"**: Pollock, "This Ghostbuster Finally Harnessed a Serious Role."

149 **"India looks fine"**: William E. Sarmento, "'Razor's Edge' Dull," *Lowell Sun*, October 29, 1984.

149 **"I consider myself"**: "Bill Murray Receives Award," *Paris News*, February 20, 1985.

150 **"He knew the local butcher"**: Author interview with Ivan Reitman, August 14, 2017.

150 **"I'm famous enough"**: Lyman, "He Ain't 'Fraid of No Ghosts."

150 **"I had a special fondness"**: Author interview with William Friedkin, October 31, 2017.

151 **"I just know what I am"**: Terri Minsky, "Chevy Chase Is Funny—Just Ask Him," *Chicago Tribune*, December 5, 1985.

151 **"I admire Mick Jagger"**: Michael Janusonis, "Author Actually Likes 'Fletch' Movie," *Chicago Tribune*, June 13, 1985.

151 **"He's a very wiseacre"**: Diane Haithman, "Chevy Chase Is a Lot Like 'Fletch,'" *Syracuse Herald American Stars Magazine*, June 9, 1985.

152 **"Andrew Bergman didn't write"**: Minsky, "Chevy Chase Is Funny."

152 **"He projects"**: Roger Ebert, "'Fletch' Works; Chase Doesn't," *Chicago Sun-Times*, May 31, 1985.

153 **"I gave my speech"**: Rena Fruchter, *I'm Chevy Chase . . . and You're Not* (Virgin Books, 2007), chapter 12.

153 **"It was not scoring very well" and following quotes in present tense**: Author interview with Amy Heckerling, March 28, 2018.

155 **"Almost unbearable"**: Marilyn Beck, "European Film Work No Treat," *Kenosha News*, December 13, 1984.

155 **"I can't say they were pals"**: Author interview with Matty Simmons, December 22, 2017.

155 **"The first was enjoyable"**: Marilyn Beck, "'Vacation,' 'Fletch' Sequels Out for Comedian Chase," *Wisconsin State Journal*, December 5, 1985.

155 **"Hollywood's latest crashed meteor"**: Paul Attanasio, "Too Much Chevy Chase: 'European Vacation' a Loser," *Washington Post*, July 30, 1985.

156 **"It's a lot easier to work"**: Merrill Shindler, "Lifestyles of the Rich and Funny," *Moviegoer*, February 1986.

156 **"He likes to focus attention"**: Dinitia Smith, "The Chase Is On," *New York Magazine*, August 23, 1993.

157 **"It's a horror story" and following quotes in present tense**: Author interview with John Landis, April 18, 2016.

157 **"In this movie"**: Shindler, "Lifestyles of the Rich and Funny."

158 **"We could see"**: Chevy Chase AMA interview on Reddit, December 8, 2014, https://www.reddit.com/r/IAmA/comments/2op1go/chevy_chase_on_ama_and_i_dont_like_it/.

160 **"'Spies' funnymen fail"**: Robert Denerstein, *Kenosha News*, December 15, 1985.

161 **"I know for a fact"**: Author interview with Dan Aykroyd, "The Ghost Writer," *Empire*, June 2016.

12: GOING WEST

163 **"This art is so different"**: Richard Corliss, "Sensational Steve Martin," *Time*, August 24, 1987.

164 **"My mind's been rejuvenated"**: Jeff Silverman, "Steve Martin Is Serious About Comedy," *Chicago Tribune*, September 23, 1987.

165 **"Mexican-Western fiesta musical"**: Ibid.

165 **"I hired two writers" and following quotes in present tense**: Author interview with Steve Martin, "Amigos Reunited," *Empire*, June 2011.

165 **"It's a strange script" and following quotes in present tense**: Author interview with John Landis, "Amigos Reunited," *Empire*, June 2011.

166 **"Chevy hid everything"**: Rena Fruchter, *I'm Chevy Chase . . . and You're Not* (Virgin Books, 2007), chapter 12.

166 **"I was the Carrot Top Amigo" and following quotes in present tense**: Author interview with Martin Short, "Amigos Reunited," *Empire*, June 2011.

166 **"How did you get so rich?"**: Quoted in Martin Short, *I Must Say: My Life as a Humble Comedy Legend* (HarperCollins, 2014), 196.

167 **Short entered his trailer**: Ibid.

168 **"What makes this film"**: Brian Hutton, "'Amigos' Comedy Is a Hit," *Joplin Globe*, December 19, 1986.

168 **"Chev, we think you've got a problem" and details**: John Blumenthal, "Playboy Interview: Chevy Chase," *Playboy*, June 1988.

168 **"I was a little like Jack Nicholson"**: Ibid.

168 **"They just started throwing pills"**: Author interview with Chevy Chase, "Amigos Reunited."

168 **"It felt like we were just shopping for ingredients" and following**: Author interview with Rick Moranis, May 24, 2013.

170 **Hughes approached him**: Details of conversation between Moranis and John Hughes provided by Moranis.

171 **"It had fourteen songs" and following quotes in present tense**: Author interview with Frank Oz, February 8, 2018.

172 **"I remember thinking"**: Author interview with Neal Scanlan, April 3, 2017.

173 **"The idea of her"**: Timothy White, "The Rumpled Anarchy of Bill Murray," *New York Times Magazine*, November 20, 1988.

174 **One day, Oz offered him**: Details of conversation between Oz and Murray provided by Oz.

175 **"one of the year's freshest"**: Michael Burkett, "'Horrors' Steals Fresh Camp from Stage," *Register*, December 19, 1986.

13: EDDIE MURPHY RAW

177 **"Son, you have an ob-leek"**: From Steve Martin interview on *Late Show with David Letterman* (CBS), November 11, 2011.

177 **"So that everywhere you walk"**: David Rensin, "Playboy Interview: Eddie Murphy," *Playboy*, February 1, 1990.

178 **"There was something about him"**: Ibid.

178 **"While I was playing"**: Gerri Hirshey, "The Black Pack," *Vanity Fair*, July 1, 1988.

178 **"I figured someone would"**: Rensin, "Playboy Interview: Eddie Murphy."

179 **"I like to see the hookers"**: Bill Zehme, "Eddie Murphy: Call Him Money," *Rolling Stone*, August 24, 1989.

179 **"Love is no punk, boy"**: Ibid.

180 **"All the flak he got for *The Razor's Edge*"**: Ibid.

180 **"We didn't have meetings"**: Author interview with Steve Meerson, May 11, 2016.

180 **"There was a scene"**: Author interview with Peter Krikes, May 11, 2016.

181 **"This is the first script"**: David T. Friendly, "Action-Comedy Is Next for Murphy," *Los Angeles Times*, June 15, 1985.

181 **"M-E-G-O"**: From Pierce O'Donnell and Dennis McDougal, *Final Subtraction: How Hollywood Really Does Business* (Doubleday, 1992), 160.

181 **"Eddie and John Hughes" and following quotes in present tense:** Author interview with Dennis Feldman, May 1, 2017.

182 **"He rides on the outside"**: Elvis Mitchell, "Eddie Murphy," *Interview*, September 1987.

182 **"Make me look as good"**: Ibid.

183 **"The whole joke"**: Author interview with Dan Petrie Jr., July 10, 2017.

183 **one day he got a call from Stallone:** Details of conversation between Murphy and Stallone taken from Zehme, "Eddie Murphy: Call Him Money."

184 **"A noisy, numbing"**: "Beverly Hills Cop II," *Variety*, December 31, 1986.

184 **"*Beverly Hills Cop II* was probably" and following:** Zehme, "Eddie Murphy: Call Him Money."

184 **"I don't know, man"**: From Rensin, "Playboy Interview: Eddie Murphy."

184 **"You had a black man":** Mitchell, "Eddie Murphy."

186 **"He's instinctual":** Bill Zehme, "Robin Williams: The Rolling Stone Interview," *Rolling Stone*, February 25, 1988.

187 **"Out of all the movies I did":** Hirshey, "The Black Pack," *Vanity Fair*, 1988.

187 **"When Eddie first told me" and following quotes in present tense:** Author interview with John Landis, April 18, 2016.

189 **"What happens when people put my business in the street?":** Details taken from Rensin, "Playboy Interview: Eddie Murphy."

189 **"The motherfucker was on his fucking toes":** Ibid.

190 **"Murphy's colossal comedic gifts":** Duane Byrge, "Coming to America," *Hollywood Reporter*, June 24, 1988.

190 **"I know what I wrote":** Cyndi Stivers, "Murphy's Law," *Premiere*, August 1992.

190 **"I feel old, real old":** Rensin, "Playboy Interview: Eddie Murphy."

14: PARTNERS IN CRIME

191 **"The family history" and following quotes in present tense:** Author interview with Carl Reiner, June 15, 2016.

192 **"John would walk":** Author interview with Walter Hill, October 25, 2016.

193 **"The shaggy moptop":** Patrick McGilligan, "*Playgirl*'s Seventh Annual 10 Sexiest Men," *Playgirl*, September 1985.

193 **"I just cried with laughter":** Patrick Goldstein, "John Candy's Ready to Take Control," *Los Angeles Times*, August 28, 1986.

194 **"At that point":** Kirk Honeycutt, *John Hughes: A Life in Film* (Race Point, 2015), 140.

194 **"We'd look into each other's eyes":** Ibid.

194 **"I thought it'd be funny":** William Ham, "John Hughes: Straight Outta Sherman," *Lollipop*, Issue 47, 2003.

195 **"We already had some" and following:** Frank Sanello, "It's Actors Steve Martin and . . . John Candy," *Joplin Globe*, November 20, 1987.

196 **"Apparently a couple of times":** Dan Aykroyd on *The Tonight Show Starring Johnny Carson* (NBC), June 25, 1987.

196 **"It was a perfectly ordinary Sunday":** Skit from *Saturday Night Live* (NBC), Season 2, Episode 3, October 2, 1976.

197 **"We were role-playing":** Paul Rosenfield, "Dum De Dum Dum," *Premiere*, July–August 1987.

198 **"Aykroyd's voice":** Ibid.

198 **"I went up to the black tower":** Ibid.

198 **"One of the biggest problems":** Marilyn Beck, "Aykroyd: Modern-Day Joe Friday," *Kenosha News*, October 17, 1986.

199 **"It was choreographed":** Author interview with Tom Hanks for *Empire Online*, December 12, 2013.

199 **"Universal Pictures credits that video":** From Dan Aykroyd webchat for *Empire Online*, February 14, 2012.

199 **"I really enjoyed it" and following:** Aykroyd on *The Tonight Show Starring Johnny Carson* (NBC), 1987.

200 **"This picture is so small":** Tom Shales, "Steve Martin on the Up and Up," *Washington Post*, June 19, 1987.

200 **"It had to be designed" and following quotes in present tense:** Author interview with Fred Schepisi, June 9, 2017.

202 **"What makes *Roxanne* so wonderful":** Roger Ebert, "Roxanne," June 19, 1987.

202 **"They got lured out of the movie" and following quotes in present tense:** Author interview with Dale Launer, May 31, 2017.

203 **"It was really down to the wire" and following quotes in present tense:** Author interview with Frank Oz, February 8, 2018.

203 **"It was one of the happiest films":** Author interview with Michael Caine for *Empire*, March 2, 2018.

203 **"*Dirty Rotten Scoundrels* was one" and following quotes in present tense:** Author interview with Steve Martin, "In Conversation with Steve Martin," *Empire*, March 2009.

205 **"I think it's very easy":** Gene Siskel, "All of Steve," *Chicago Tribune*, January 20, 1987.

15: "WE'RE BACK!"

207 **"I was told he would stop" and following quotes in present tense:** Author interview with Richard Donner, July 1, 2017.

208 **"A crumb, a pig":** Timothy White, "The Rumpled Anarchy of Bill Murray," *New York Times Magazine*, November 20, 1988.

209 **"*Scrooged* was a miserable gig":** Ian Spelling, "Bill Murray Ain't Afraid of No Ghosts," *Starlog*, March 1989.

210 **"Who makes millions of movies":** Patrick Goldstein, "'Ghostbusters II': Return of the Money-Making Slime," *Rolling Stone*, June 1, 1989.

210 **"in the dollars-and-cents":** Ibid.

211 **"I think walking into the meeting":** Ibid.

211 **"just too horrible for a movie":** Adam Eisenberg, "Ghostbusters Revisited," *Cinefex*, November 1989.

212 **"The script is nowhere near ready" and following:** Spelling, "Bill Murray Ain't Afraid of No Ghosts."

212 **"Shooting anywhere in New York"**: Eisenberg, "Ghostbusters Revisited."

213 **"When we had the uniforms on"**: Ibid.

213 **"They poured buckets"**: Ibid.

213 **"He has a better chance"**: Goldstein, "'Ghostbusters II': Return of the Money-Making Slime."

214 **"Come on, you gotta admit"**: Ibid.

214 **"We had nearly 180 shots"**: Eisenberg, "Ghostbusters Revisited."

214 **"Those special-effects guys"**: Martyn Palmer, "The World According to Bill Murray," *The Mail on Sunday*, February 6, 2010.

214 **"This movie is a total disappointment"**: Roger Ebert on *Siskel & Ebert* (Reelz), June 24, 1989.

214 **"All the acting parts"**: Author interview with Ivan Reitman, August 14, 2017.

215 **"I think it holds up"**: Author interview with Dan Aykroyd, "The Ghost Writer," *Empire*, June 2016.

215 **"It was just awful"**: Chevy Chase on *The Barbara Walters Special* (ABC), March 26, 1990.

215 **"We were told that"**: Ibid.

216 **"You're the first Betty Ford graduate"**: From *The Tonight Show Starring Johnny Carson* (NBC), December 12, 1986.

216 **"Chase essentially seems absent"**: Roger Ebert, "Three Amigos," *Chicago Sun-Times*, December 12, 1986.

216 **"I have thought"**: Gene Siskel on *The Tonight Show Starring Johnny Carson* (NBC), December 12, 1986.

216 **"I hope you were kind to me"**: Ebert on *The Tonight Show Starring Johnny Carson*, December 12, 1986.

216 **"So within a couple of days"**: Chevy Chase AMA interview on Reddit, December 8, 2014.

217 **"Welcome to *Monday Night Live*" and following**: from *The 59th Academy Awards* (ABC), March 30, 1987.

218 **"Good evening, Hollywood phonies" and following**: from *The 60th Academy Awards* (ABC), April 11, 1988.

218 **"The best film Chase has made"**: Siskel on *Siskel & Ebert*, May 28, 1988.

219 **"A small miracle"**: Ebert on *Siskel & Ebert*, May 28, 1988.

219 **"about as funny"**: "'Funny Farm' Not Funny at All; Chevy Chase Needs Better Stuff," *Frederick Post*, December 27, 1988.

219 **"No, I don't think so"**: Joshua Klein, "Harold Ramis," *AVClub*, March 3, 1999, https://www.avclub.com/harold-ramis-1798207996.

219 **"He was funny" and following quotes in present tense**: Author interview with Allan Arkush, March 11, 2018.

221 **"This thing is just Joke City"**: Siskel on *Siskel & Ebert*, March 18, 1989.

221 **"Too often he just"**: Ebert on *Siskel & Ebert*, March 18, 1989.

221 **"I feel I'm going"**: Chase on *The Barbara Walters Special*, 1990.

221 **"John was the fastest typist" and following quotes in present tense**: Author interview with Jeremiah Chechik, July 2, 2017.

16: EXIT THE NICE GUYS

227 **"There were two phases" and following quotes in present tense**: Author interview with Rick Moranis, May 24, 2013.

228 **"He's a lovely human being"**: Author interview with Trevor Albert, June 16, 2017.

229 **"The title says it all"**: Moranis on *Late Night with David Letterman* (NBC), June 21, 1989.

229 **"You drive on the lot"**: Moranis on *Late Night with David Letterman* (NBC), October 6, 1989.

229 **"You can put it"**: Moranis on *Late Night with David Letterman* (NBC), August 10, 1990.

233 **"Loved him"**: Author interview with Steve Martin, "In Conversation with Steve Martin," *Empire*, March 2009.

233 **"I remember on *Uncle Buck*" and following quotes in present tense:** Author interview with Bob Crane, July 7, 2017.

234 **"There was a harder edge"**: Marilyn Moss, "John Candy Is Delirious," *Box Office*, March 1991.

234 **"Candy once again"**: Dave Kerh, "John Candy Is Back in a Role Just His Size," *Chicago Tribune*, August 16, 1989.

235 **"That was a wonderful experience" and following quotes in present tense:** Author interview with Dave Thomas, September 13, 2017.

235 **"John has a way"**: Frank Sanello, "John Candy: Actor," *Empire*, October 1991.

17: GETTING SERIOUS

242 **"It's very ugly"**: David Sheff, "Playboy Interview: Steve Martin," *Playboy*, January 1993.

242 **"Victoria wanted children"**: Author interview with Carl Reiner, June 15, 2016.

243 **"The number of funny"**: Steve Martin, *Born Standing Up* (Scribner, 2007), 19.

243 **"What I liked"**: Gail Buchalter, "It's Love. That's Serious," *Parade*, April 28, 1991.

244 "Whenever I'd visited" and following quotes in present tense: Author interview with Mick Jackson, August 2, 2017.

246 "There's an extra chill": Elaine Dutka, "A Side Order of Steve Martin," *Los Angeles Times*, February 3, 1991.

246 "The lack of subtlety": Roger Ebert, *Chicago Sun-Times*, February 8, 1991.

247 "We're a couple forever": Sheff, "Playboy Interview: Steve Martin."

247 "I was very screwed up": David Wild, "Steve Martin: The Rolling Stone Interview," *Rolling Stone*, September 1999.

248 "Eddie Murphy is our Kellogg's": "Franchising Is Key in New Hollywood," *Santa Cruz Sentinel*, June 7, 1989.

249 "*Harlem Nights* was the first time": Cyndi Stivers, "Murphy's Law," *Premiere*, August 1992.

249 "It was a nice payday": Mark Dinning, "Nick Nolte: Hall of Fame—The Maverick Series," *Empire*, March 2003.

249 "I don't think we got the script right": Author interview with Walter Hill, October 25, 2016.

249 "I was fucked up": Stivers, "Murphy's Law."

250 "I want to go back": Ibid.

250 "It's a movie": Maureen Dowd, "He's Never Been Happier, or More Glum," *New York Times*, June 28, 1992.

251 "Eddie might show up": Ibid.

251 "The audience cheers": Ibid.

251 when he received a call: Details of phone call between John Landis and Sherry Lansing taken from author interview with Landis.

252 "There's no reason": Bill Zehme, "Eddie Murphy: Call Him Money," *Rolling Stone*, August 24, 1989.

252 **"Joel and I visited" and following quotes in present tense:** Author interview with Steven E. de Souza, June 25, 2016.

253 **"The picture was in trouble" and following quotes in present tense:** Author interview with John Landis, April 18, 2016.

254 **"Eddie needs to shoot off":** Richard Schickel, "Eddie Who?," *Time*, June 6, 1994.

255 **"We want this movie":** James Greene Jr., "Drugs, Death and That Wig: An Oral History of 'Vampire in Brooklyn,'" *Hopes&Fears*, October 27, 2015, http://www.hopesandfears.com/hopes/culture/film/216583-vampire-in-brooklyn-oral-history.

18: TIME OUT

257 **"I felt the mattress depress":** David Sheff, "Playboy Interview: Dan Aykroyd," *Playboy*, August 1993.

258 **"I was taken to see" and following quotes in present tense**: Author interview with Dan Aykroyd, "The Ghost Writer," *Empire*, June 2016.

259 **"I was as complete a wreck":** Marc Shapiro, "Dan Aykroyd: Fantasy-maker," *Starlog*, March 1991.

260 **"Chevy knew it was going":** Rena Fruchter, *I'm Chevy Chase . . . and You're Not* (Virgin Books, 2007), chapter 15.

260 **"Let me preface this" and following quotes in present tense:** Author interview with Bob Crane, July 7, 2017.

261 **"What transpires":** Shapiro, "Dan Aykroyd: Fantasymaker."

262 **"Most of the jokes":** Owen Gleiberman, "Nothing but Trouble," *Entertainment Weekly*, March 1, 1991.

263 **"One of the great things":** Chevy Chase on *The Chevy Chase Show* (Fox), September 17, 1993.

263 **"What are you doing with yourself"**: Chevy Chase on *The Chevy Chase Show* (Fox), September 7, 1993.

264 **"The shows weren't good"**: John Carmody, "The TV Column," *Washington Post*, October 7, 1993.

264 **"He came in"**: Author interview with Steven E. de Souza, June 25, 2016.

265 **"The only person I had in mind" and following quotes in present tense**: Author interview with Danny Rubin, June 28, 2017.

266 **"We were left there" and following quotes in present tense**: Author interview with Trevor Albert, June 16, 2017.

269 **"Bill's a big guy" and following quotes in present tense**: Author interview with Stephen Tobolowsky, June 24, 2017.

270 **"He's raging, angry"** Judd Apatow, *Sick in the Head* (Random House, 2015), 126.

271 **"Bill destroys all meaning"**: Ibid., 128.

272 **"Just haven't had the time"**: David Friedman, "They Came at Him Like Bees," *Pacific Stars and Stripes*, March 13, 1993.

273 **"Such a fiendishly clever premise"**: Robert W. Butler, *Kansas City Star*, February 13, 1993.

273 **"The story's premise"**: Janet Maslin, "Bill Murray Battles Pittsburgh Time Warp," *New York Times*, February 12, 1993.

273 **"Murray returns"**: Todd Camp, *Fort Worth Star-Telegram*, February 13, 1993.

274 **"I think it's an extraordinary movie"**: Bill Murray on *Squawk Box* (CNBC), February 10, 2017.

EPILOGUE

275 **"Toga! Toga!" and following:** Bill Murray and Chevy Chase on *Saturday Night Live* (NBC), Season 24, Episode 14, February 20, 1999.

278 **"Beverly's hilarious":** Chevy Chase on "Clark & Ellen" featurette for *Vacation*, 2015.

278 **"The villain was based":** Author interview with Dan Aykroyd, "The Ghost Writer," *Empire*, June 2016.

279 **"Why would I retire?":** Author interview with Rick Moranis, May 24, 2013.

279 **"Tired of sitting on my butt":** Steve Martin, *The Ten, Make That Nine, Habits of Very Organized People. Make That Ten: The Tweets of Steve Martin* (Grand Central Publishing, 2012), 98.

INDEX

ABOUT THE AUTHOR

NICK DE SEMLYEN is a film journalist who has written for publications including *Rolling Stone*, *Stuff*, and *Time Out*. He is the features editor for *Empire*, the world's biggest movie magazine.